SPIDER-MAN 2099

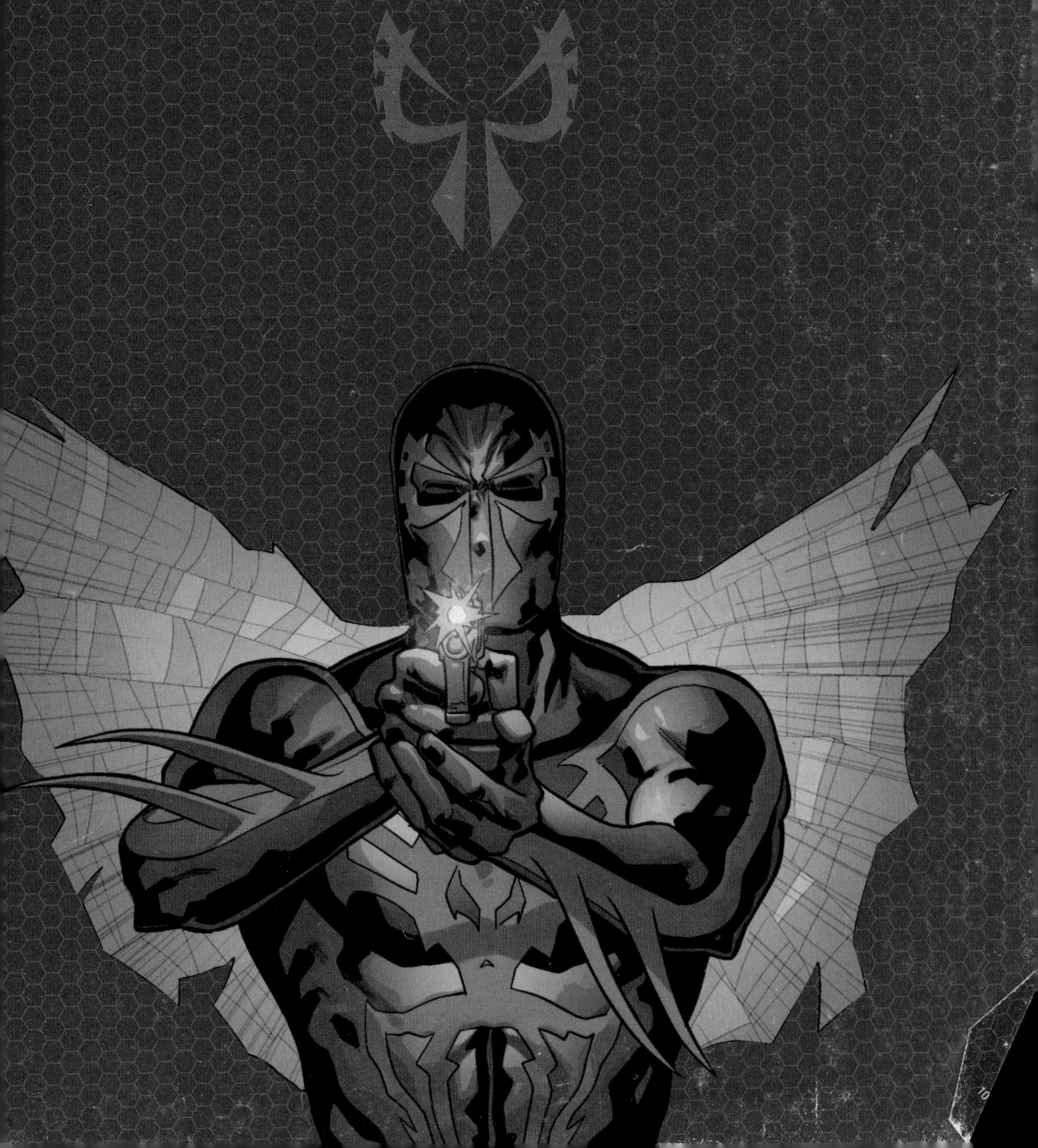

SPIDER-MAN 2099

WRITER
PETER DAVID

ARTIST
WILL SLINEY

COLOR ARTISTS
ANTONIO FABELA
WITH **ANDRES MOSSA** (#12)

LETTERER
VC'S JOE CARAMAGN.

COVER ART
FRANCESCO MATTINA

EDITORS
ELLIE PYLE & DEVIN LEWIS

SENIOR EDITOR
NICK LOWE

SPIDER-MAN CREATED BY
STAN LEE & STEVE DITKO

Collection Editor: Sarah Brunstad • Associate Managing Editor: Alex Starbuck
Editors, Special Projects: Jennifer Grünwald & Mark D. Beazley • Senior Editor, Special Projects: Jeff Youngquist
SVP Print, Sales & Marketing: David Gabriel • Book Design: Jeff Powell

Editor in Chief: Axel Alonso • Chief Creative Officer: Joe Quesada • Publisher: Dan Buckley • Executive Producer: Alan Fine

SPIDER-MAN 2099 VOL. 2: SPIDER-VERSE. Contains material originally published in magazine form as SPIDER-MAN 2099 #6-12. First printing 2015. ISBN# 978-0-7851-9080-6. Published by MARVEL WORLd.
a subsidiary of MARVEL ENTERTAINMENT, LLC. OFFICE OF PUBLICATION: 135 West 50th Street, New York, NY 10020. Copyright © 2015 MARVEL No similarity between any of the names, characters, persons, an
tions in this magazine with those of any living or dead person or institution is intended, and any such similarity which may exist is purely coincidental. **Printed in the U.S.A.** ALAN FINE, President, Marvel Entertai
BUCKLEY, President, TV, Publishing and Brand Management; JOE QUESADA, Chief Creative Officer; TOM BREVOORT, SVP of Publishing; DAVID BOGART, SVP of Operations & Procurement, Publishing; C.B. CEB
International Development & Brand Management; DAVID GABRIEL, SVP Print, Sales & Marketing; JIM O'KEEFE, VP of Operations & Logistics; DAN CARR, Executive Director of Publishing Technology; SUSAN CRE
Operations Manager; ALEX MORALES, Publishing Operations Manager; STAN LEE, Chairman Emeritus. For information regarding advertising in Marvel Comics or on Marvel.com, please contact Jonathan Rhe
Custom Solutions & Ad Sales, at jrheingold@marvel.com. For Marvel subscription inquiries, please call 800-217-9158. **Manufactured between 5/22/2015 and 6/29/2015 by R.R. DONNELLEY, INC., SALE**

9 8 7 6 5 4 3 2 1

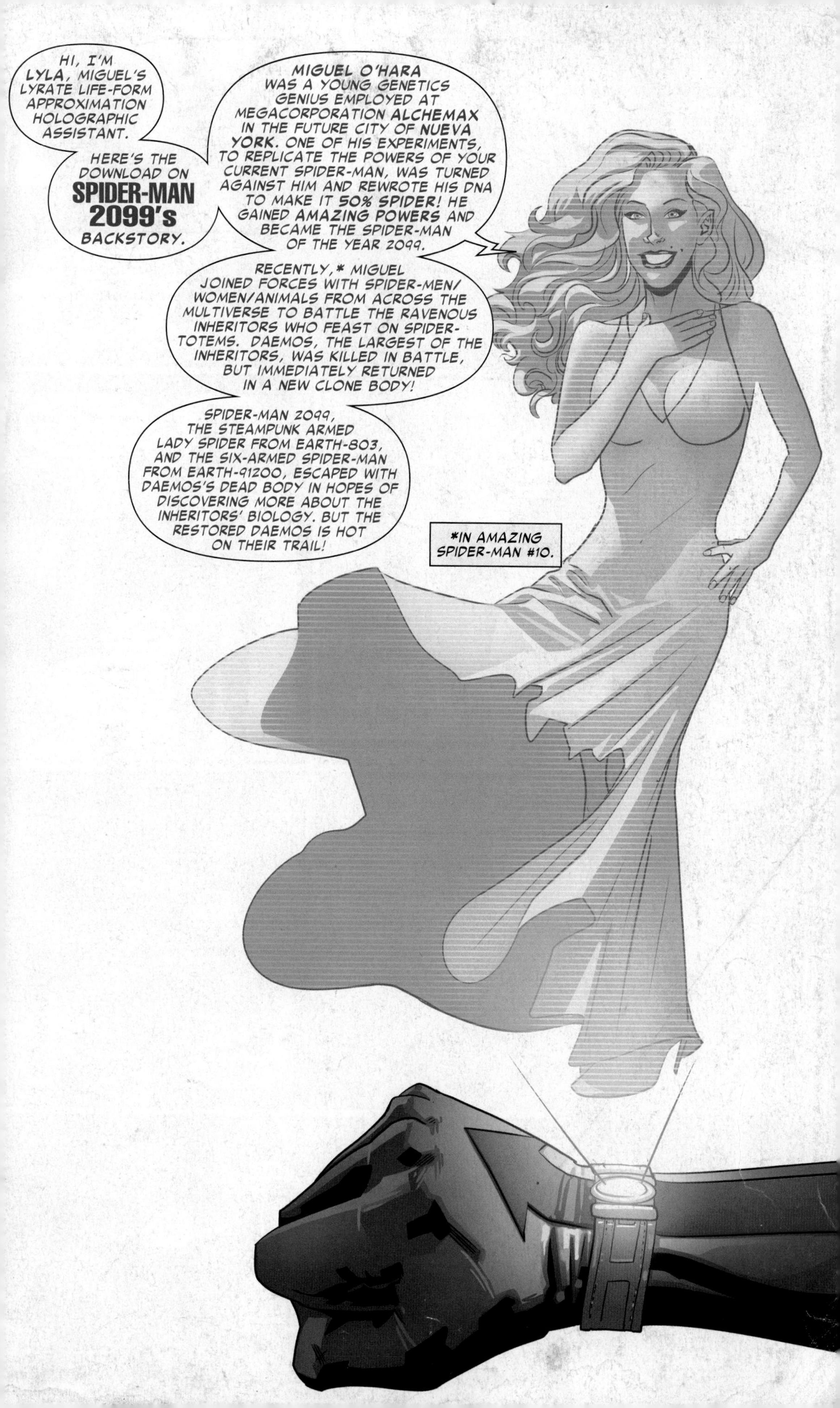

HI, I'M LYLA, MIGUEL'S LYRATE LIFE-FORM APPROXIMATION HOLOGRAPHIC ASSISTANT.
HERE'S THE DOWNLOAD ON SPIDER-MAN 2099's BACKSTORY.
MIGUEL O'HARA WAS A YOUNG GENETICS GENIUS EMPLOYED AT MEGACORPORATION ALCHEMAX IN THE FUTURE CITY OF NUEVA YORK. ONE OF HIS EXPERIMENTS, TO REPLICATE THE POWERS OF YOUR CURRENT SPIDER-MAN, WAS TURNED AGAINST HIM AND REWROTE HIS DNA TO MAKE IT 50% SPIDER! HE GAINED AMAZING POWERS AND BECAME THE SPIDER-MAN OF THE YEAR 2099.
RECENTLY,* MIGUEL JOINED FORCES WITH SPIDER-MEN/ WOMEN/ANIMALS FROM ACROSS THE MULTIVERSE TO BATTLE THE RAVENOUS INHERITORS WHO FEAST ON SPIDER-TOTEMS. DAEMOS, THE LARGEST OF THE INHERITORS, WAS KILLED IN BATTLE, BUT IMMEDIATELY RETURNED IN A NEW CLONE BODY!
SPIDER-MAN 2099, THE STEAMPUNK ARMED LADY SPIDER FROM EARTH-803, AND THE SIX-ARMED SPIDER-MAN FROM EARTH-91200, ESCAPED WITH DAEMOS'S DEAD BODY IN HOPES OF DISCOVERING MORE ABOUT THE INHERITORS' BIOLOGY. BUT THE RESTORED DAEMOS IS HOT ON THEIR TRAIL!
*IN AMAZING SPIDER-MAN #10.

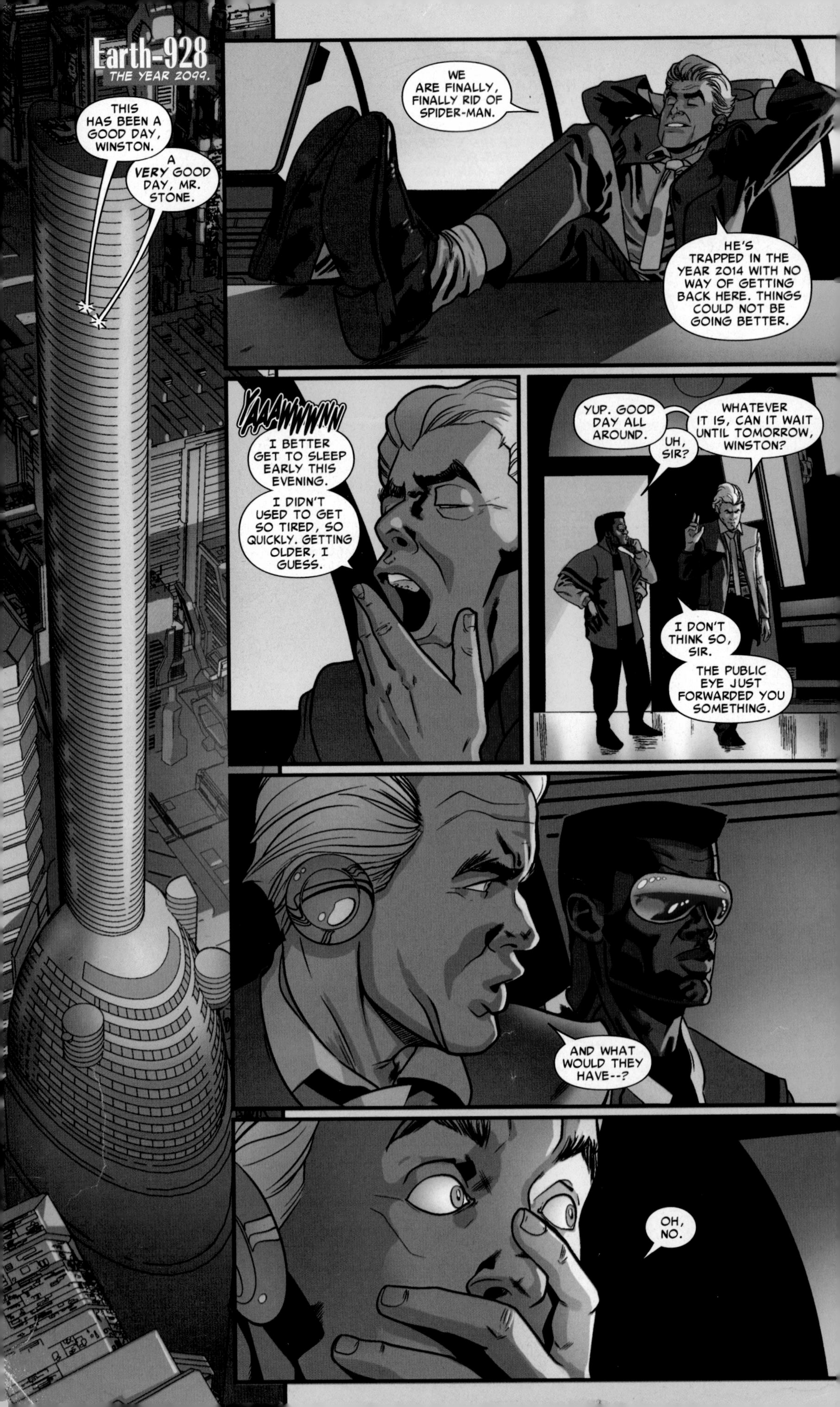
Earth-928
THE YEAR 2099.
THIS HAS BEEN A GOOD DAY, WINSTON.
A VERY GOOD DAY, MR. STONE.
WE ARE FINALLY, FINALLY RID OF SPIDER-MAN.
HE'S TRAPPED IN THE YEAR 2014 WITH NO WAY OF GETTING BACK HERE. THINGS COULD NOT BE GOING BETTER.
YAAAWWWNN
I BETTER GET TO SLEEP EARLY THIS EVENING.
I DIDN'T USED TO GET SO TIRED, SO QUICKLY. GETTING OLDER, I GUESS.
YUP. GOOD DAY ALL AROUND.
UH, SIR?
WHATEVER IT IS, CAN IT WAIT UNTIL TOMORROW, WINSTON?
I DON'T THINK SO, SIR.
THE PUBLIC EYE JUST FORWARDED YOU SOMETHING.
AND WHAT WOULD THEY HAVE--?
OH, NO.

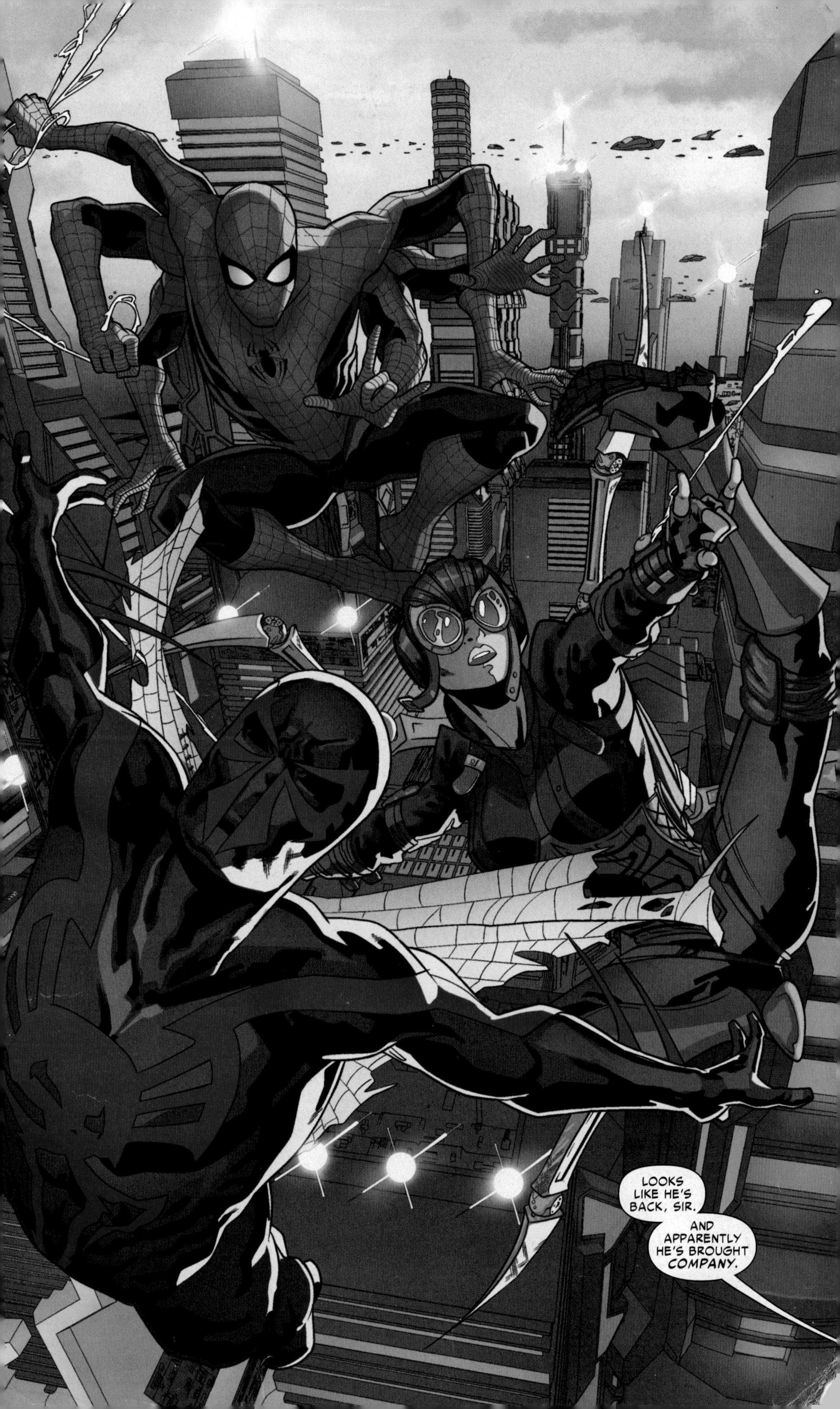
LOOKS LIKE HE'S BACK, SIR.
AND APPARENTLY HE'S BROUGHT COMPANY.

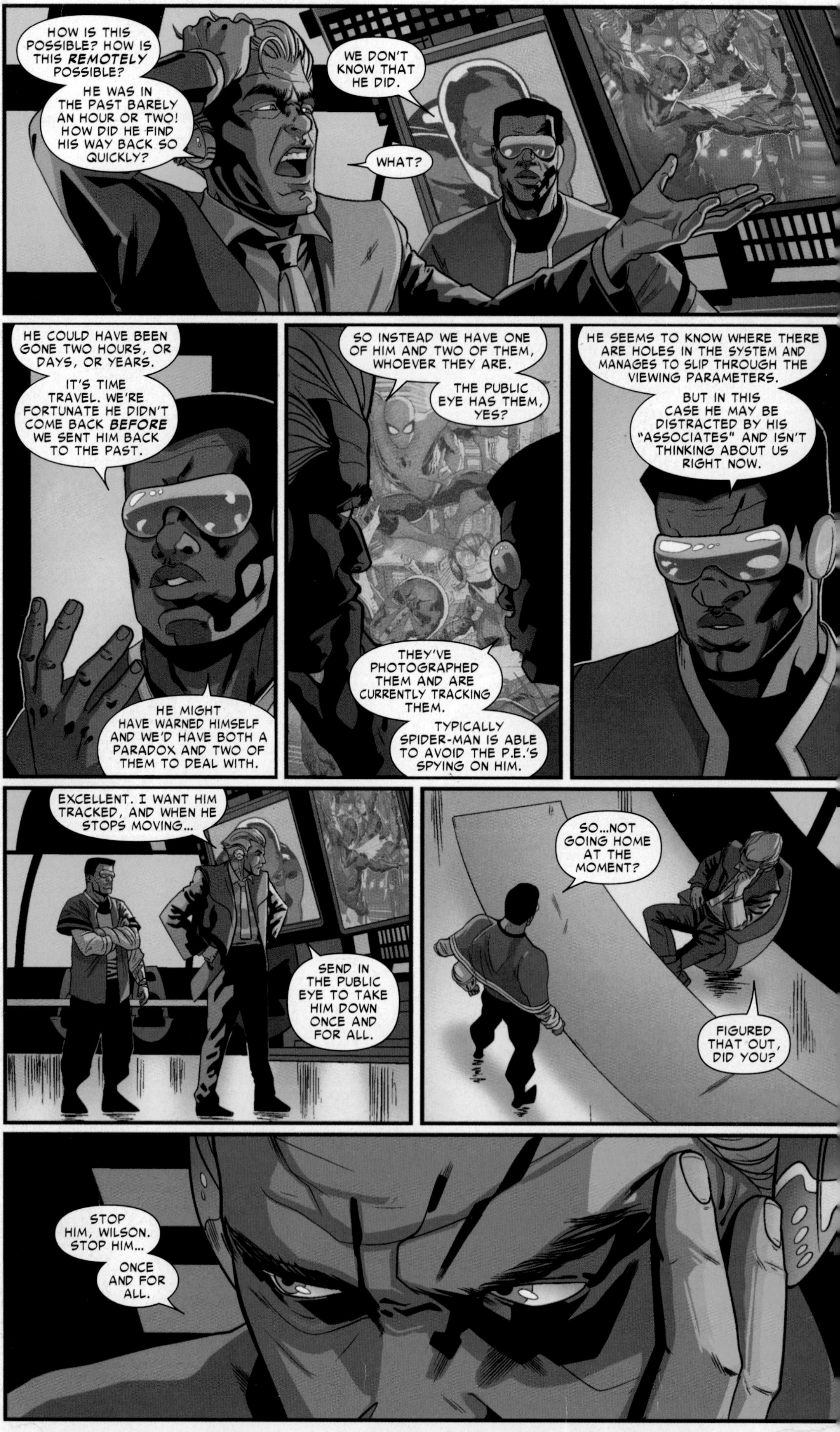
HOW IS THIS POSSIBLE? HOW IS THIS *REMOTELY* POSSIBLE?
HE WAS IN THE PAST BARELY AN HOUR OR TWO! HOW DID HE FIND HIS WAY BACK SO QUICKLY?
WE DON'T KNOW THAT HE DID.
WHAT?
HE COULD HAVE BEEN GONE TWO HOURS, OR DAYS, OR YEARS.
IT'S TIME TRAVEL. WE'RE FORTUNATE HE DIDN'T COME BACK *BEFORE* WE SENT HIM BACK TO THE PAST.
HE MIGHT HAVE WARNED HIMSELF AND WE'D HAVE BOTH A PARADOX AND TWO OF THEM TO DEAL WITH.
SO INSTEAD WE HAVE ONE OF HIM AND TWO OF THEM, WHOEVER THEY ARE.
THE PUBLIC EYE HAS THEM, YES?
THEY'VE PHOTOGRAPHED THEM AND ARE CURRENTLY TRACKING THEM.
TYPICALLY SPIDER-MAN IS ABLE TO AVOID THE P.E.'S SPYING ON HIM.
HE SEEMS TO KNOW WHERE THERE ARE HOLES IN THE SYSTEM AND MANAGES TO SLIP THROUGH THE VIEWING PARAMETERS.
BUT IN THIS CASE HE MAY BE DISTRACTED BY HIS "ASSOCIATES" AND ISN'T THINKING ABOUT US RIGHT NOW.
EXCELLENT. I WANT HIM TRACKED, AND WHEN HE STOPS MOVING...
SEND IN THE PUBLIC EYE TO TAKE HIM DOWN ONCE AND FOR ALL.
SO...NOT GOING HOME AT THE MOMENT?
FIGURED THAT OUT, DID YOU?
STOP HIM, WILSON. STOP HIM...
ONCE AND FOR ALL.

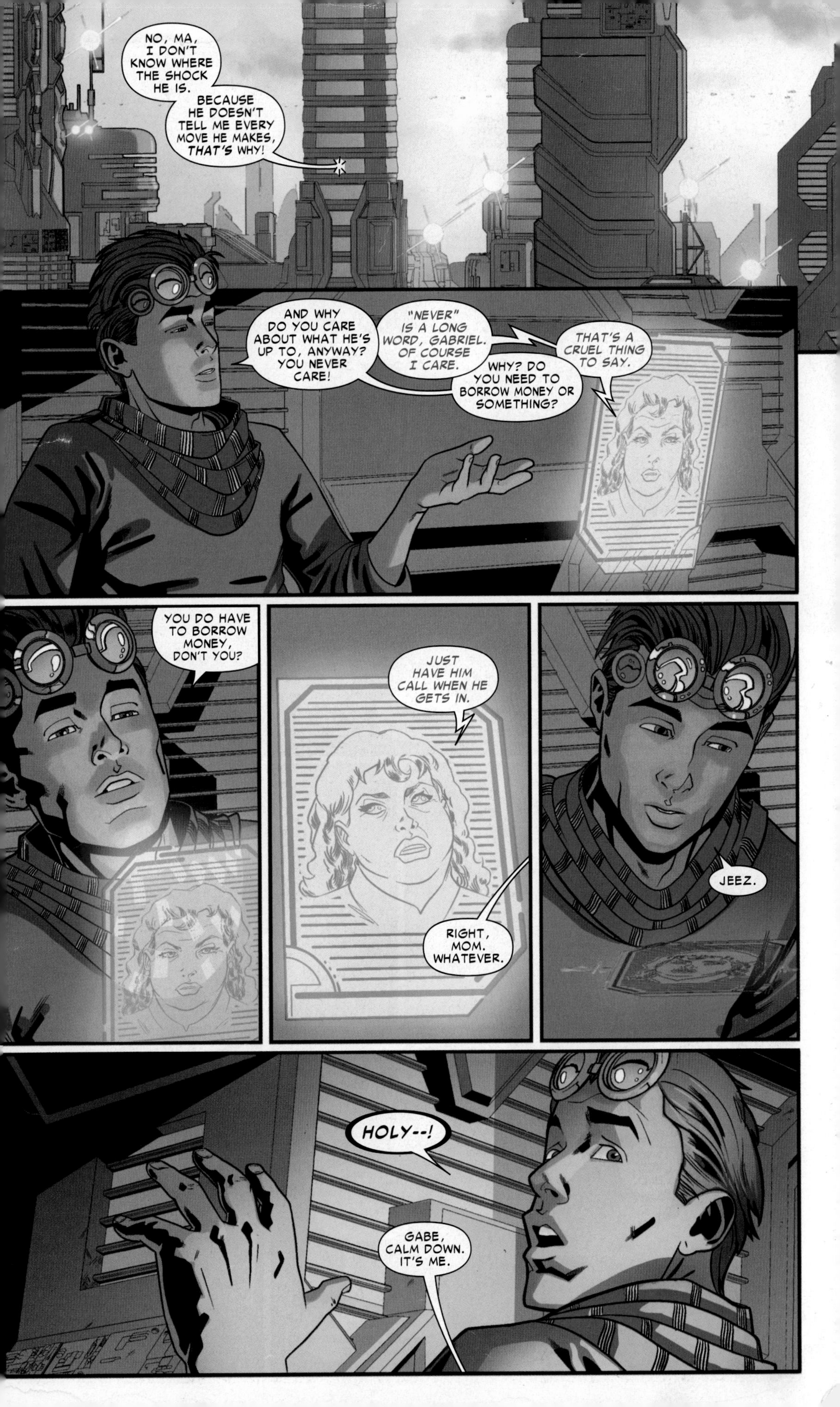
NO, MA, I DON'T KNOW WHERE THE SHOCK HE IS.
BECAUSE HE DOESN'T TELL ME EVERY MOVE HE MAKES, *THAT'S* WHY!
AND WHY DO YOU CARE ABOUT WHAT HE'S UP TO, ANYWAY? YOU NEVER CARE!
"NEVER" IS A LONG WORD, GABRIEL. OF COURSE I CARE.
THAT'S A CRUEL THING TO SAY.
WHY? DO YOU NEED TO BORROW MONEY OR SOMETHING?
YOU DO HAVE TO BORROW MONEY, DON'T YOU?
JUST HAVE HIM CALL WHEN HE GETS IN.
RIGHT, MOM. WHATEVER.
JEEZ.
HOLY--!
GABE, CALM DOWN. IT'S ME.

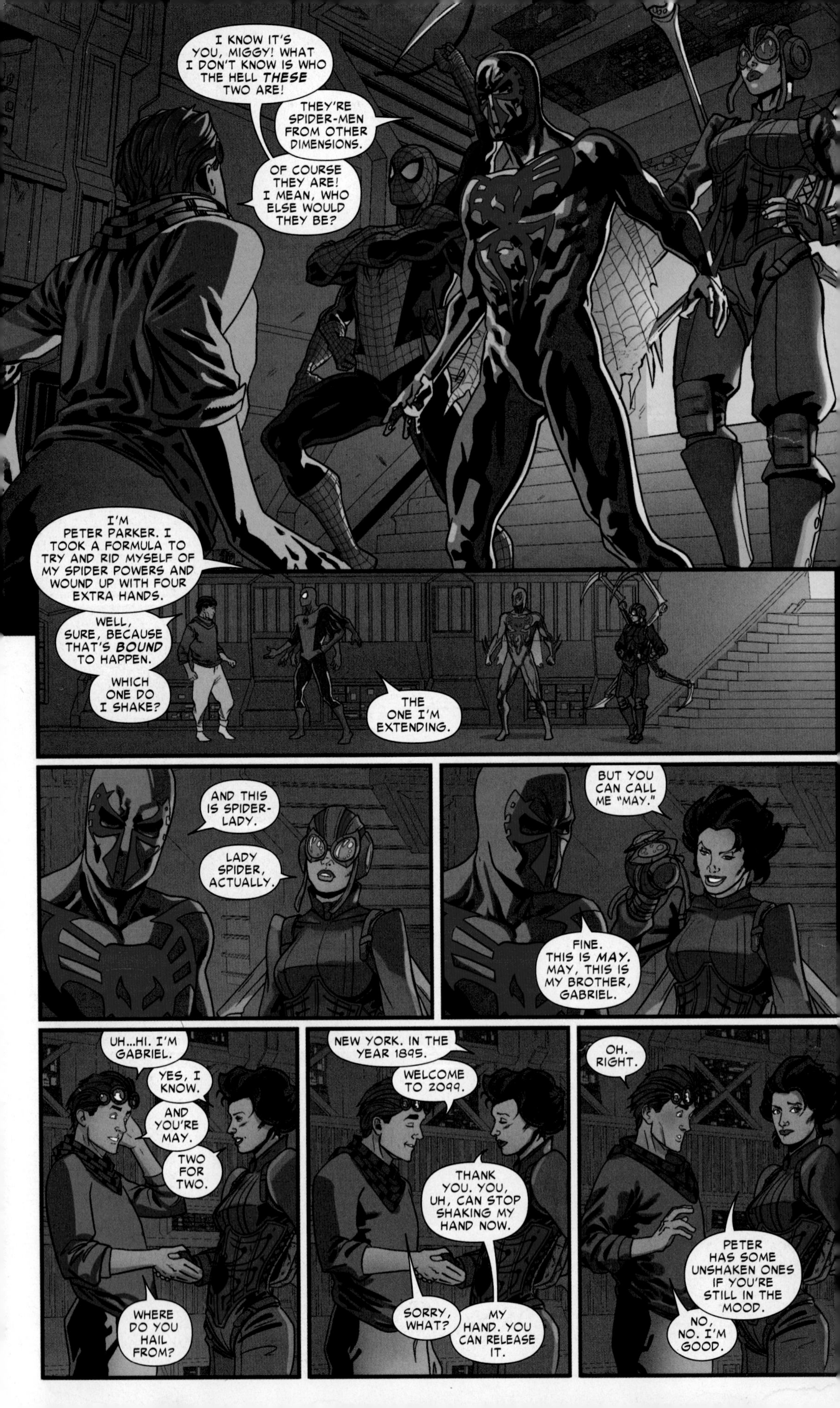
I KNOW IT'S YOU, MIGGY! WHAT I DON'T KNOW IS WHO THE HELL *THESE* TWO ARE!
THEY'RE SPIDER-MEN FROM OTHER DIMENSIONS.
OF COURSE THEY ARE! I MEAN, WHO ELSE WOULD THEY BE?
I'M PETER PARKER. I TOOK A FORMULA TO TRY AND RID MYSELF OF MY SPIDER POWERS AND WOUND UP WITH FOUR EXTRA HANDS.
WELL, SURE, BECAUSE THAT'S *BOUND* TO HAPPEN.
WHICH ONE DO I SHAKE?
THE ONE I'M EXTENDING.
AND THIS IS SPIDER-LADY.
LADY SPIDER, ACTUALLY.
BUT YOU CAN CALL ME "MAY."
FINE. THIS IS *MAY*. MAY, THIS IS MY BROTHER, GABRIEL.
UH...HI. I'M GABRIEL.
YES, I KNOW.
AND YOU'RE MAY.
TWO FOR TWO.
WHERE DO YOU HAIL FROM?
NEW YORK. IN THE YEAR 1895.
WELCOME TO 2099.
THANK YOU. YOU, UH, CAN STOP SHAKING MY HAND NOW.
SORRY, WHAT?
MY HAND. YOU CAN RELEASE IT.
OH. RIGHT.
PETER HAS SOME UNSHAKEN ONES IF YOU'RE STILL IN THE MOOD.
NO, NO. I'M GOOD.

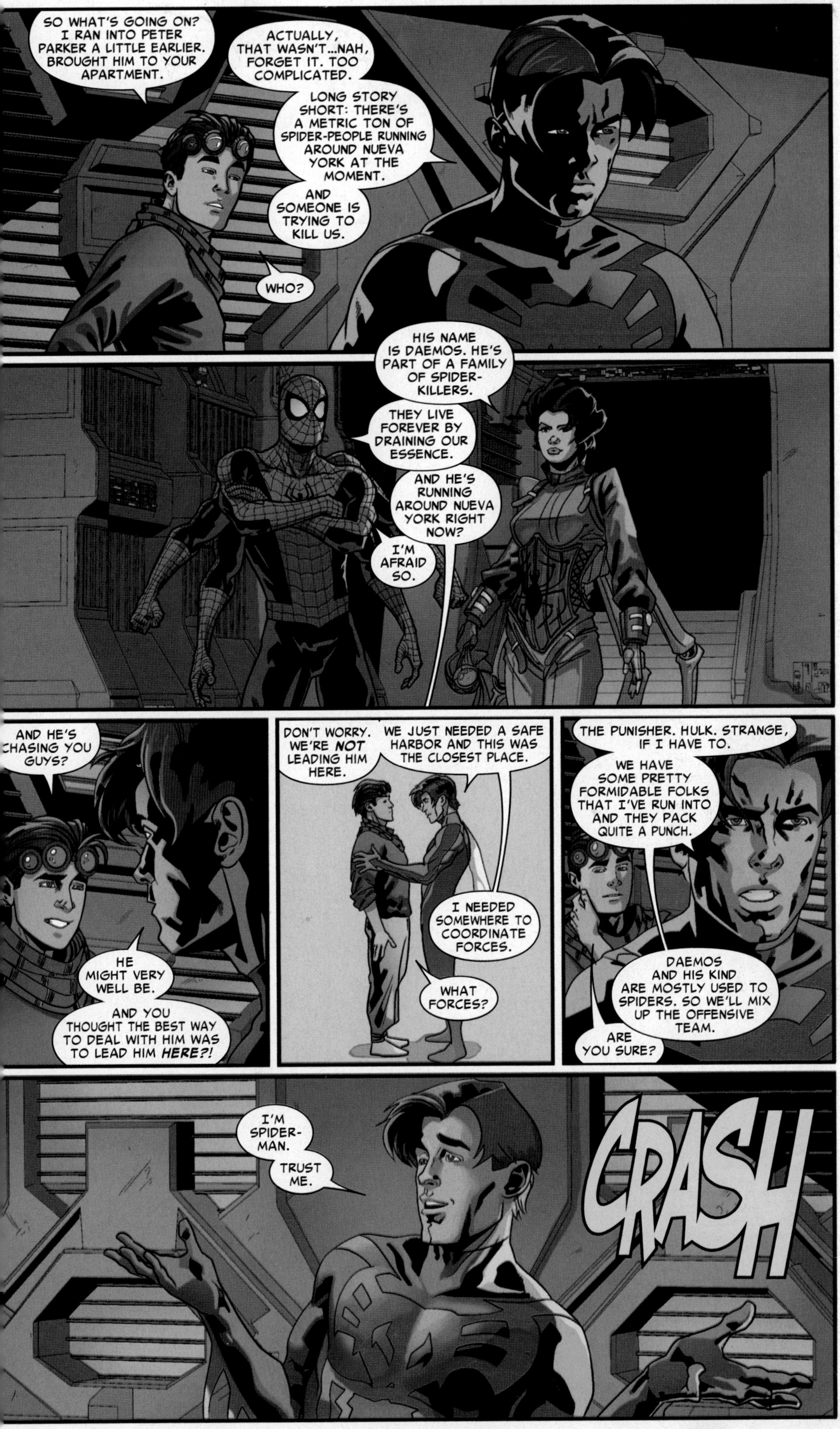

SO WHAT'S GOING ON? I RAN INTO PETER PARKER A LITTLE EARLIER. BROUGHT HIM TO YOUR APARTMENT.
ACTUALLY, THAT WASN'T...NAH, FORGET IT. TOO COMPLICATED.
LONG STORY SHORT: THERE'S A METRIC TON OF SPIDER-PEOPLE RUNNING AROUND NUEVA YORK AT THE MOMENT.
AND SOMEONE IS TRYING TO KILL US.
WHO?
HIS NAME IS DAEMOS. HE'S PART OF A FAMILY OF SPIDER-KILLERS.
THEY LIVE FOREVER BY DRAINING OUR ESSENCE.
AND HE'S RUNNING AROUND NUEVA YORK RIGHT NOW?
I'M AFRAID SO.
AND HE'S CHASING YOU GUYS?
HE MIGHT VERY WELL BE.
AND YOU THOUGHT THE BEST WAY TO DEAL WITH HIM WAS TO LEAD HIM *HERE?!*
DON'T WORRY. WE'RE *NOT* LEADING HIM HERE.
WE JUST NEEDED A SAFE HARBOR AND THIS WAS THE CLOSEST PLACE.
I NEEDED SOMEWHERE TO COORDINATE FORCES.
WHAT FORCES?
THE PUNISHER. HULK. STRANGE, IF I HAVE TO.
WE HAVE SOME PRETTY FORMIDABLE FOLKS THAT I'VE RUN INTO AND THEY PACK QUITE A PUNCH.
DAEMOS AND HIS KIND ARE MOSTLY USED TO SPIDERS. SO WE'LL MIX UP THE OFFENSIVE TEAM.
ARE YOU SURE?
I'M SPIDER-MAN.
TRUST ME.
CRASH

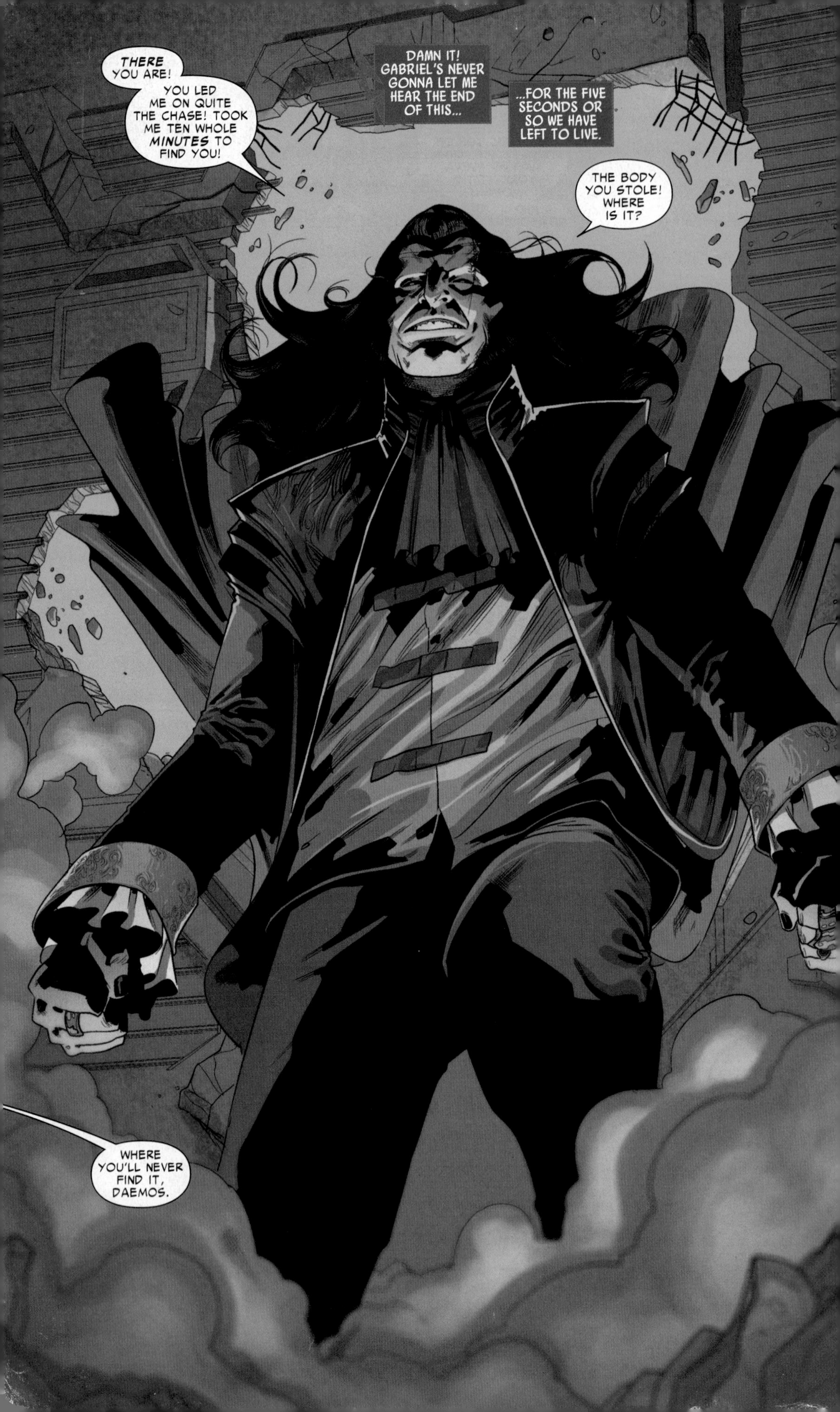
THERE YOU ARE!
YOU LED ME ON QUITE THE CHASE! TOOK ME TEN WHOLE MINUTES TO FIND YOU!
DAMN IT! GABRIEL'S NEVER GONNA LET ME HEAR THE END OF THIS...
...FOR THE FIVE SECONDS OR SO WE HAVE LEFT TO LIVE.
THE BODY YOU STOLE! WHERE IS IT?
WHERE YOU'LL NEVER FIND IT, DAEMOS.

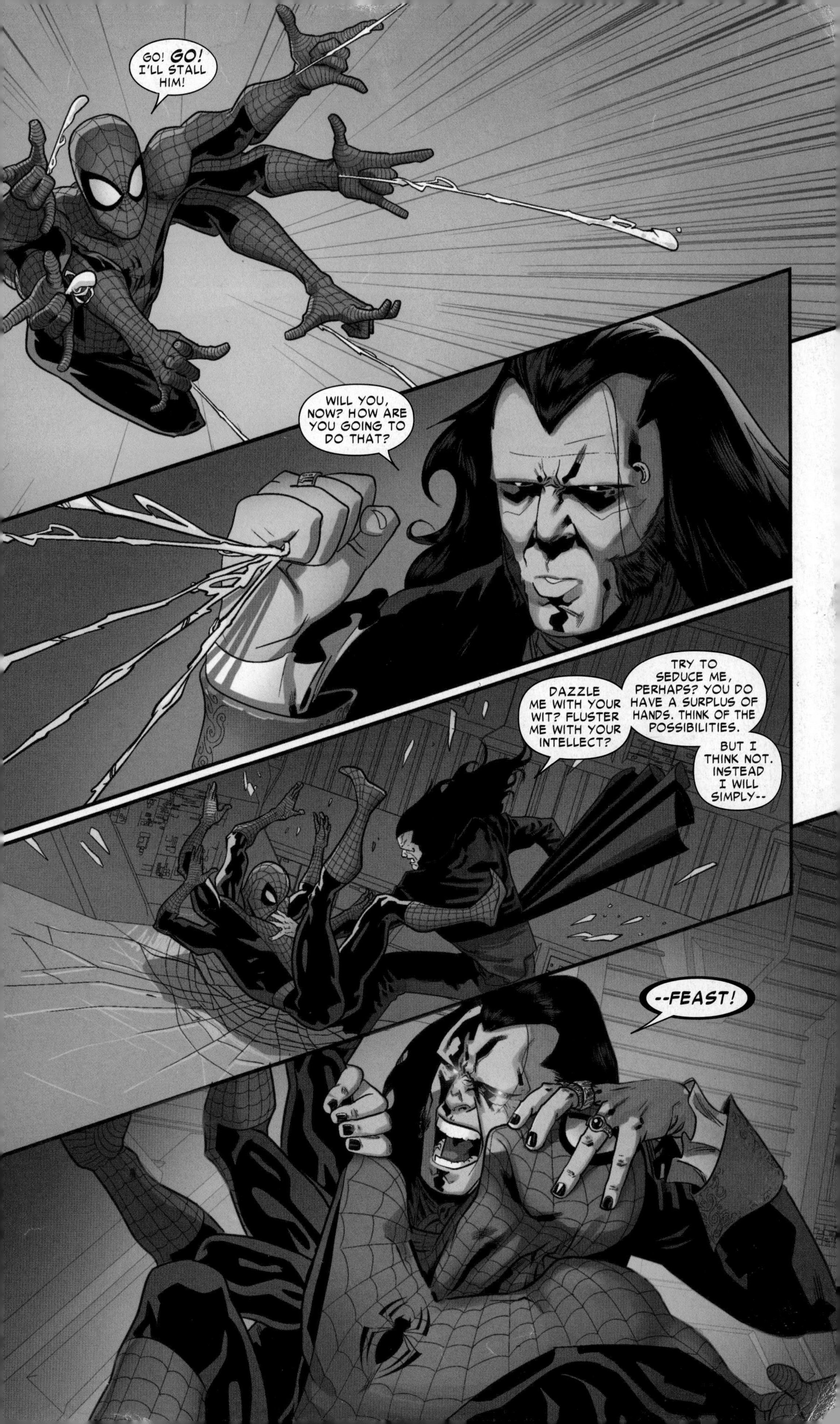
GO! GO! I'LL STALL HIM!
WILL YOU, NOW? HOW ARE YOU GOING TO DO THAT?
DAZZLE ME WITH YOUR WIT? FLUSTER ME WITH YOUR INTELLECT?
TRY TO SEDUCE ME, PERHAPS? YOU DO HAVE A SURPLUS OF HANDS. THINK OF THE POSSIBILITIES.
BUT I THINK NOT. INSTEAD I WILL SIMPLY--
--FEAST!

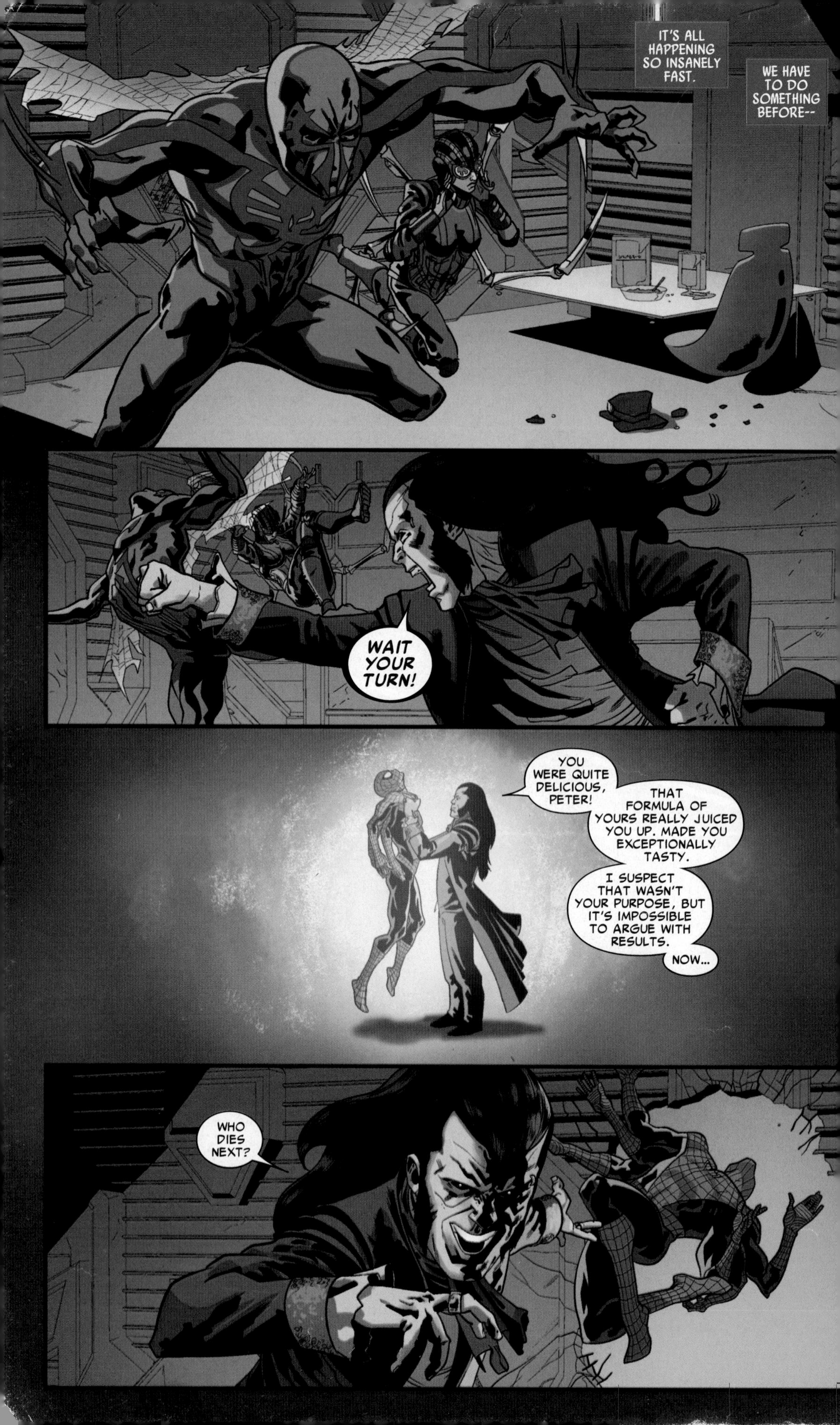
IT'S ALL HAPPENING SO INSANELY FAST.
WE HAVE TO DO SOMETHING BEFORE--
WAIT YOUR TURN!
YOU WERE QUITE DELICIOUS, PETER!
THAT FORMULA OF YOURS REALLY JUICED YOU UP. MADE YOU EXCEPTIONALLY TASTY.
I SUSPECT THAT WASN'T YOUR PURPOSE, BUT IT'S IMPOSSIBLE TO ARGUE WITH RESULTS.
NOW...
WHO DIES NEXT?

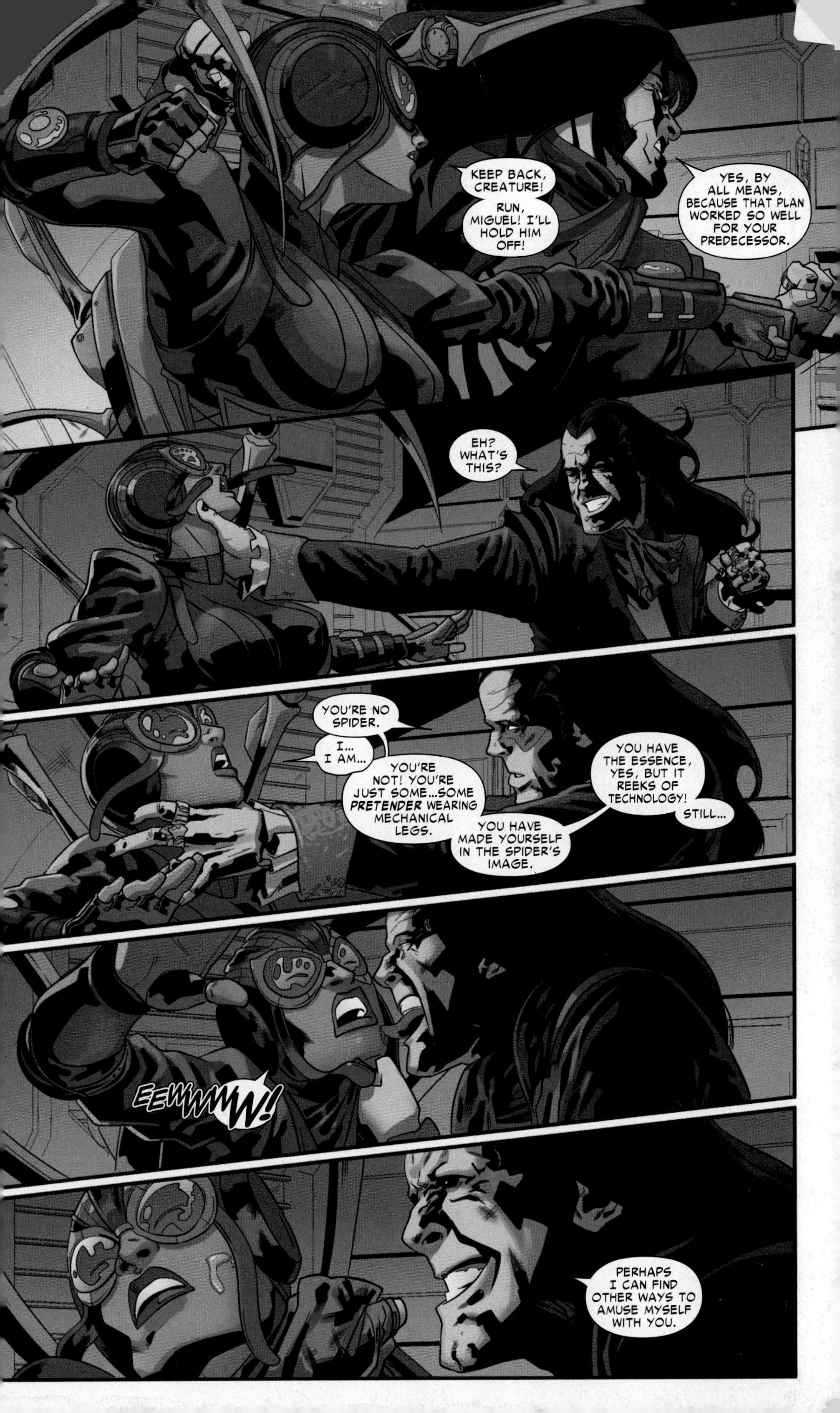
KEEP BACK, CREATURE!
RUN, MIGUEL! I'LL HOLD HIM OFF!
YES, BY ALL MEANS, BECAUSE THAT PLAN WORKED SO WELL FOR YOUR PREDECESSOR.
EH? WHAT'S THIS?
YOU'RE NO SPIDER.
I... I AM...
YOU'RE NOT! YOU'RE JUST SOME...SOME PRETENDER WEARING MECHANICAL LEGS.
YOU HAVE MADE YOURSELF IN THE SPIDER'S IMAGE.
YOU HAVE THE ESSENCE, YES, BUT IT REEKS OF TECHNOLOGY!
STILL...
EEWWWW!
PERHAPS I CAN FIND OTHER WAYS TO AMUSE MYSELF WITH YOU.

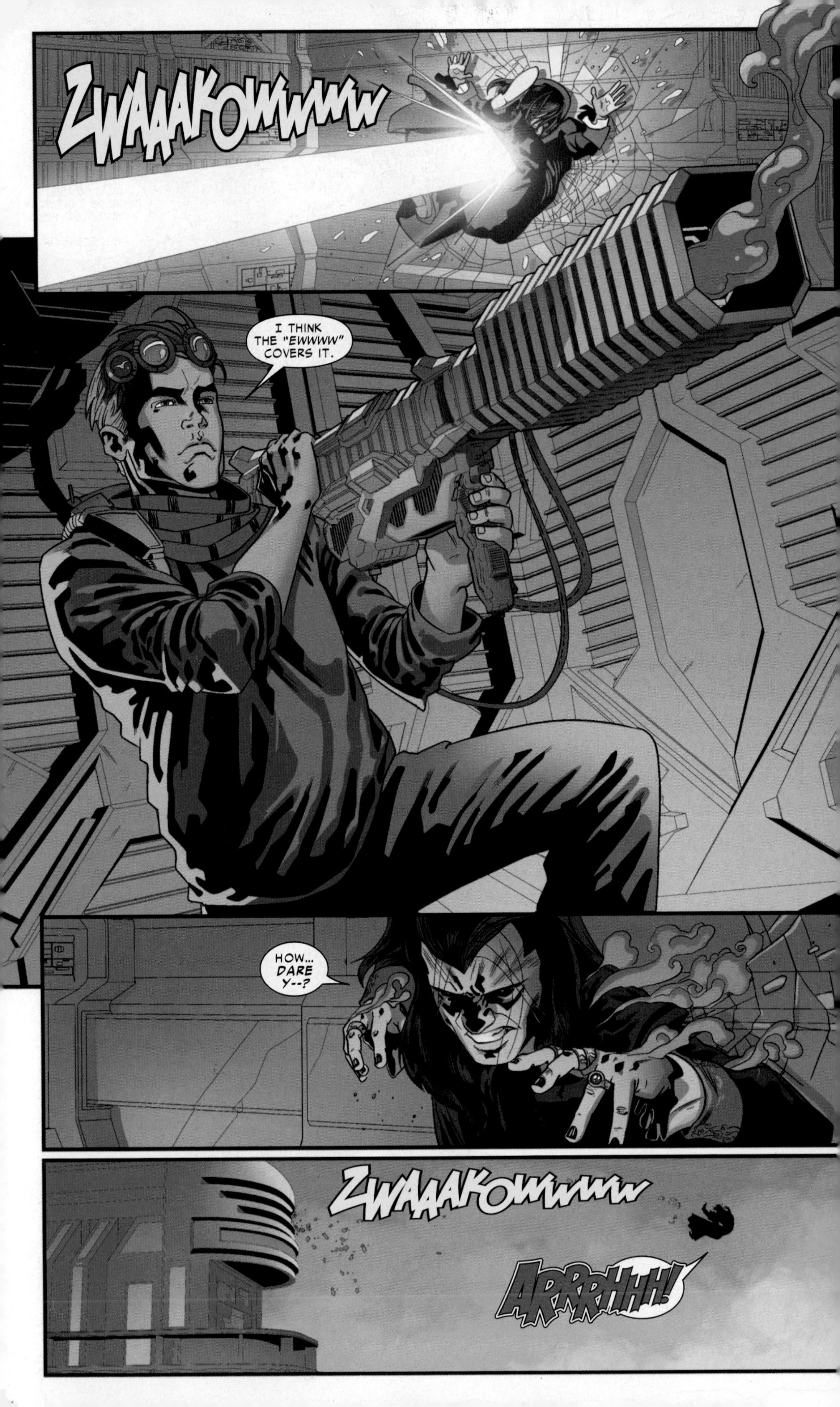
ZWAAAKOWWWWW
I THINK THE "EWWWW" COVERS IT.
HOW... DARE Y--?
ZWAAAKOWWWWW
ARRRHHH!

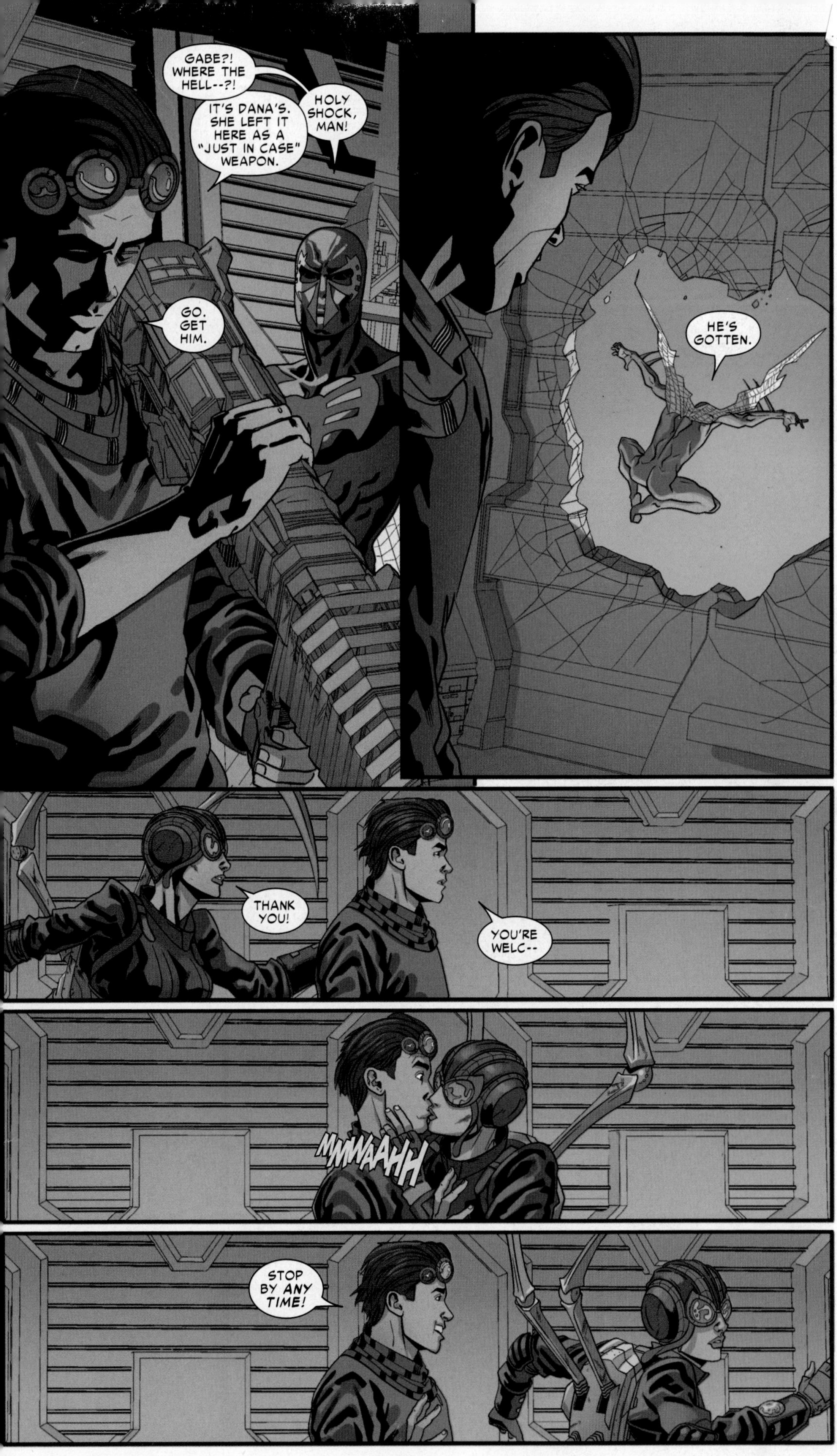
GABE?! WHERE THE HELL--?!
HOLY SHOCK, MAN!
IT'S DANA'S. SHE LEFT IT HERE AS A "JUST IN CASE" WEAPON.
GO. GET HIM.
HE'S GOTTEN.
THANK YOU!
YOU'RE WELC--
MMWAAHH
STOP BY ANY TIME!

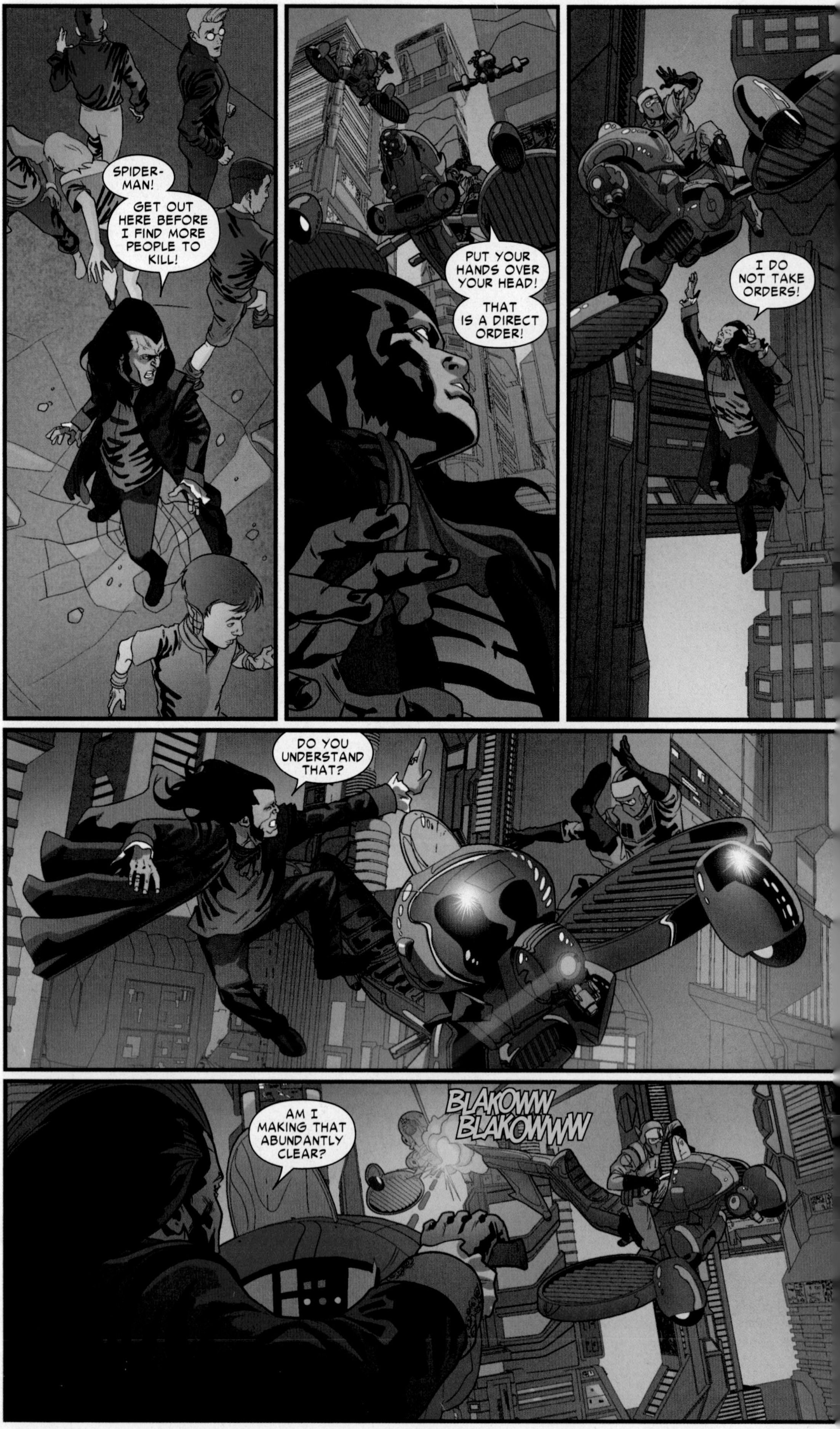
SPIDER-MAN!
GET OUT HERE BEFORE I FIND MORE PEOPLE TO KILL!
PUT YOUR HANDS OVER YOUR HEAD!
THAT IS A DIRECT ORDER!
I DO NOT TAKE ORDERS!
DO YOU UNDERSTAND THAT?
AM I MAKING THAT ABUNDANTLY CLEAR?
BLAKOWW
BLAKOWWW

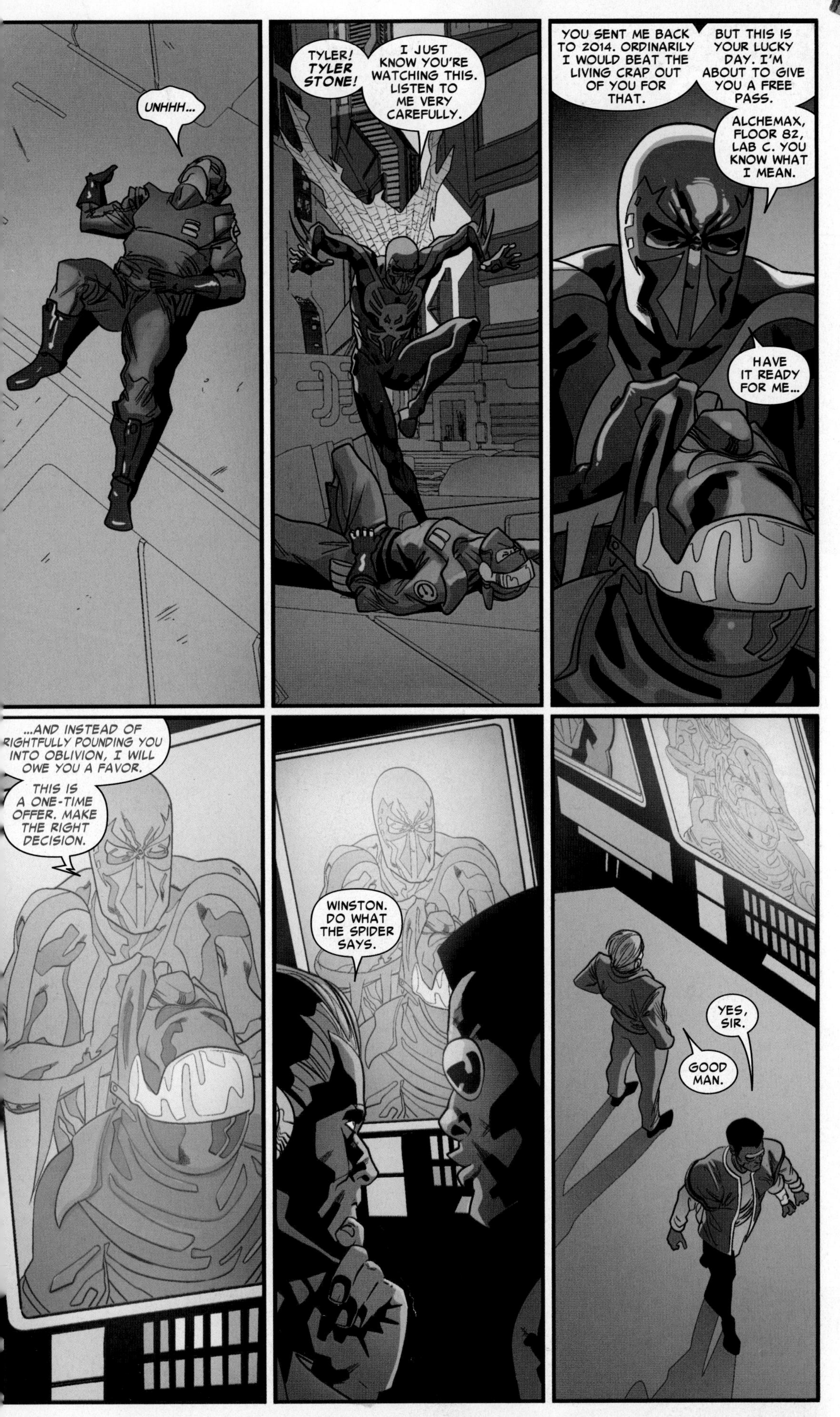
UNHHH...
TYLER! TYLER STONE!
I JUST KNOW YOU'RE WATCHING THIS. LISTEN TO ME VERY CAREFULLY.
YOU SENT ME BACK TO 2014. ORDINARILY I WOULD BEAT THE LIVING CRAP OUT OF YOU FOR THAT.
BUT THIS IS YOUR LUCKY DAY. I'M ABOUT TO GIVE YOU A FREE PASS.
ALCHEMAX, FLOOR 82, LAB C. YOU KNOW WHAT I MEAN.
HAVE IT READY FOR ME...
...AND INSTEAD OF RIGHTFULLY POUNDING YOU INTO OBLIVION, I WILL OWE YOU A FAVOR.
THIS IS A ONE-TIME OFFER. MAKE THE RIGHT DECISION.
WINSTON. DO WHAT THE SPIDER SAYS.
YES, SIR.
GOOD MAN.

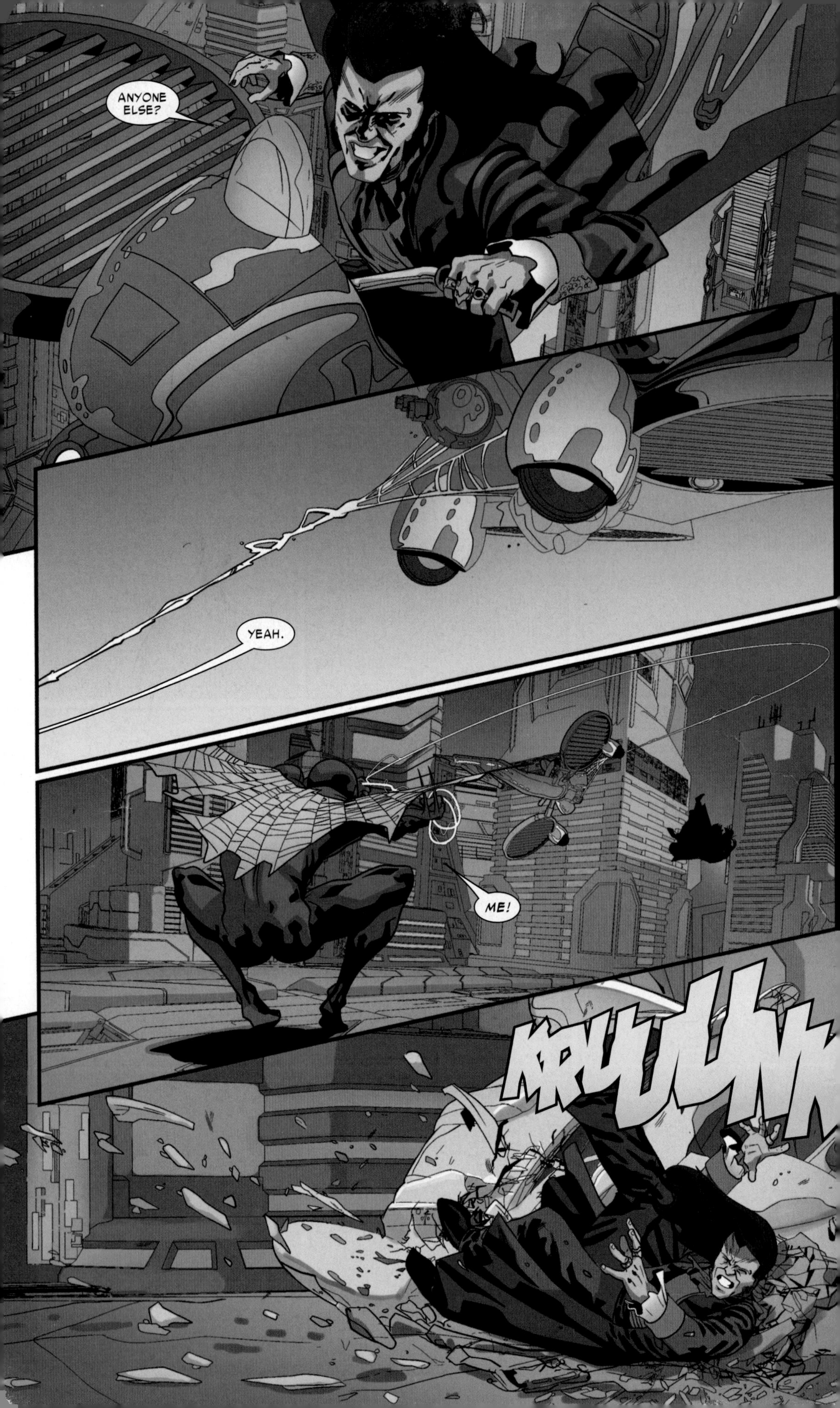
ANYONE ELSE?
YEAH.
ME!
KRUUNK

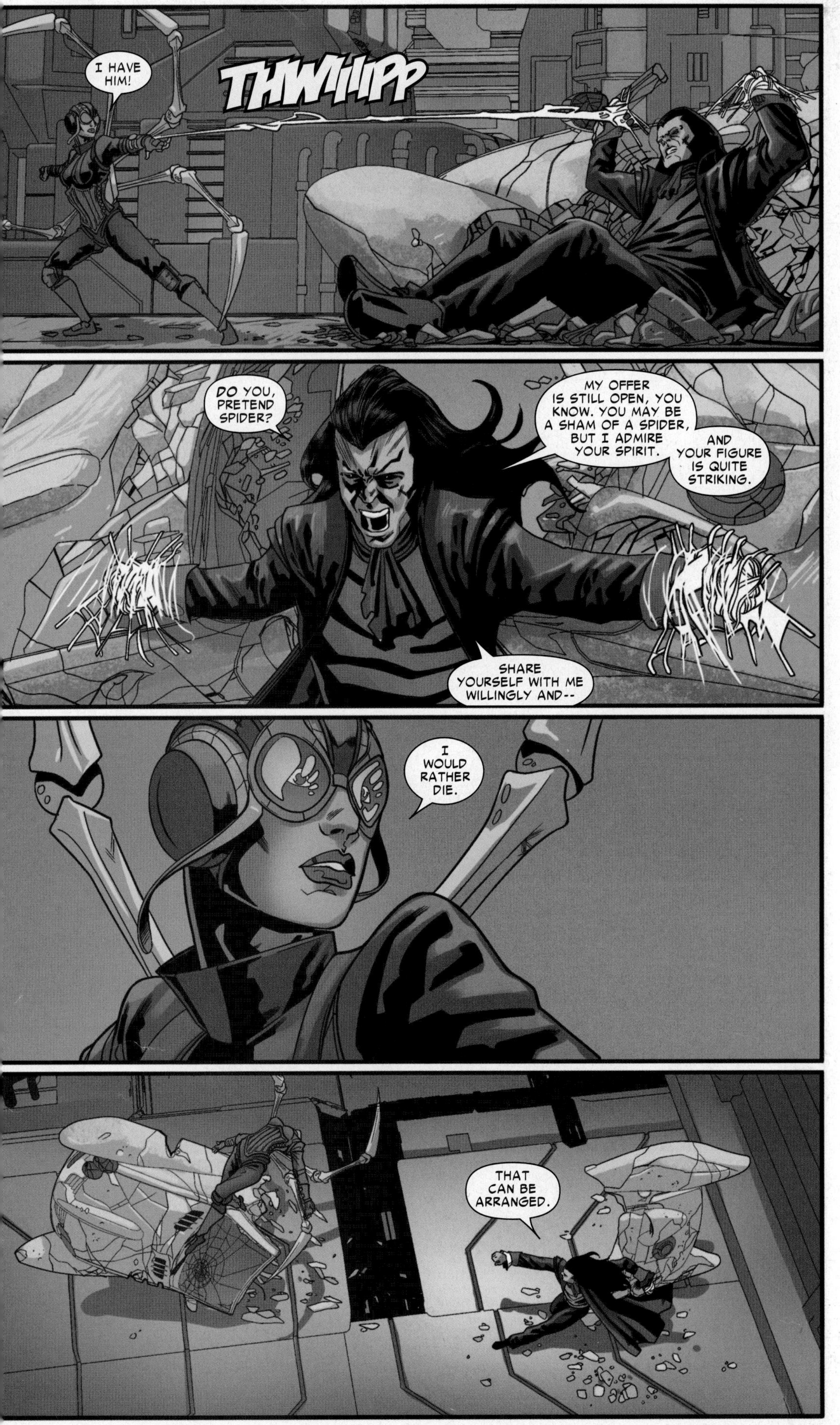

I HAVE HIM!
THWIIIPP
DO YOU, PRETEND SPIDER?
MY OFFER IS STILL OPEN, YOU KNOW. YOU MAY BE A SHAM OF A SPIDER, BUT I ADMIRE YOUR SPIRIT.
AND YOUR FIGURE IS QUITE STRIKING.
SHARE YOURSELF WITH ME WILLINGLY AND--
I WOULD RATHER DIE.
THAT CAN BE ARRANGED.

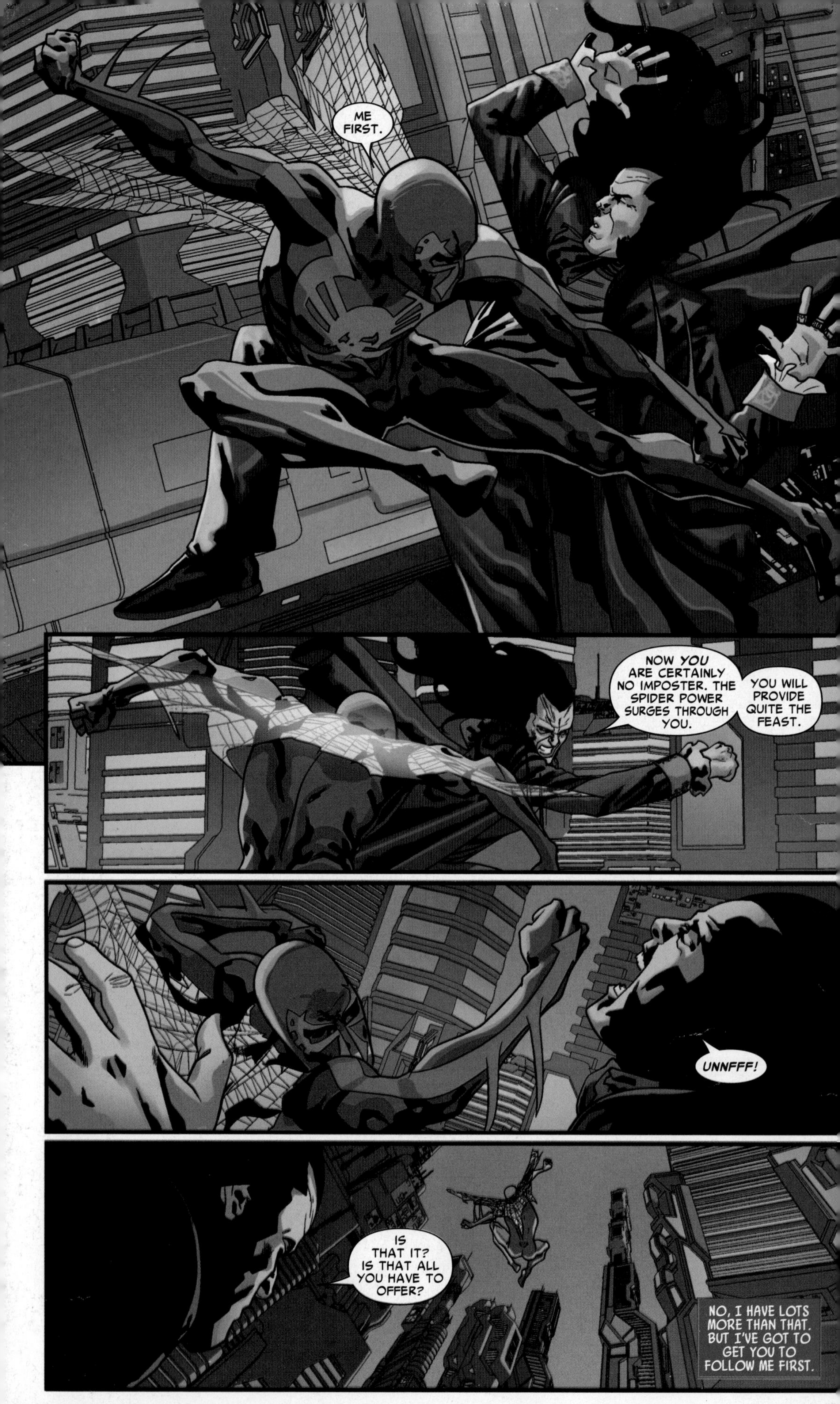
ME FIRST.
NOW YOU ARE CERTAINLY NO IMPOSTER. THE SPIDER POWER SURGES THROUGH YOU.
YOU WILL PROVIDE QUITE THE FEAST.
UNNFFF!
IS THAT IT? IS THAT ALL YOU HAVE TO OFFER?
NO, I HAVE LOTS MORE THAN THAT. BUT I'VE GOT TO GET YOU TO FOLLOW ME FIRST.

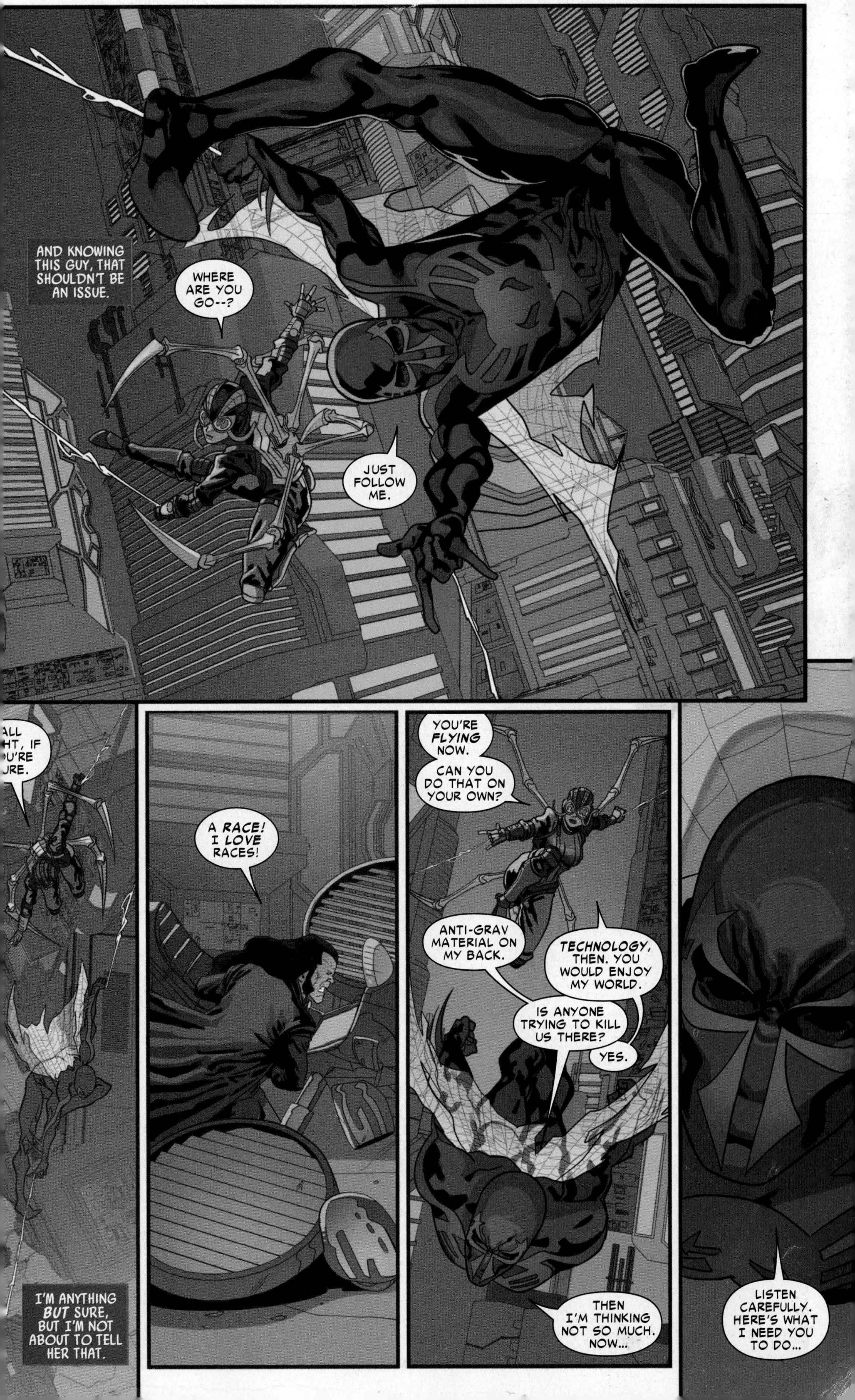

AND KNOWING THIS GUY, THAT SHOULDN'T BE AN ISSUE.
WHERE ARE YOU GO--?
JUST FOLLOW ME.
ALL RIGHT, IF YOU'RE SURE.
I'M ANYTHING *BUT* SURE, BUT I'M NOT ABOUT TO TELL HER THAT.
A *RACE!* I *LOVE* RACES!
YOU'RE *FLYING* NOW.
CAN YOU DO THAT ON YOUR OWN?
ANTI-GRAV MATERIAL ON MY BACK.
TECHNOLOGY, THEN. YOU WOULD ENJOY MY WORLD.
IS ANYONE TRYING TO KILL US THERE?
YES.
THEN I'M THINKING NOT SO MUCH. NOW...
LISTEN CAREFULLY. HERE'S WHAT I NEED YOU TO DO...

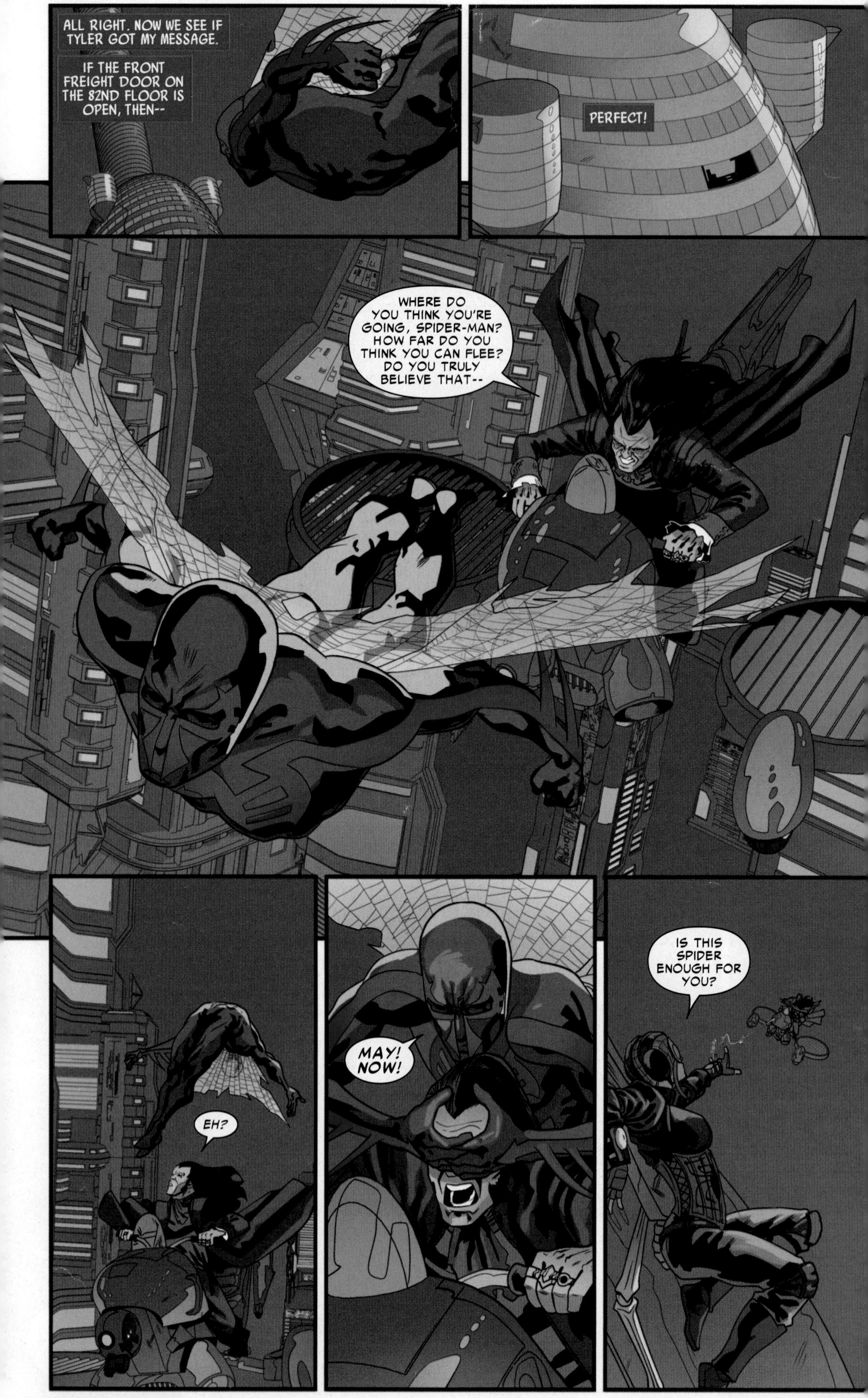

ALL RIGHT. NOW WE SEE IF TYLER GOT MY MESSAGE.
IF THE FRONT FREIGHT DOOR ON THE 82ND FLOOR IS OPEN, THEN--
PERFECT!
WHERE DO YOU THINK YOU'RE GOING, SPIDER-MAN? HOW FAR DO YOU THINK YOU CAN FLEE? DO YOU TRULY BELIEVE THAT--
EH?
MAY! NOW!
IS THIS SPIDER ENOUGH FOR YOU?

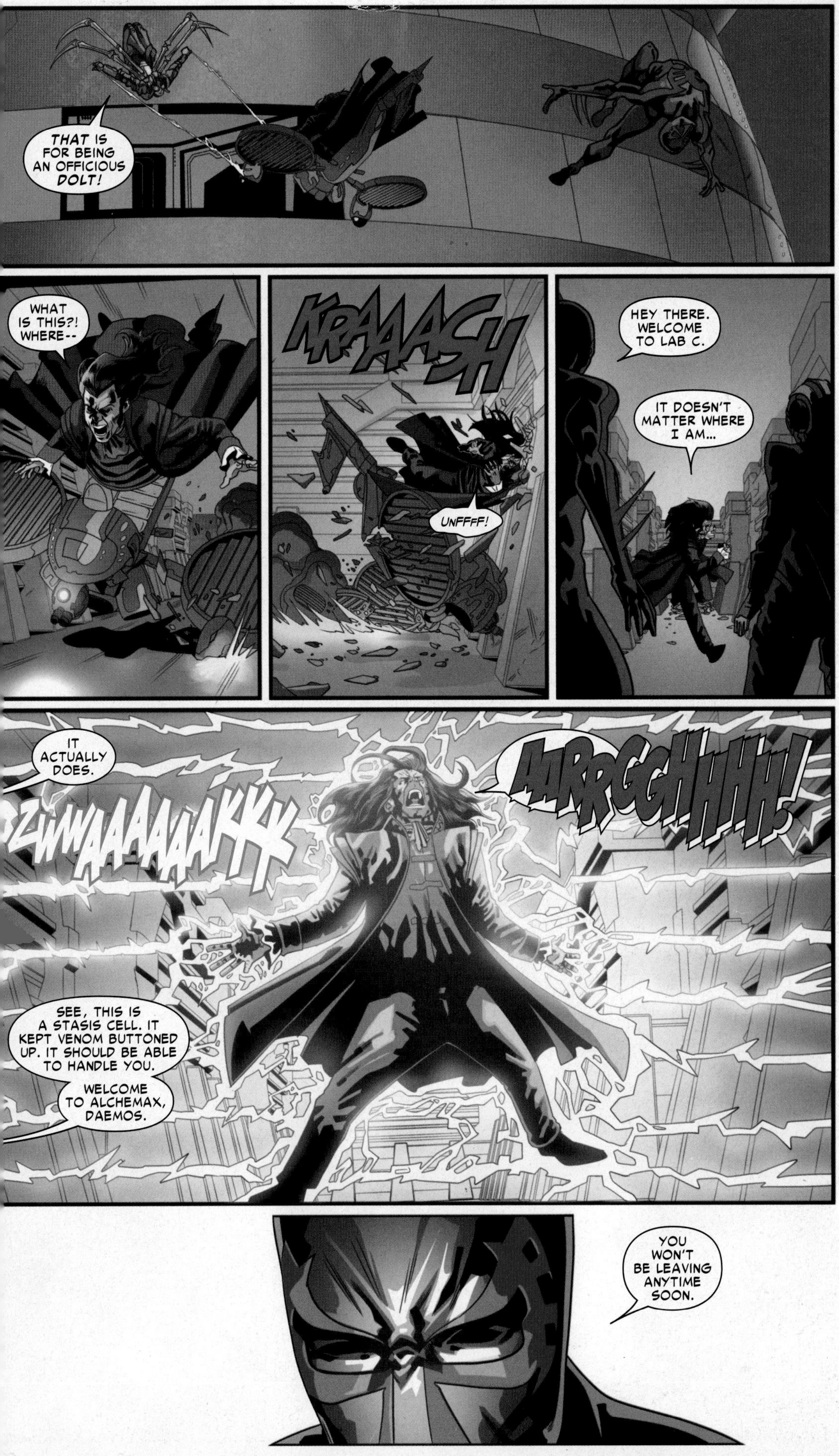
THAT IS FOR BEING AN OFFICIOUS DOLT!
WHAT IS THIS?! WHERE--
KRAAASH
UNFFFF!
HEY THERE. WELCOME TO LAB C.
IT DOESN'T MATTER WHERE I AM...
IT ACTUALLY DOES.
ZWWAAAAAAKKK
AARRGGHHHH!
SEE, THIS IS A STASIS CELL. IT KEPT VENOM BUTTONED UP. IT SHOULD BE ABLE TO HANDLE YOU.
WELCOME TO ALCHEMAX, DAEMOS.
YOU WON'T BE LEAVING ANYTIME SOON.

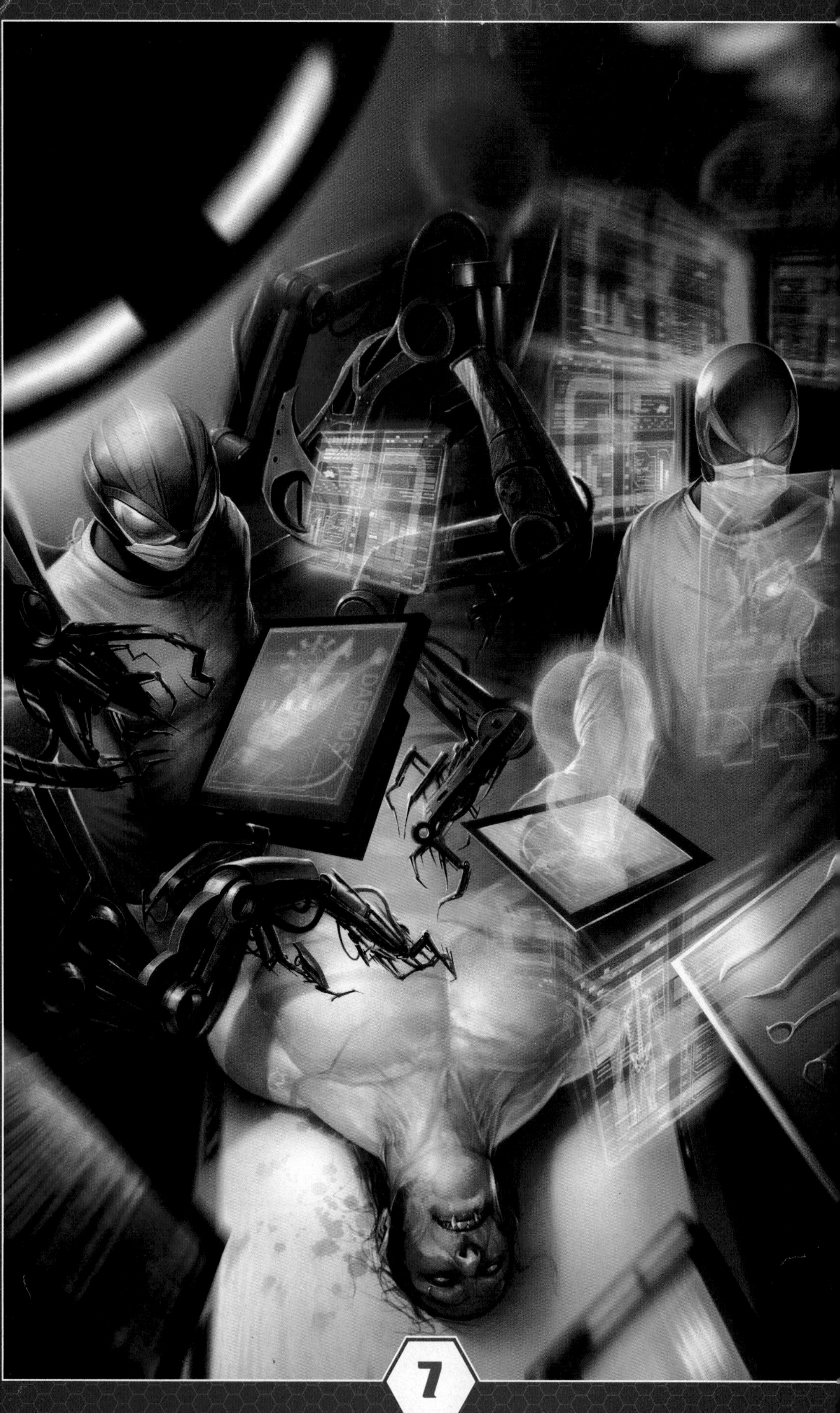

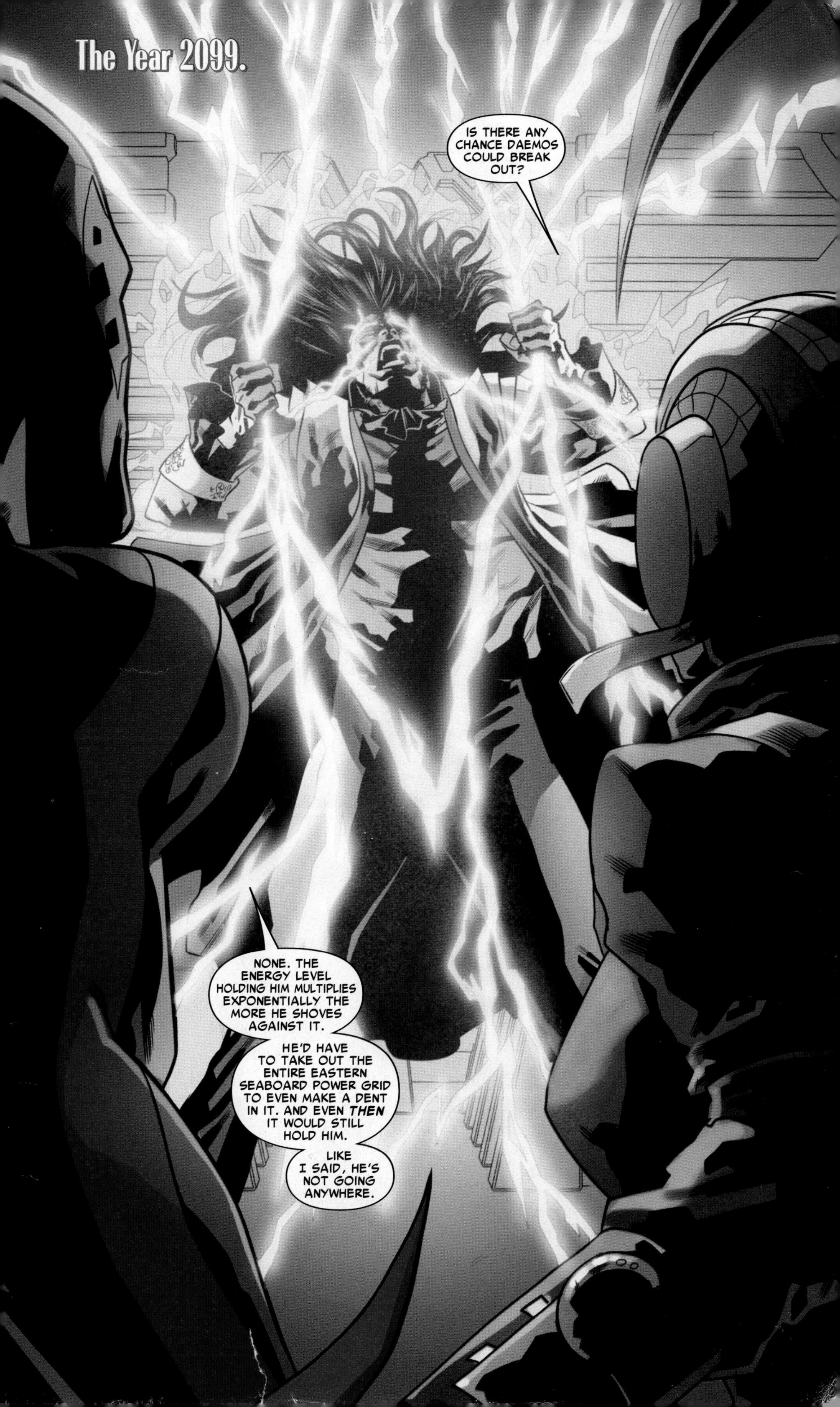
The Year 2099.
IS THERE ANY CHANCE DAEMOS COULD BREAK OUT?
NONE. THE ENERGY LEVEL HOLDING HIM MULTIPLIES EXPONENTIALLY THE MORE HE SHOVES AGAINST IT.
HE'D HAVE TO TAKE OUT THE ENTIRE EASTERN SEABOARD POWER GRID TO EVEN MAKE A DENT IN IT. AND EVEN *THEN* IT WOULD STILL HOLD HIM.
LIKE I SAID, HE'S NOT GOING ANYWHERE.

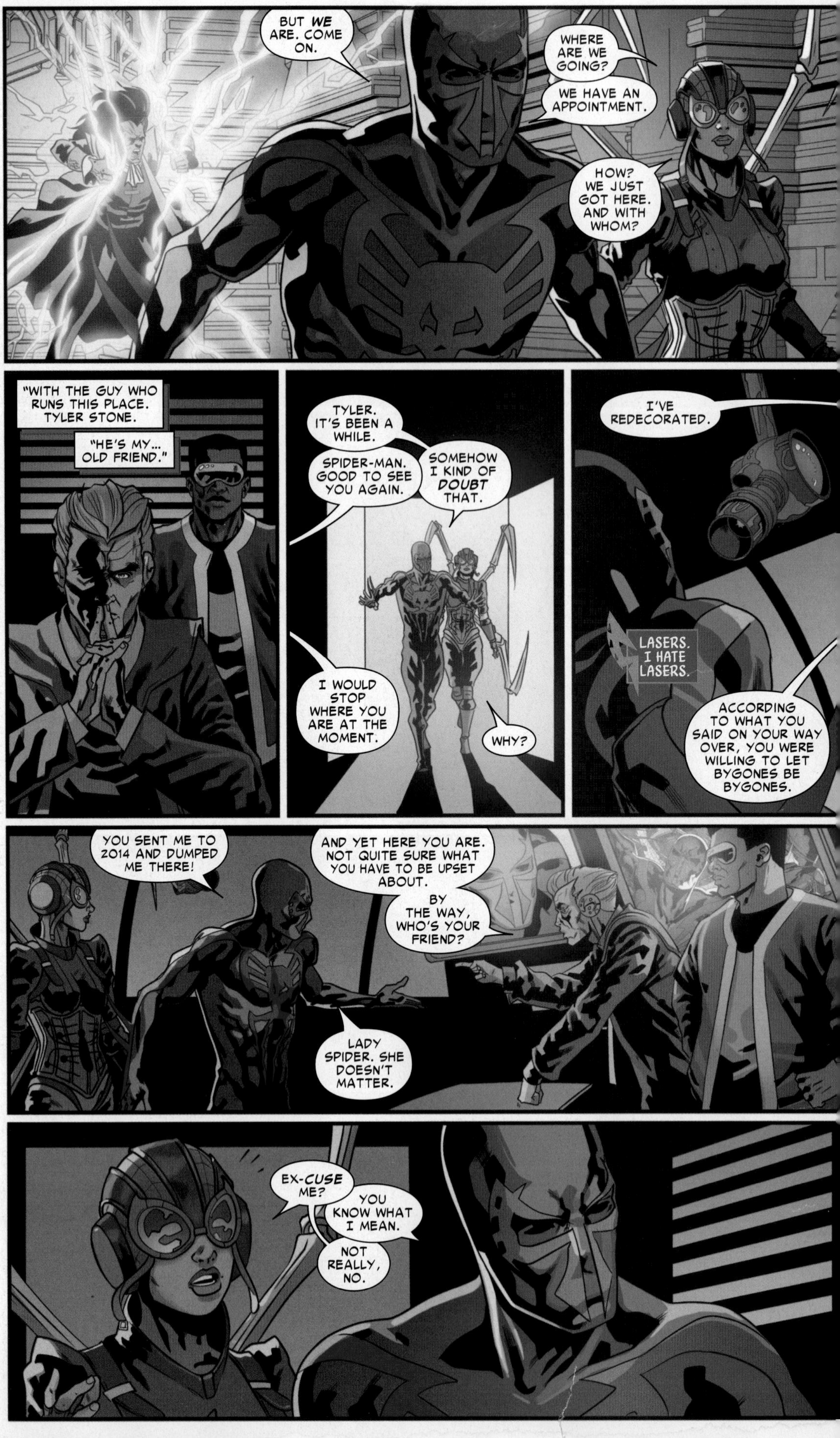
BUT WE ARE. COME ON.
WHERE ARE WE GOING?
WE HAVE AN APPOINTMENT.
HOW? WE JUST GOT HERE. AND WITH WHOM?
"WITH THE GUY WHO RUNS THIS PLACE. TYLER STONE.
"HE'S MY... OLD FRIEND."
TYLER. IT'S BEEN A WHILE.
SPIDER-MAN. GOOD TO SEE YOU AGAIN.
SOMEHOW I KIND OF DOUBT THAT.
I WOULD STOP WHERE YOU ARE AT THE MOMENT.
WHY?
I'VE REDECORATED.
LASERS. I HATE LASERS.
ACCORDING TO WHAT YOU SAID ON YOUR WAY OVER, YOU WERE WILLING TO LET BYGONES BE BYGONES.
YOU SENT ME TO 2014 AND DUMPED ME THERE!
AND YET HERE YOU ARE. NOT QUITE SURE WHAT YOU HAVE TO BE UPSET ABOUT.
BY THE WAY, WHO'S YOUR FRIEND?
LADY SPIDER. SHE DOESN'T MATTER.
EX-CUSE ME?
YOU KNOW WHAT I MEAN.
NOT REALLY, NO.

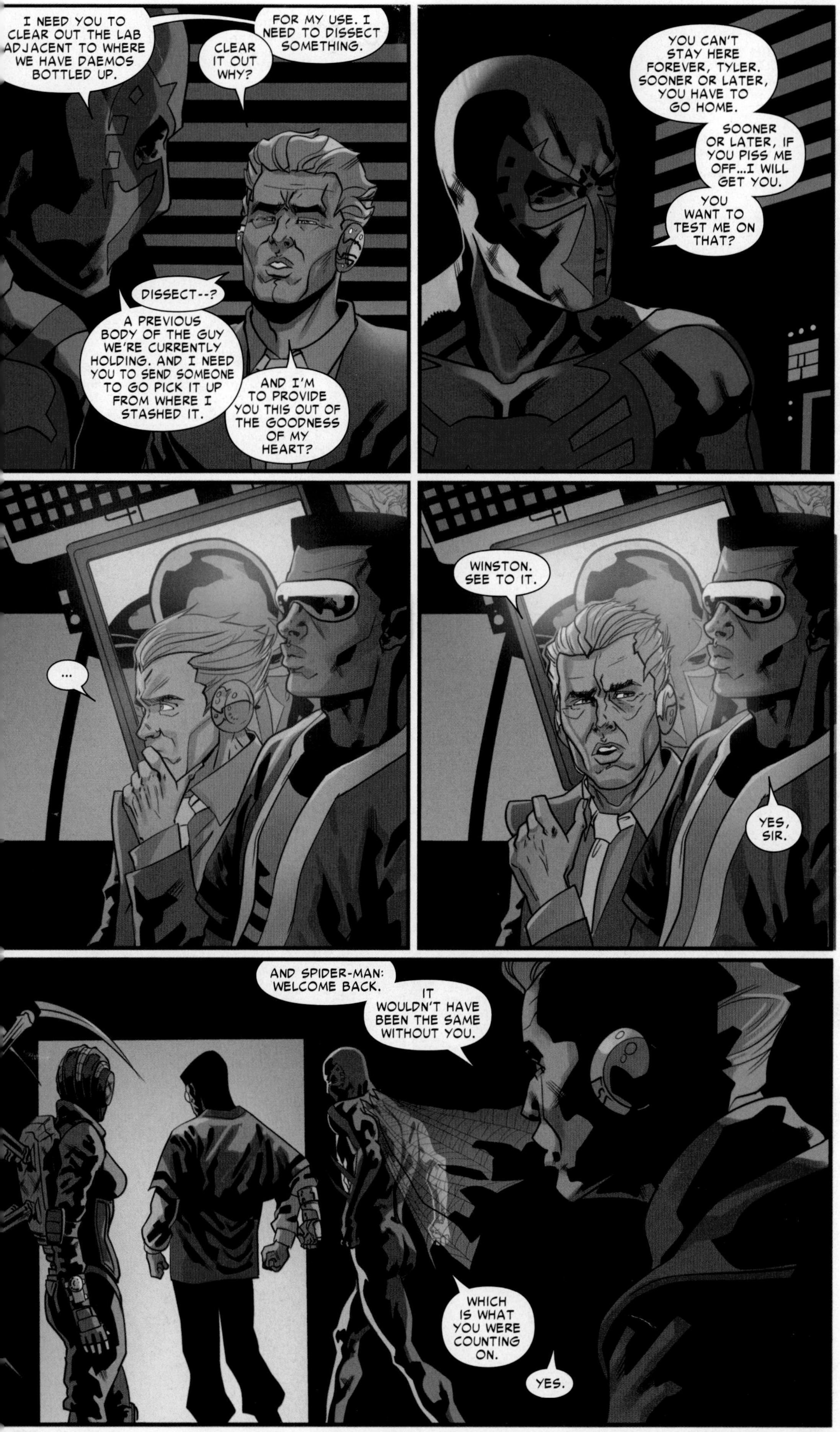
I NEED YOU TO CLEAR OUT THE LAB ADJACENT TO WHERE WE HAVE DAEMOS BOTTLED UP.
CLEAR IT OUT WHY?
FOR MY USE. I NEED TO DISSECT SOMETHING.
DISSECT--?
A PREVIOUS BODY OF THE GUY WE'RE CURRENTLY HOLDING. AND I NEED YOU TO SEND SOMEONE TO GO PICK IT UP FROM WHERE I STASHED IT.
AND I'M TO PROVIDE YOU THIS OUT OF THE GOODNESS OF MY HEART?
YOU CAN'T STAY HERE FOREVER, TYLER. SOONER OR LATER, YOU HAVE TO GO HOME.
SOONER OR LATER, IF YOU PISS ME OFF...I WILL GET YOU.
YOU WANT TO TEST ME ON THAT?
...
WINSTON. SEE TO IT.
YES, SIR.
AND SPIDER-MAN: WELCOME BACK.
IT WOULDN'T HAVE BEEN THE SAME WITHOUT YOU.
WHICH IS WHAT YOU WERE COUNTING ON.
YES.

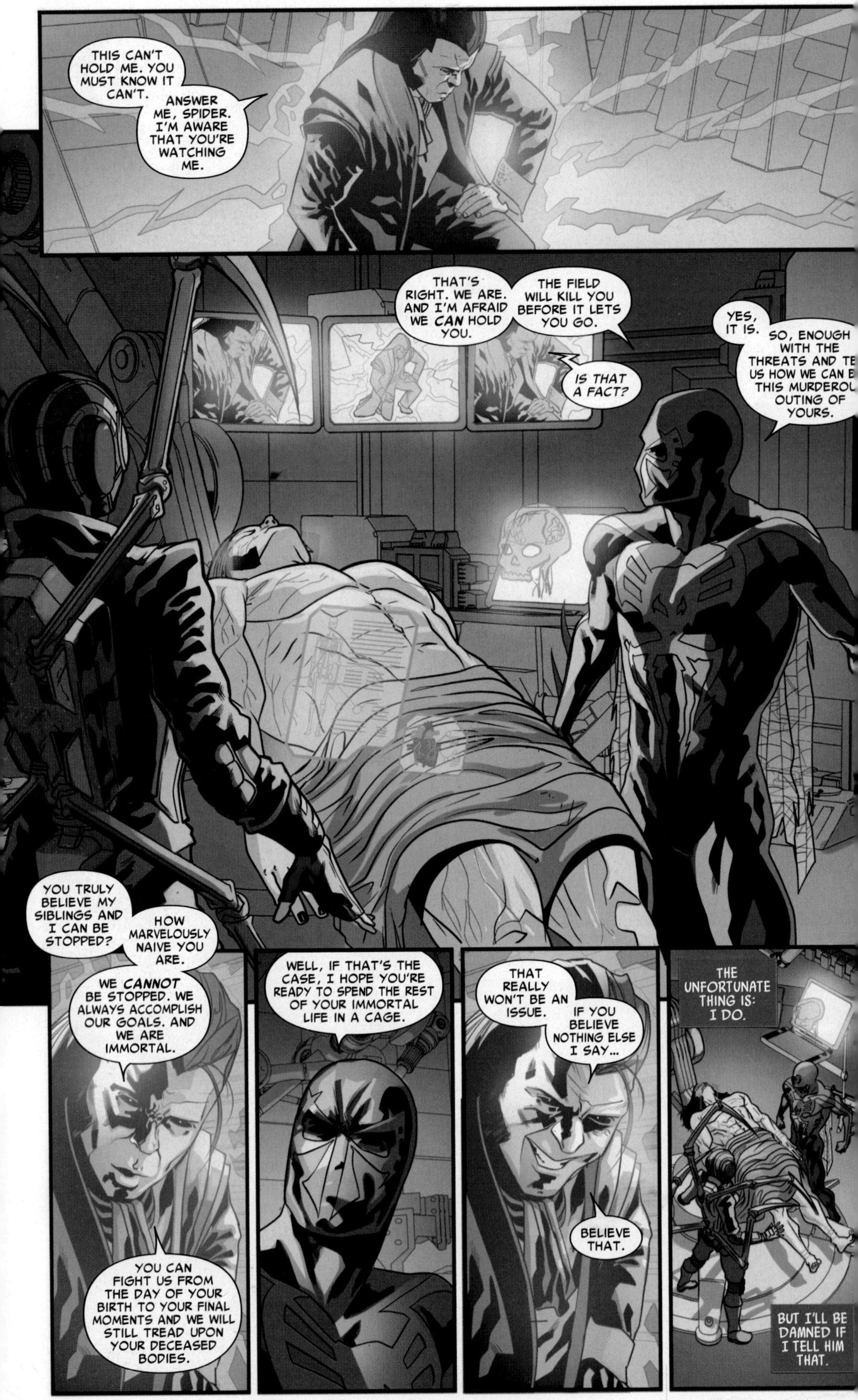
THIS CAN'T HOLD ME. YOU MUST KNOW IT CAN'T.
ANSWER ME, SPIDER. I'M AWARE THAT YOU'RE WATCHING ME.
THAT'S RIGHT. WE ARE. AND I'M AFRAID WE CAN HOLD YOU.
THE FIELD WILL KILL YOU BEFORE IT LETS YOU GO.
IS THAT A FACT?
YES, IT IS.
SO, ENOUGH WITH THE THREATS AND TE US HOW WE CAN E THIS MURDEROU OUTING OF YOURS.
YOU TRULY BELIEVE MY SIBLINGS AND I CAN BE STOPPED?
HOW MARVELOUSLY NAIVE YOU ARE.
WE CANNOT BE STOPPED. WE ALWAYS ACCOMPLISH OUR GOALS. AND WE ARE IMMORTAL.
YOU CAN FIGHT US FROM THE DAY OF YOUR BIRTH TO YOUR FINAL MOMENTS AND WE WILL STILL TREAD UPON YOUR DECEASED BODIES.
WELL, IF THAT'S THE CASE, I HOPE YOU'RE READY TO SPEND THE REST OF YOUR IMMORTAL LIFE IN A CAGE.
THAT REALLY WON'T BE AN ISSUE.
IF YOU BELIEVE NOTHING ELSE I SAY...
BELIEVE THAT.
THE UNFORTUNATE THING IS: I DO.
BUT I'LL BE DAMNED IF I TELL HIM THAT.

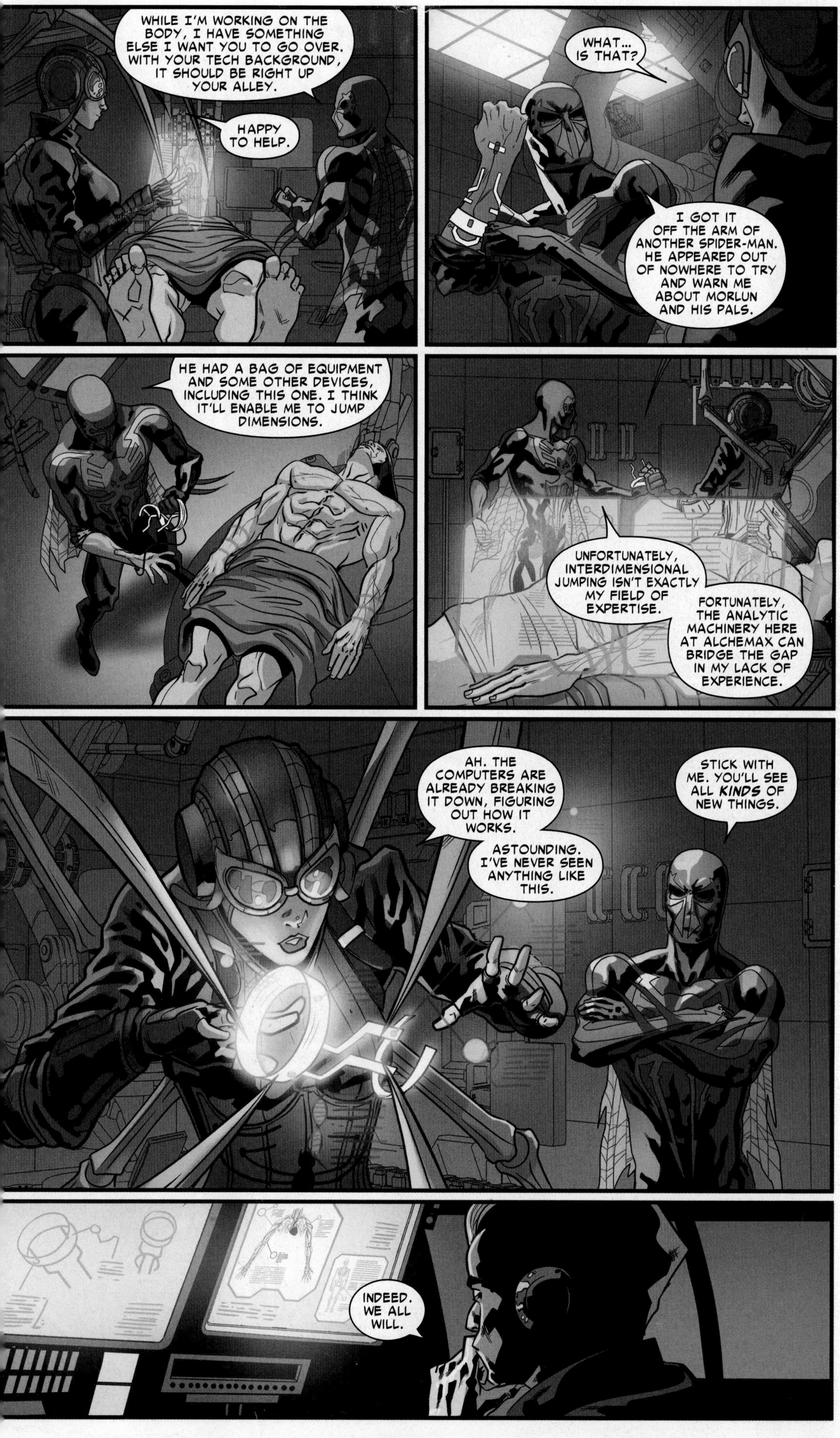
WHILE I'M WORKING ON THE BODY, I HAVE SOMETHING ELSE I WANT YOU TO GO OVER. WITH YOUR TECH BACKGROUND, IT SHOULD BE RIGHT UP YOUR ALLEY.
HAPPY TO HELP.
WHAT... IS THAT?
I GOT IT OFF THE ARM OF ANOTHER SPIDER-MAN. HE APPEARED OUT OF NOWHERE TO TRY AND WARN ME ABOUT MORLUN AND HIS PALS.
HE HAD A BAG OF EQUIPMENT AND SOME OTHER DEVICES, INCLUDING THIS ONE. I THINK IT'LL ENABLE ME TO JUMP DIMENSIONS.
UNFORTUNATELY, INTERDIMENSIONAL JUMPING ISN'T EXACTLY MY FIELD OF EXPERTISE.
FORTUNATELY, THE ANALYTIC MACHINERY HERE AT ALCHEMAX CAN BRIDGE THE GAP IN MY LACK OF EXPERIENCE.
AH. THE COMPUTERS ARE ALREADY BREAKING IT DOWN, FIGURING OUT HOW IT WORKS.
ASTOUNDING. I'VE NEVER SEEN ANYTHING LIKE THIS.
STICK WITH ME. YOU'LL SEE ALL KINDS OF NEW THINGS.
INDEED. WE ALL WILL.

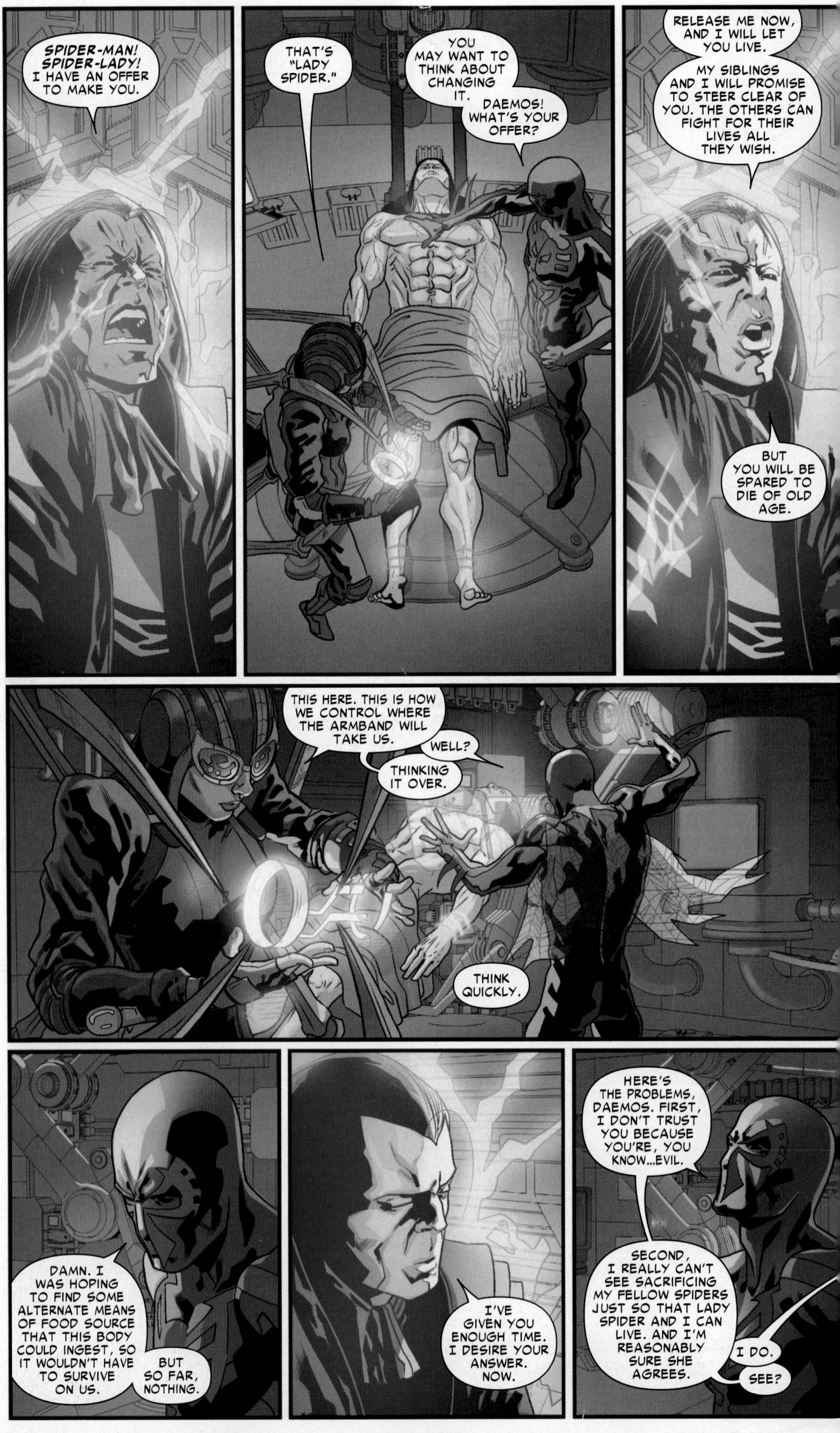
SPIDER-MAN! SPIDER-LADY! I HAVE AN OFFER TO MAKE YOU.
THAT'S "LADY SPIDER."
YOU MAY WANT TO THINK ABOUT CHANGING IT.
DAEMOS! WHAT'S YOUR OFFER?
RELEASE ME NOW, AND I WILL LET YOU LIVE.
MY SIBLINGS AND I WILL PROMISE TO STEER CLEAR OF YOU. THE OTHERS CAN FIGHT FOR THEIR LIVES ALL THEY WISH.
BUT YOU WILL BE SPARED TO DIE OF OLD AGE.
THIS HERE. THIS IS HOW WE CONTROL WHERE THE ARMBAND WILL TAKE US.
WELL?
THINKING IT OVER.
THINK QUICKLY.
DAMN. I WAS HOPING TO FIND SOME ALTERNATE MEANS OF FOOD SOURCE THAT THIS BODY COULD INGEST, SO IT WOULDN'T HAVE TO SURVIVE ON US.
BUT SO FAR, NOTHING.
I'VE GIVEN YOU ENOUGH TIME. I DESIRE YOUR ANSWER. NOW.
HERE'S THE PROBLEMS, DAEMOS. FIRST, I DON'T TRUST YOU BECAUSE YOU'RE, YOU KNOW...EVIL.
SECOND, I REALLY CAN'T SEE SACRIFICING MY FELLOW SPIDERS JUST SO THAT LADY SPIDER AND I CAN LIVE. AND I'M REASONABLY SURE SHE AGREES.
I DO.
SEE?

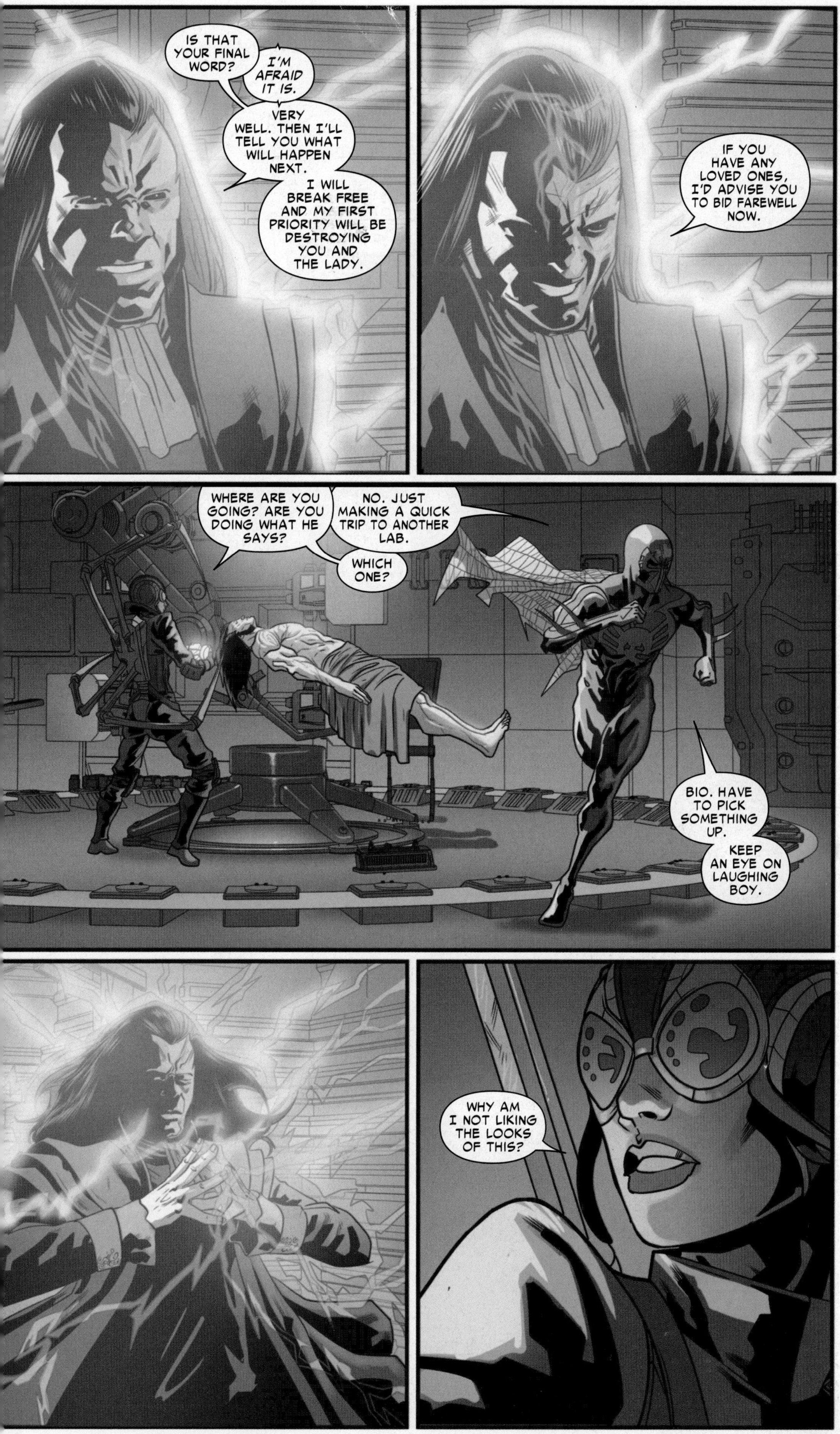
IS THAT YOUR FINAL WORD?
I'M AFRAID IT IS.
VERY WELL. THEN I'LL TELL YOU WHAT WILL HAPPEN NEXT.
I WILL BREAK FREE AND MY FIRST PRIORITY WILL BE DESTROYING YOU AND THE LADY.
IF YOU HAVE ANY LOVED ONES, I'D ADVISE YOU TO BID FAREWELL NOW.
WHERE ARE YOU GOING? ARE YOU DOING WHAT HE SAYS?
NO. JUST MAKING A QUICK TRIP TO ANOTHER LAB.
WHICH ONE?
BIO. HAVE TO PICK SOMETHING UP.
KEEP AN EYE ON LAUGHING BOY.
WHY AM I NOT LIKING THE LOOKS OF THIS?

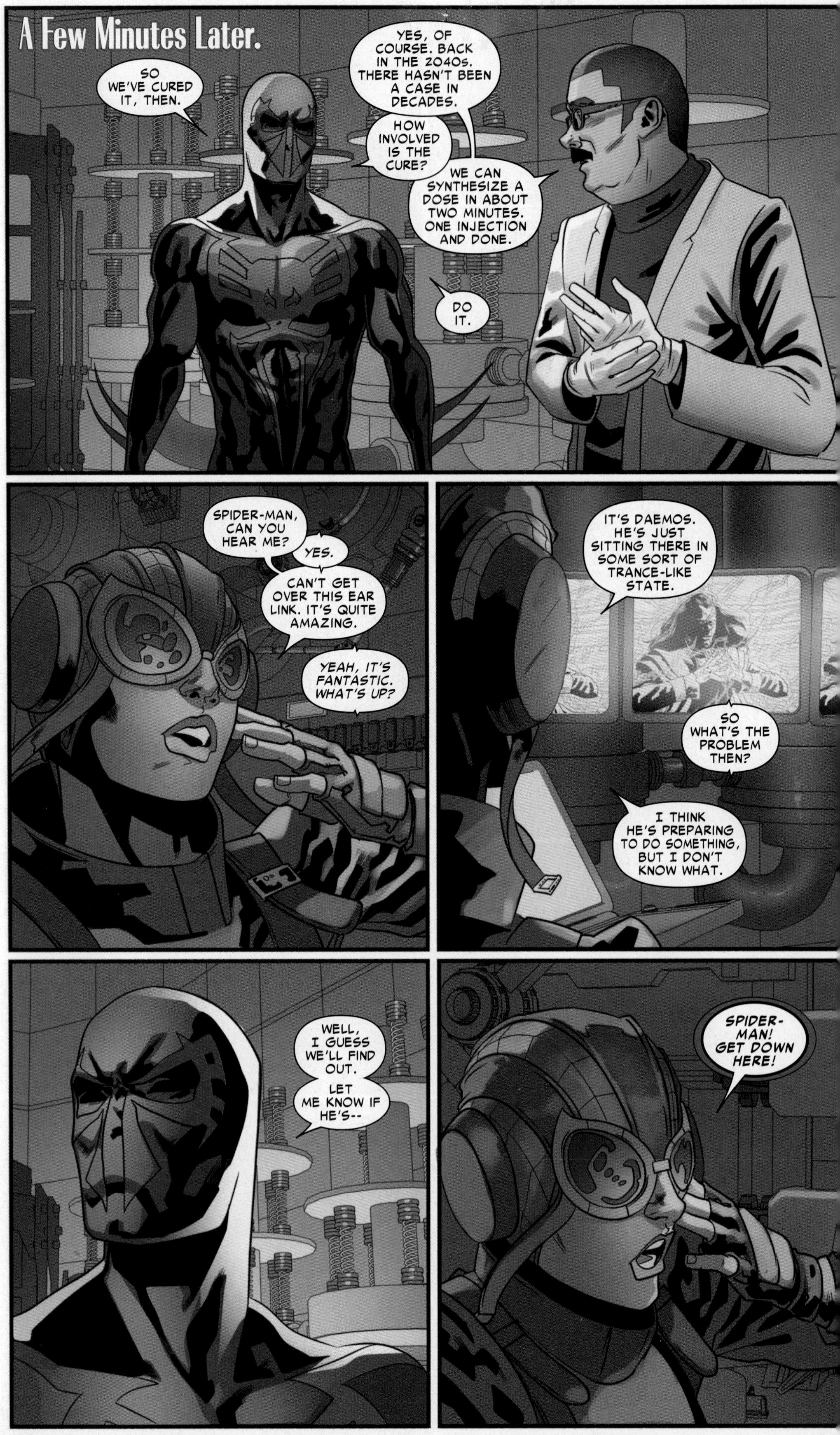
A Few Minutes Later.
SO WE'VE CURED IT, THEN.
YES, OF COURSE. BACK IN THE 2040s. THERE HASN'T BEEN A CASE IN DECADES.
HOW INVOLVED IS THE CURE?
WE CAN SYNTHESIZE A DOSE IN ABOUT TWO MINUTES. ONE INJECTION AND DONE.
DO IT.
SPIDER-MAN, CAN YOU HEAR ME?
YES.
CAN'T GET OVER THIS EAR LINK. IT'S QUITE AMAZING.
YEAH, IT'S FANTASTIC. WHAT'S UP?
IT'S DAEMOS. HE'S JUST SITTING THERE IN SOME SORT OF TRANCE-LIKE STATE.
SO WHAT'S THE PROBLEM THEN?
I THINK HE'S PREPARING TO DO SOMETHING, BUT I DON'T KNOW WHAT.
WELL, I GUESS WE'LL FIND OUT.
LET ME KNOW IF HE'S--
SPIDER-MAN! GET DOWN HERE!

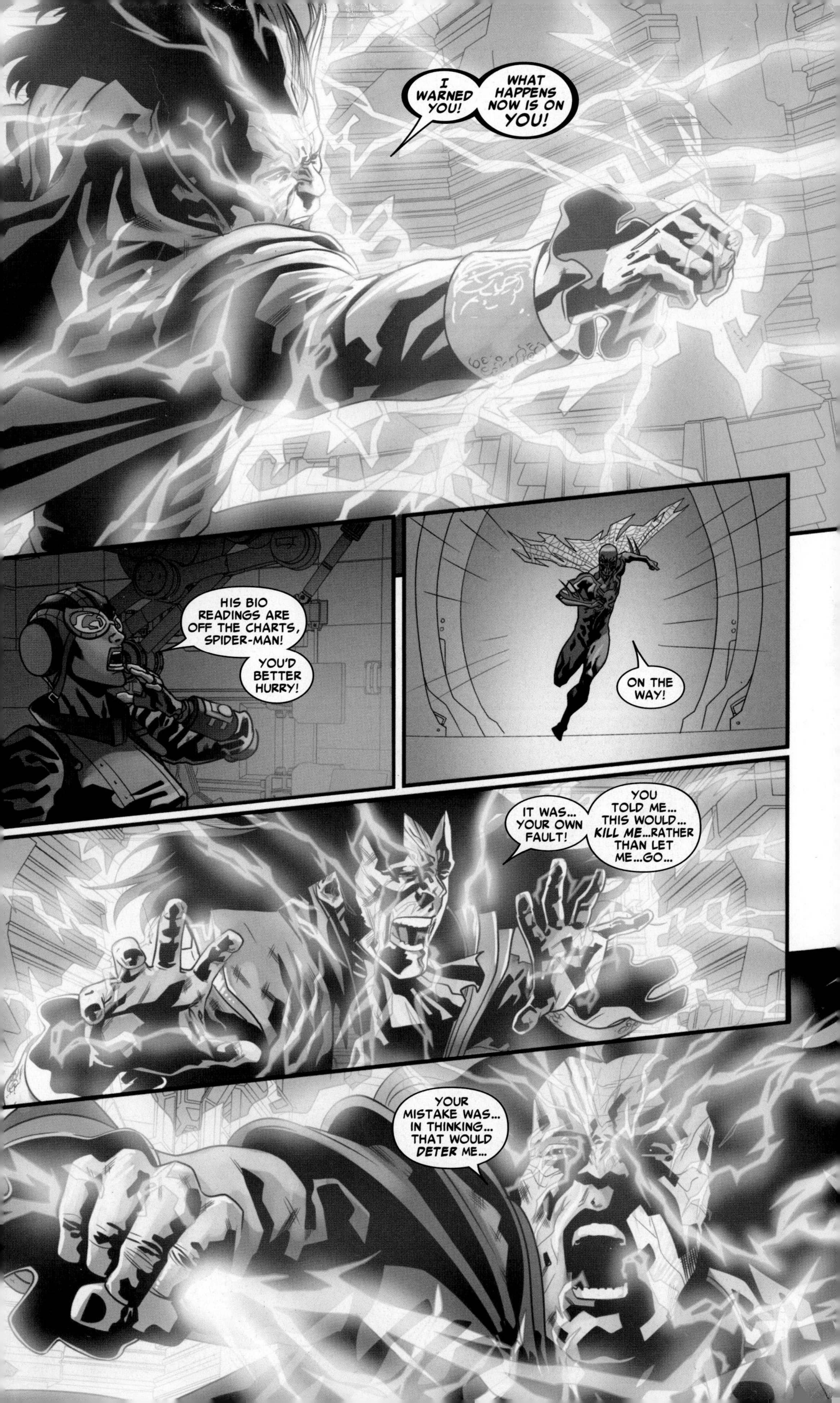

I WARNED YOU!
WHAT HAPPENS NOW IS ON YOU!
HIS BIO READINGS ARE OFF THE CHARTS, SPIDER-MAN!
YOU'D BETTER HURRY!
ON THE WAY!
IT WAS... YOUR OWN FAULT!
YOU TOLD ME... THIS WOULD... KILL ME...RATHER THAN LET ME...GO...
YOUR MISTAKE WAS... IN THINKING... THAT WOULD DETER ME...

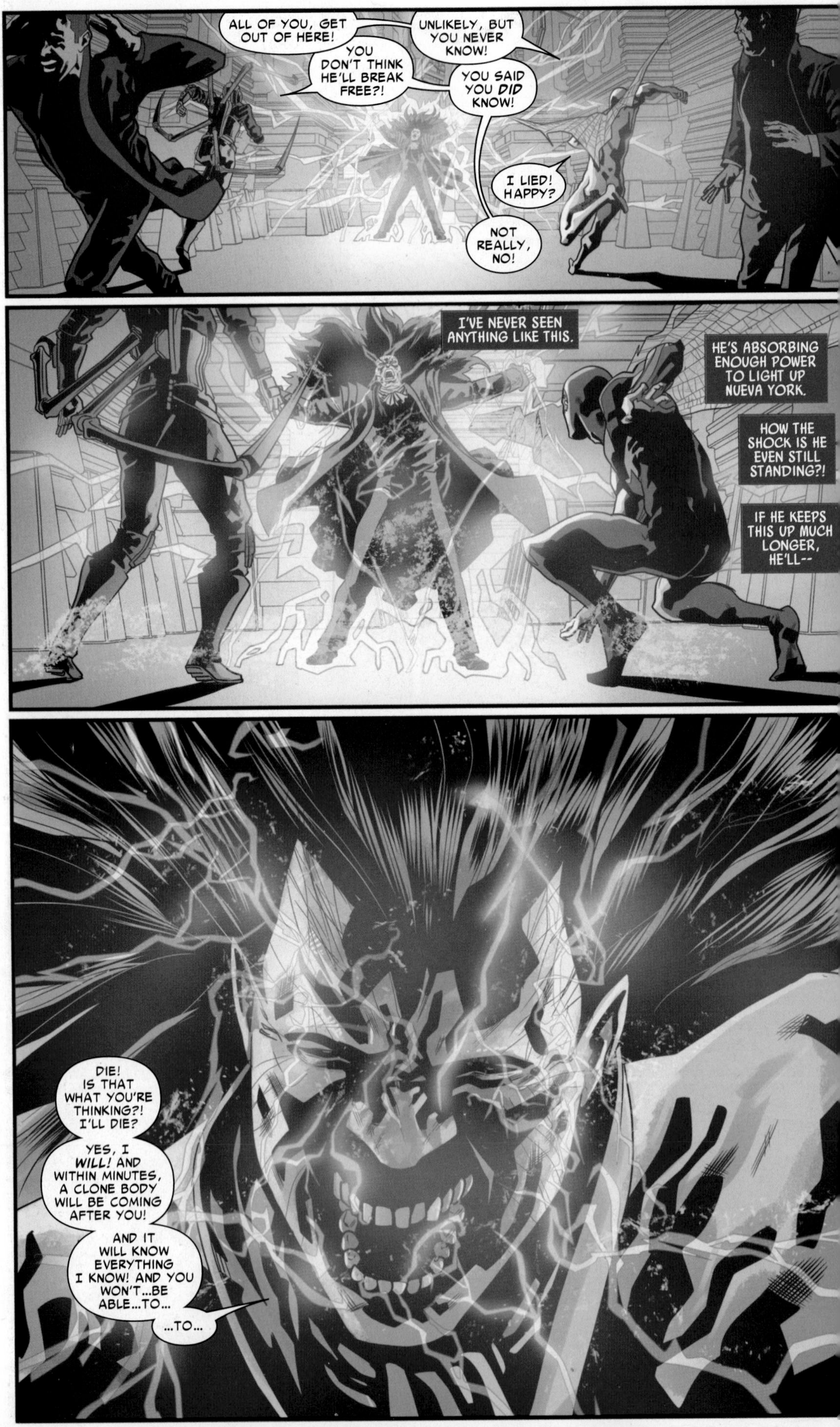
ALL OF YOU, GET OUT OF HERE!
UNLIKELY, BUT YOU NEVER KNOW!
YOU DON'T THINK HE'LL BREAK FREE?!
YOU SAID YOU DID KNOW!
I LIED! HAPPY?
NOT REALLY, NO!
I'VE NEVER SEEN ANYTHING LIKE THIS.
HE'S ABSORBING ENOUGH POWER TO LIGHT UP NUEVA YORK.
HOW THE SHOCK IS HE EVEN STILL STANDING?!
IF HE KEEPS THIS UP MUCH LONGER, HE'LL--
DIE! IS THAT WHAT YOU'RE THINKING?! I'LL DIE?
YES, I WILL! AND WITHIN MINUTES, A CLONE BODY WILL BE COMING AFTER YOU!
AND IT WILL KNOW EVERYTHING I KNOW! AND YOU WON'T...BE ABLE...TO...
...TO...

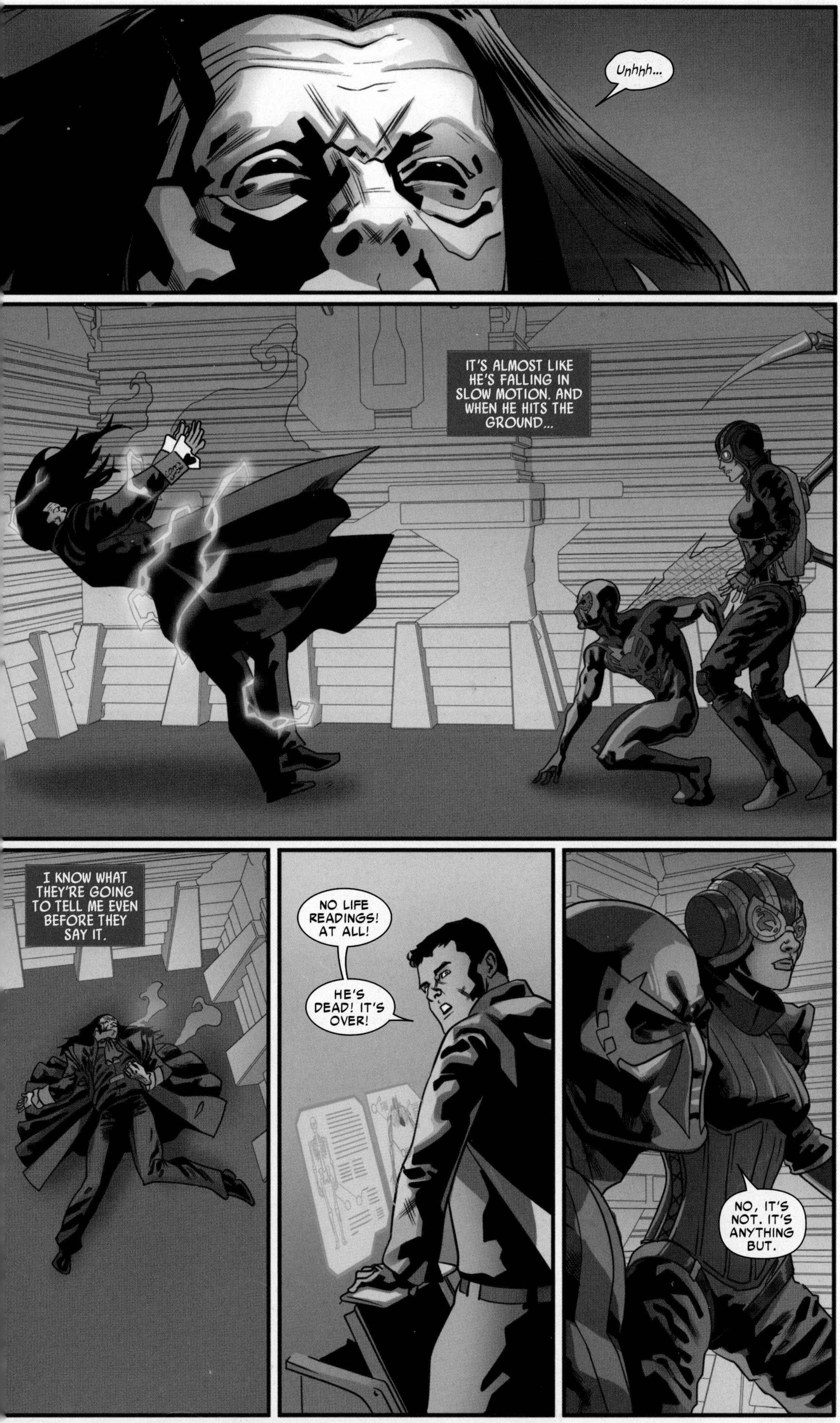

Unhhh...
IT'S ALMOST LIKE HE'S FALLING IN SLOW MOTION. AND WHEN HE HITS THE GROUND...
I KNOW WHAT THEY'RE GOING TO TELL ME EVEN BEFORE THEY SAY IT.
NO LIFE READINGS! AT ALL!
HE'S DEAD! IT'S OVER!
NO, IT'S NOT. IT'S ANYTHING BUT.

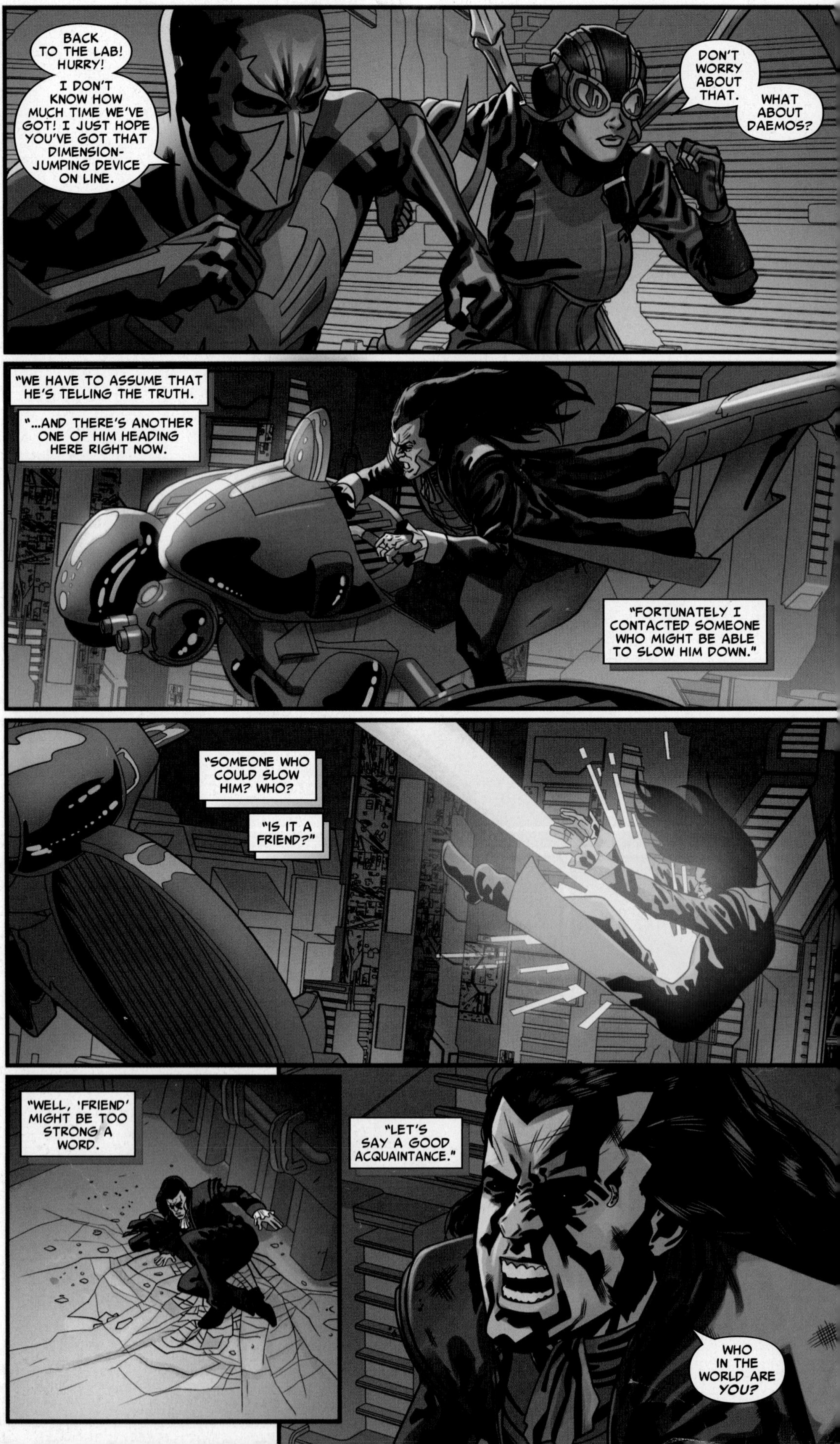
BACK TO THE LAB! HURRY!
I DON'T KNOW HOW MUCH TIME WE'VE GOT! I JUST HOPE YOU'VE GOT THAT DIMENSION-JUMPING DEVICE ON LINE.
DON'T WORRY ABOUT THAT.
WHAT ABOUT DAEMOS?
"WE HAVE TO ASSUME THAT HE'S TELLING THE TRUTH.
"...AND THERE'S ANOTHER ONE OF HIM HEADING HERE RIGHT NOW.
"FORTUNATELY I CONTACTED SOMEONE WHO MIGHT BE ABLE TO SLOW HIM DOWN."
"SOMEONE WHO COULD SLOW HIM? WHO?
"IS IT A FRIEND?"
"WELL, 'FRIEND' MIGHT BE TOO STRONG A WORD.
"LET'S SAY A GOOD ACQUAINTANCE."
WHO IN THE WORLD ARE YOU?

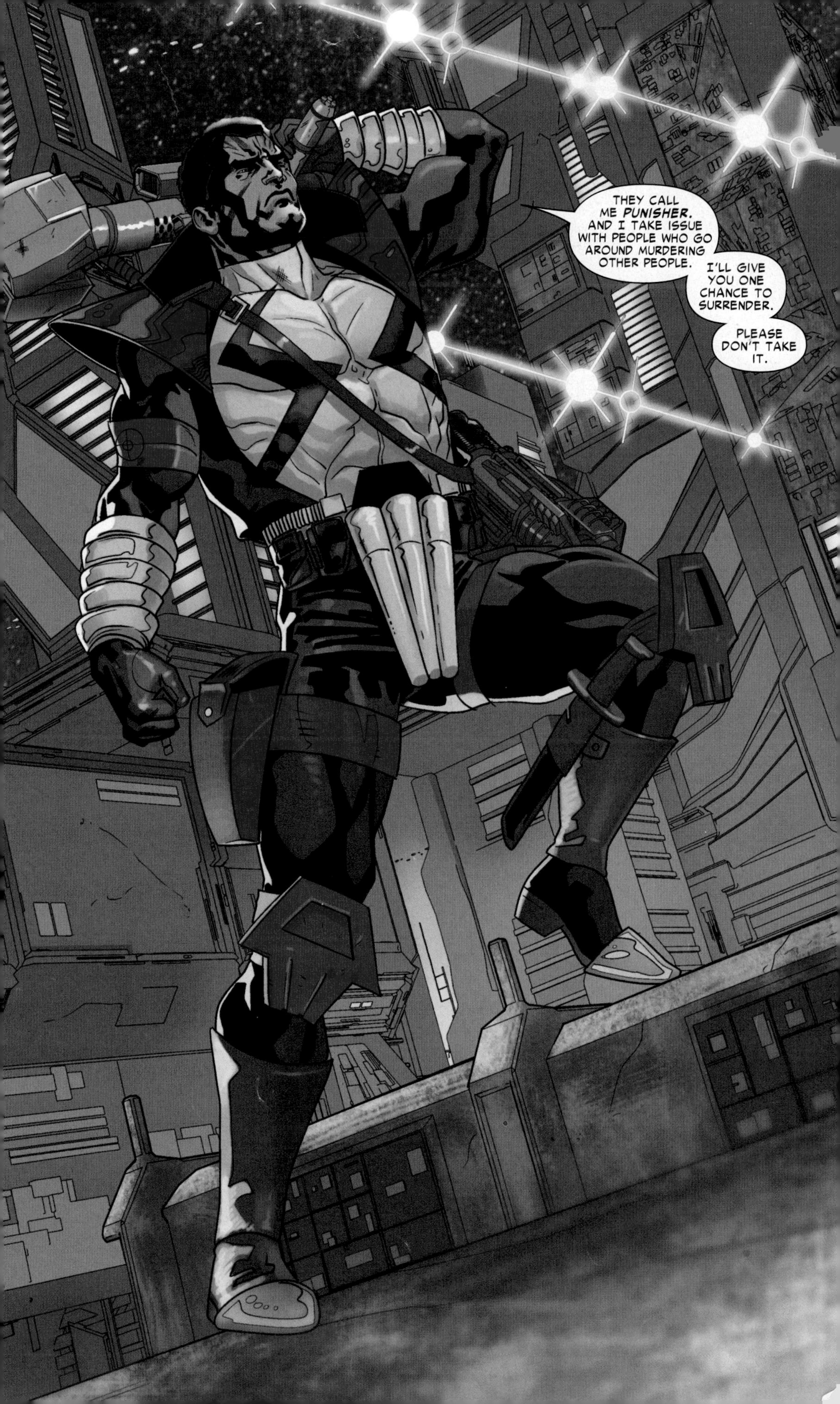
THEY CALL ME ***PUNISHER.*** AND I TAKE ISSUE WITH PEOPLE WHO GO AROUND MURDERING OTHER PEOPLE.
I'LL GIVE YOU ONE CHANCE TO SURRENDER.
PLEASE DON'T TAKE IT.

HAPPILY!

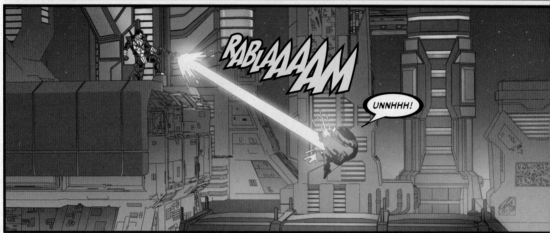

RABLAAAAAM

UNNHHH!

QUITE... THE WEAPON... YOU HAVE...

BUT SOONER OR LATER, YOU WILL RUN OUT OF AMMO...

...OR EVEN WORSE...

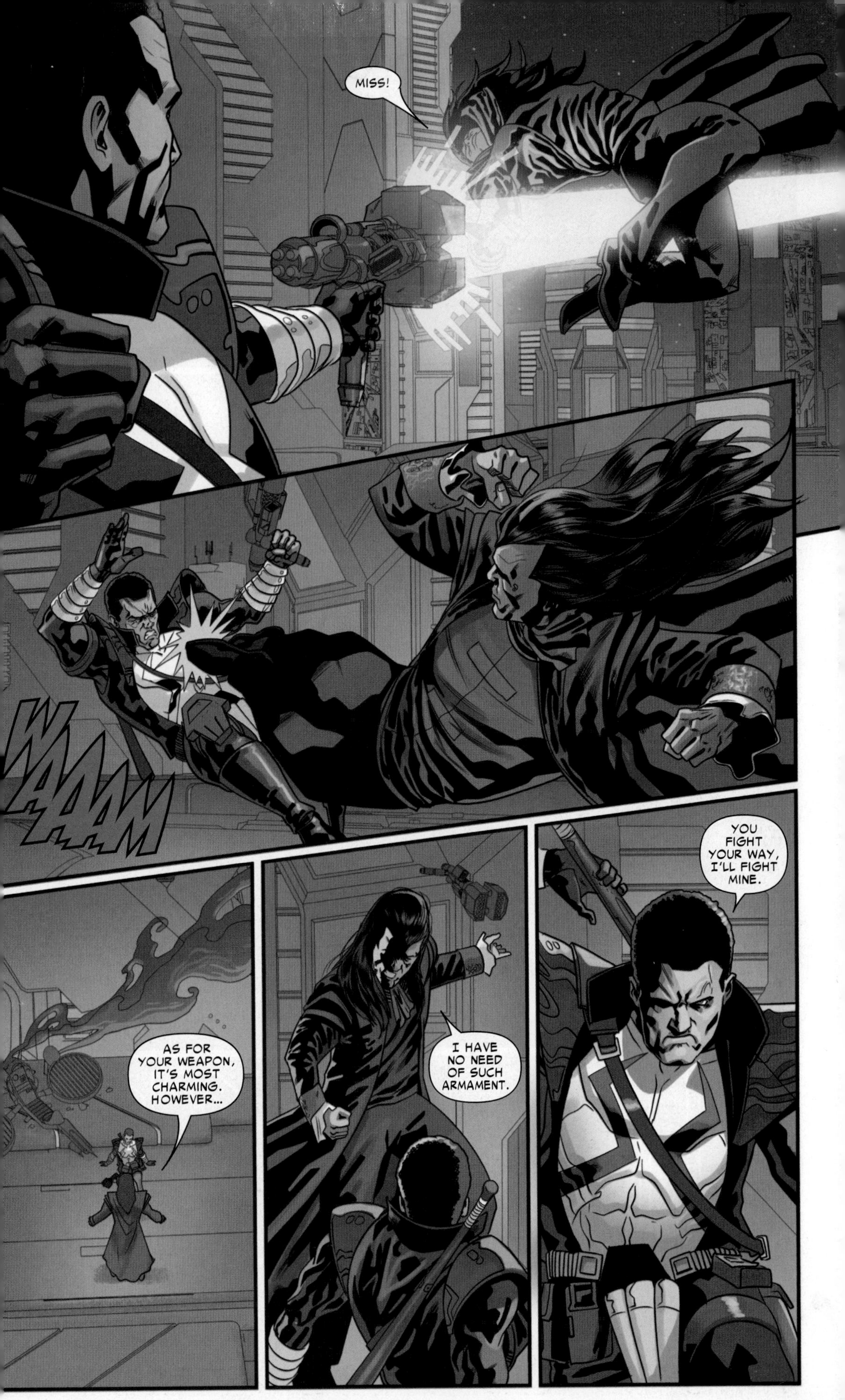
MISS!
WAAAM
AS FOR YOUR WEAPON, IT'S MOST CHARMING. HOWEVER...
I HAVE NO NEED OF SUCH ARMAMENT.
YOU FIGHT YOUR WAY, I'LL FIGHT MINE.

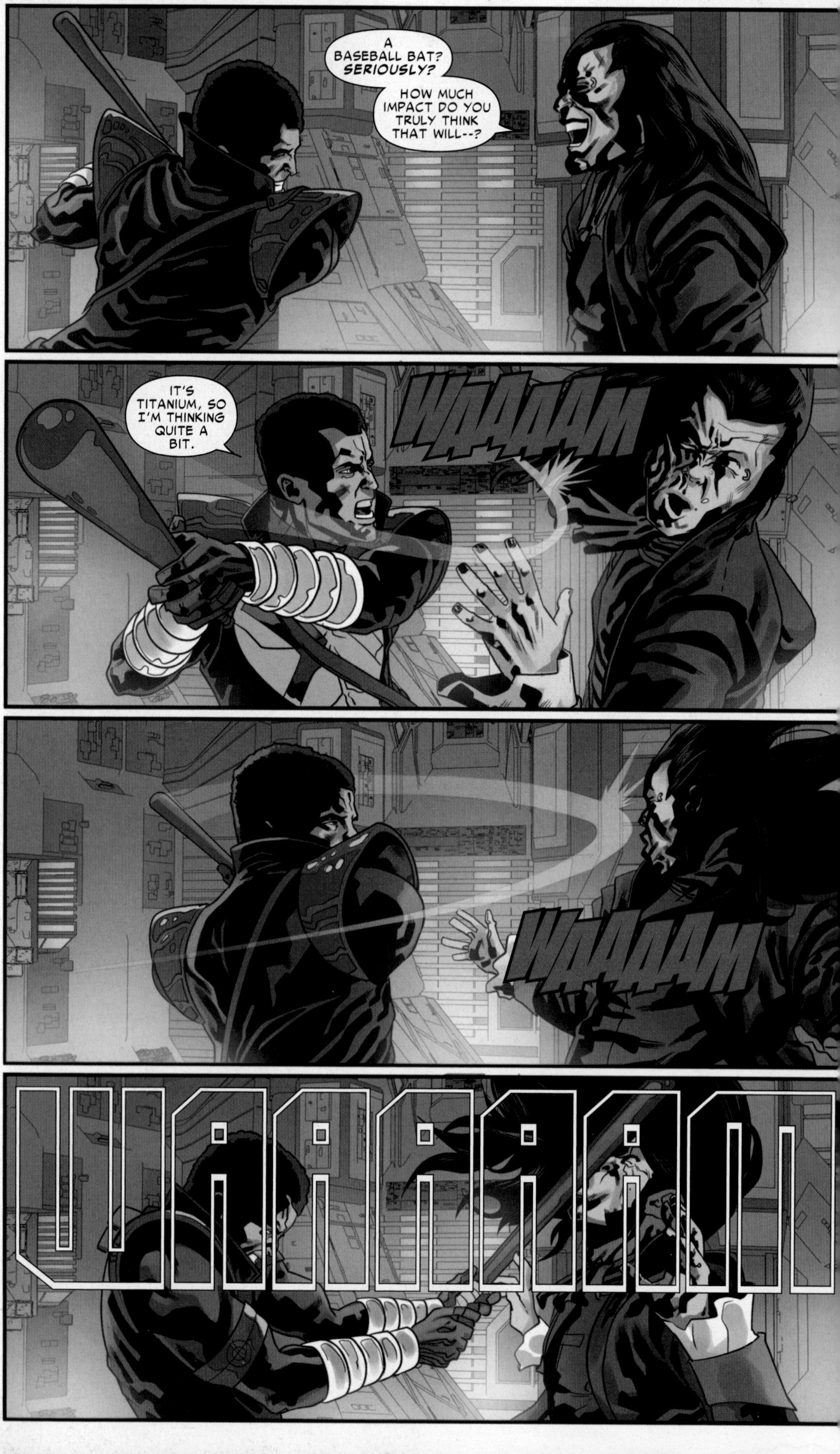
A BASEBALL BAT? SERIOUSLY?
HOW MUCH IMPACT DO YOU TRULY THINK THAT WILL--?
IT'S TITANIUM, SO I'M THINKING QUITE A BIT.
WAAAAM
WAAAAM

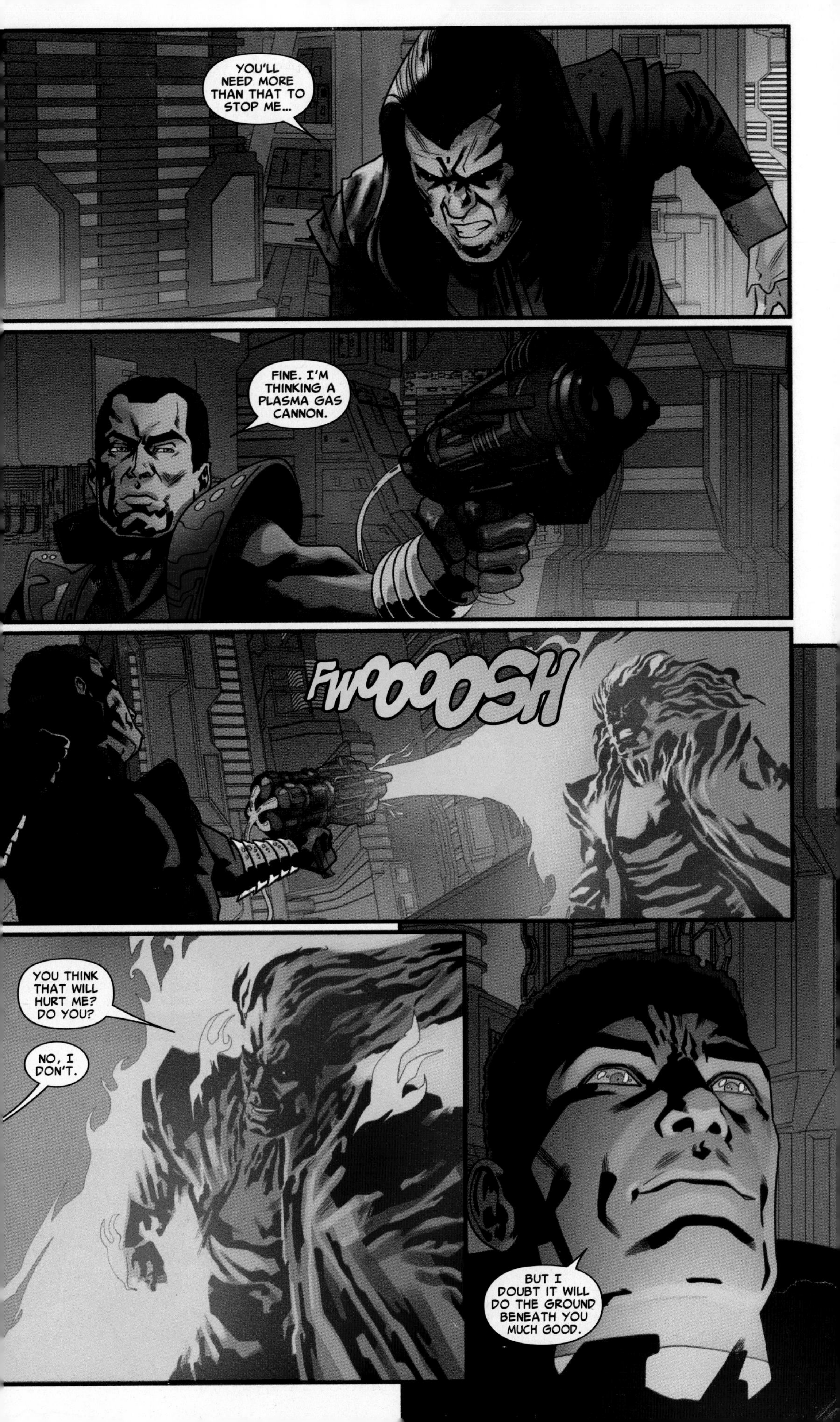
YOU'LL NEED MORE THAN THAT TO STOP ME...
FINE. I'M THINKING A PLASMA GAS CANNON.
FWOOOOSH
YOU THINK THAT WILL HURT ME? DO YOU?
NO, I DON'T.
BUT I DOUBT IT WILL DO THE GROUND BENEATH YOU MUCH GOOD.

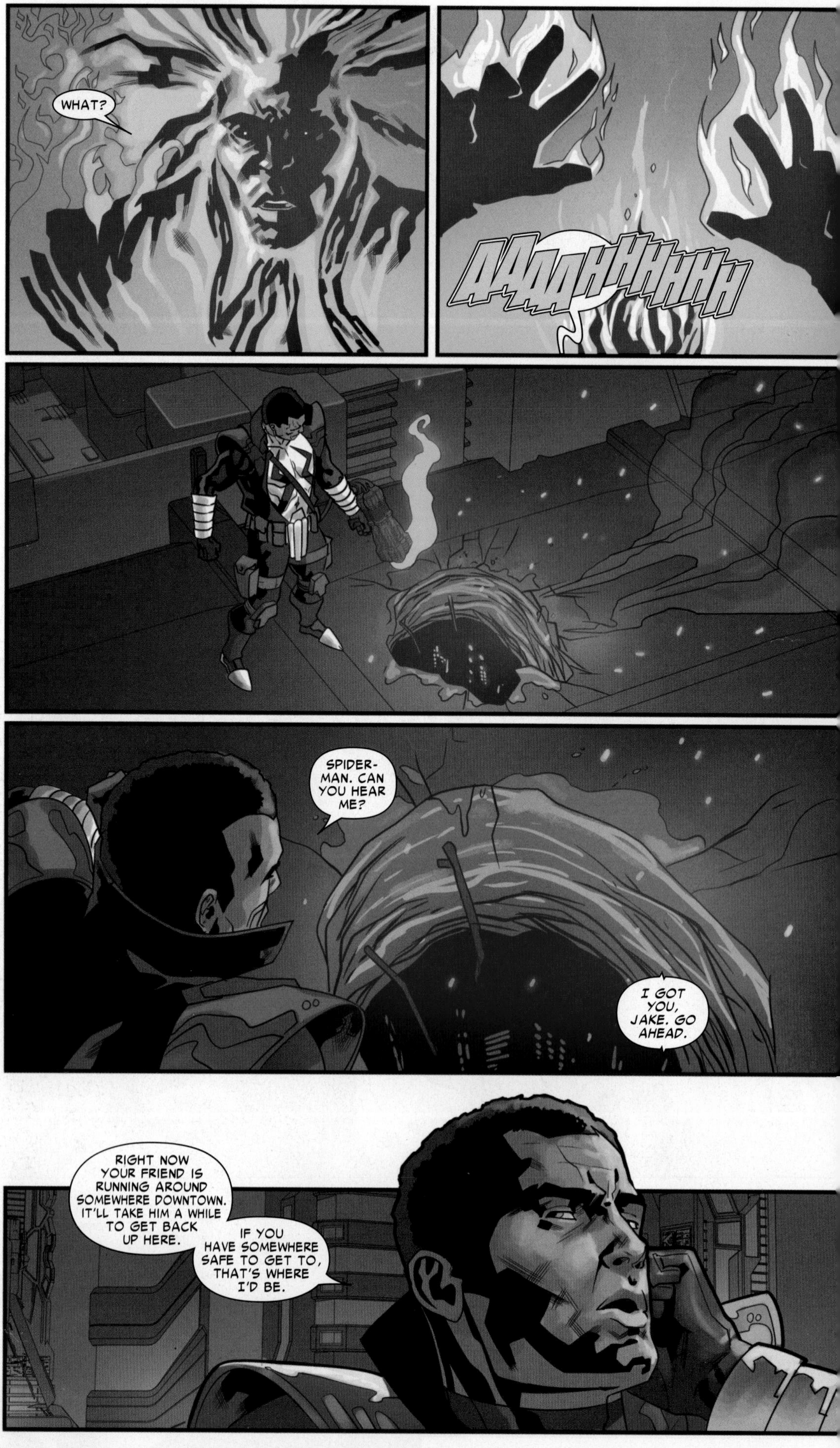
WHAT?
AAAAHHHHHH
SPIDER-MAN. CAN YOU HEAR ME?
I GOT YOU, JAKE. GO AHEAD.
RIGHT NOW YOUR FRIEND IS RUNNING AROUND SOMEWHERE DOWNTOWN. IT'LL TAKE HIM A WHILE TO GET BACK UP HERE.
IF YOU HAVE SOMEWHERE SAFE TO GET TO, THAT'S WHERE I'D BE.

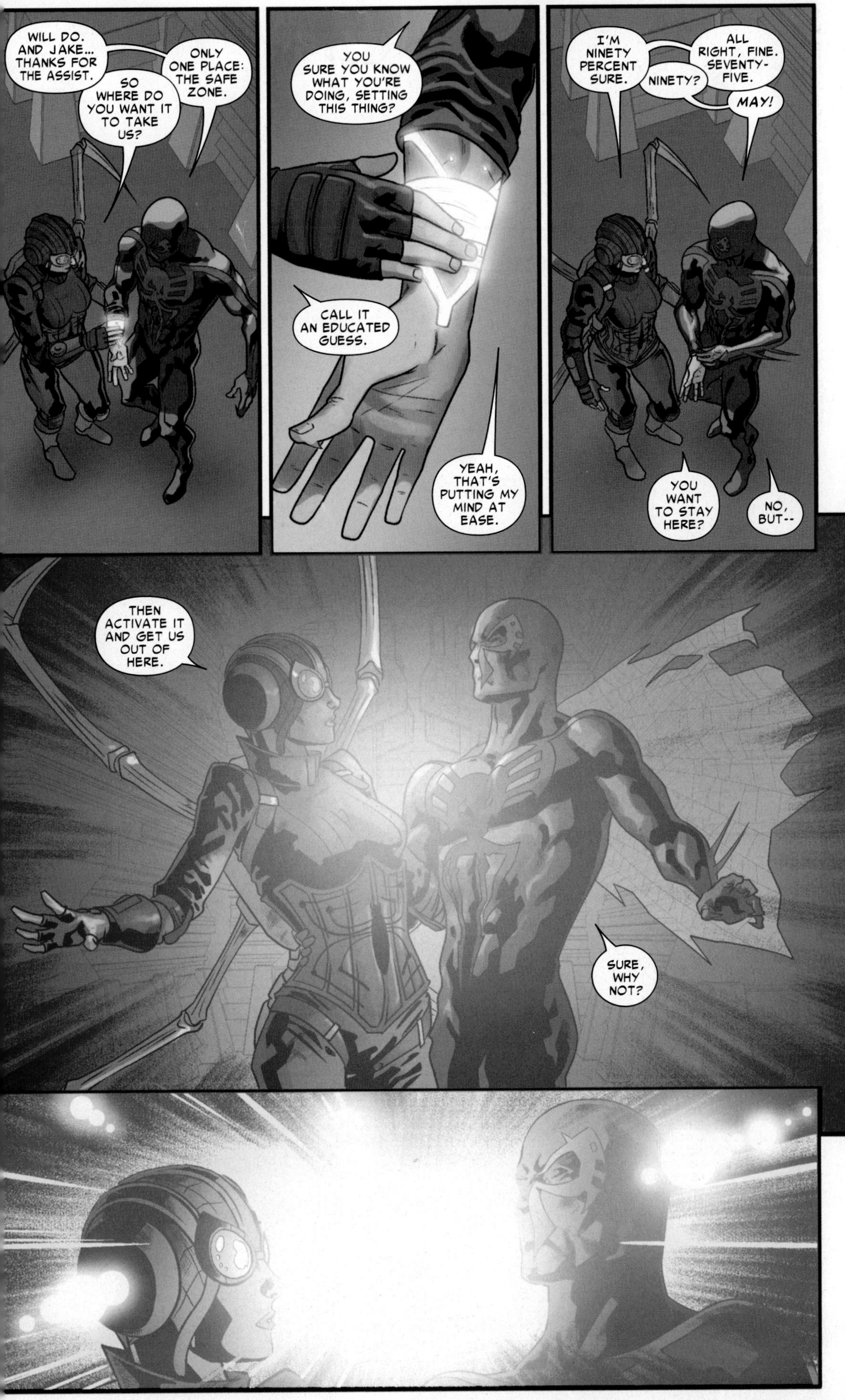
WILL DO. AND JAKE... THANKS FOR THE ASSIST.
SO WHERE DO YOU WANT IT TO TAKE US?
ONLY ONE PLACE: THE SAFE ZONE.
YOU SURE YOU KNOW WHAT YOU'RE DOING, SETTING THIS THING?
CALL IT AN EDUCATED GUESS.
YEAH, THAT'S PUTTING MY MIND AT EASE.
I'M NINETY PERCENT SURE.
NINETY?
ALL RIGHT, FINE. SEVENTY-FIVE.
MAY!
YOU WANT TO STAY HERE?
NO, BUT--
THEN ACTIVATE IT AND GET US OUT OF HERE.
SURE, WHY NOT?

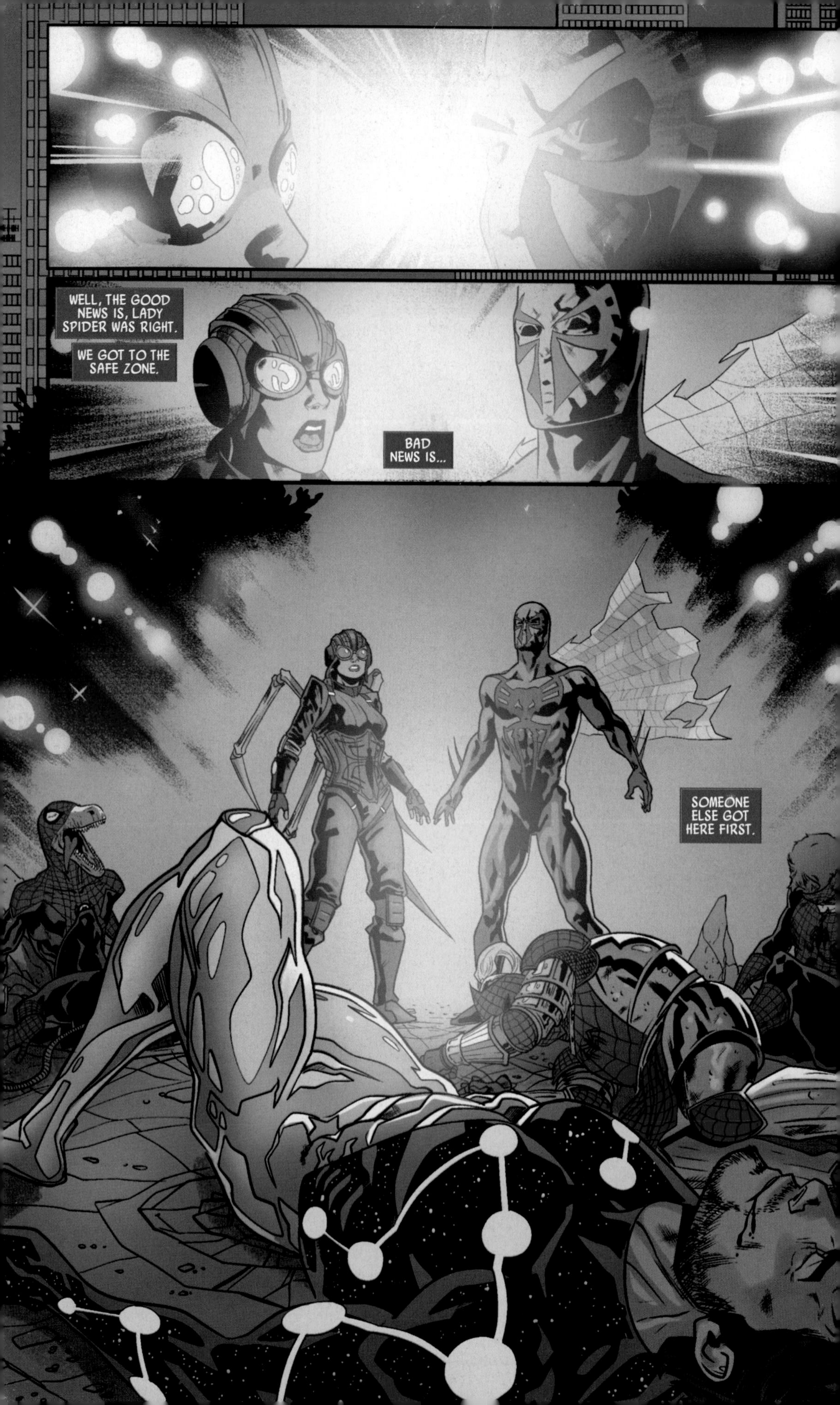
WELL, THE GOOD NEWS IS, LADY SPIDER WAS RIGHT.
WE GOT TO THE SAFE ZONE.
BAD NEWS IS...
SOMEONE ELSE GOT HERE FIRST.

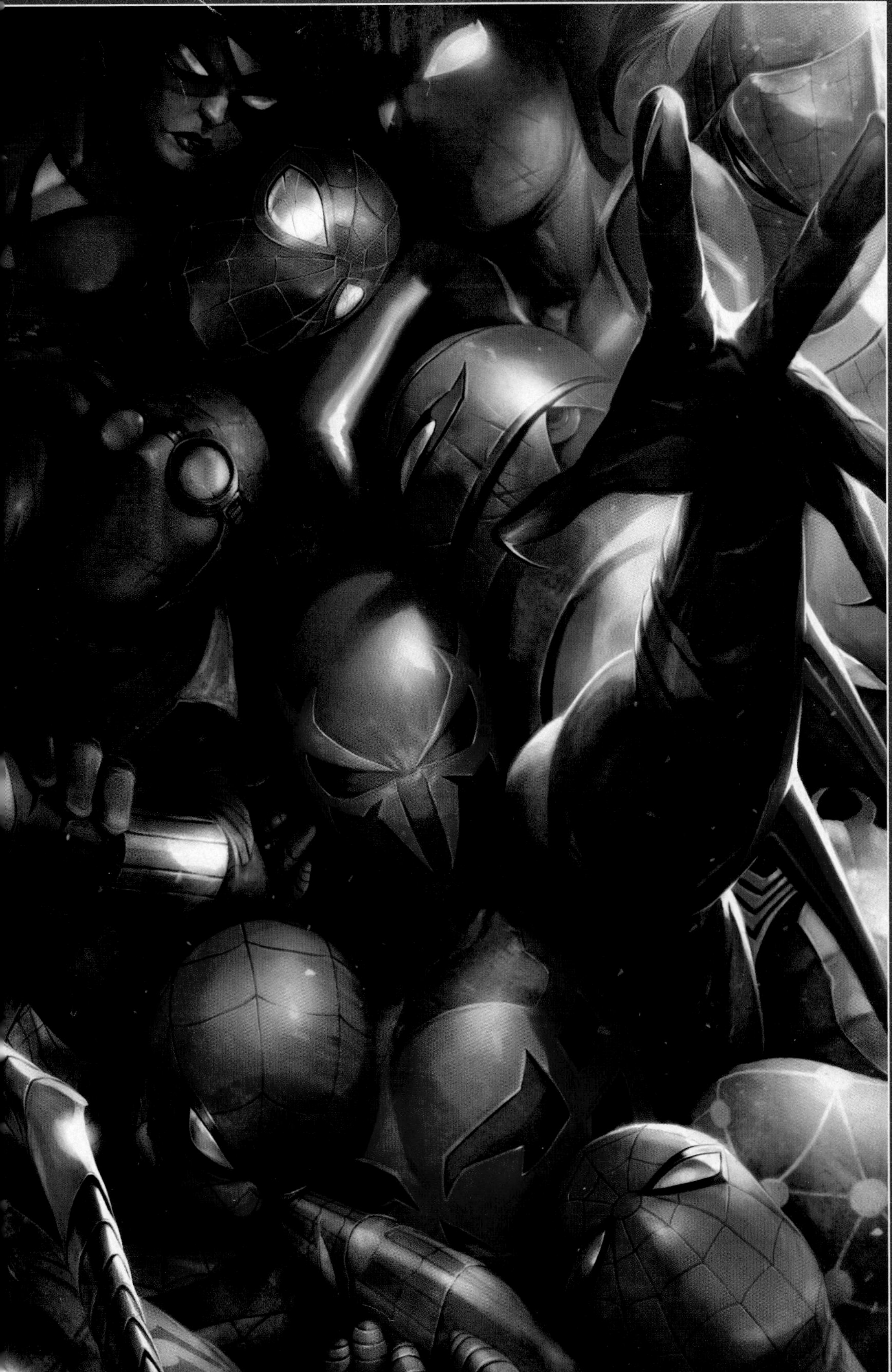

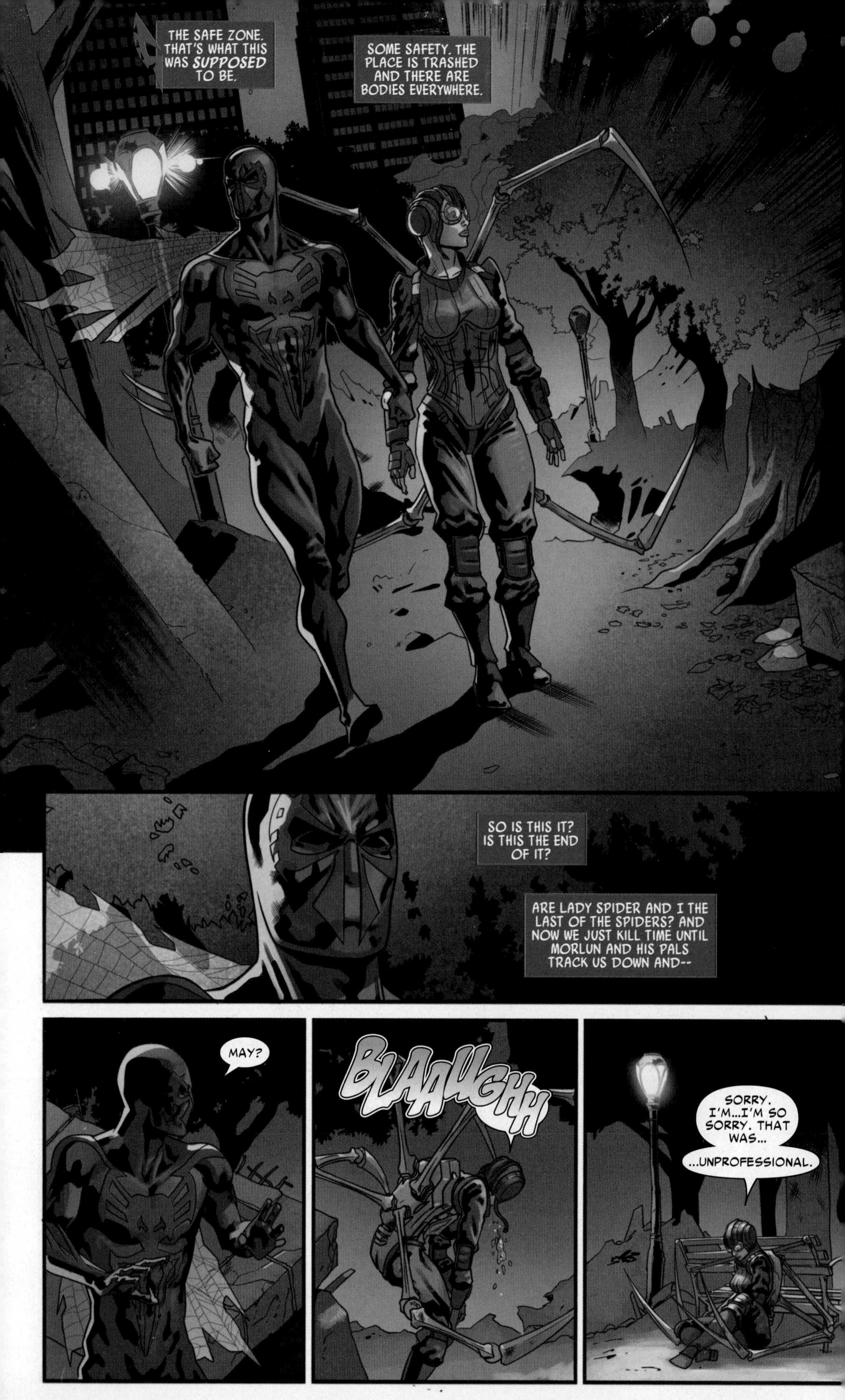

THE SAFE ZONE. THAT'S WHAT THIS WAS *SUPPOSED* TO BE.
SOME SAFETY. THE PLACE IS TRASHED AND THERE ARE BODIES EVERYWHERE.
SO IS THIS IT? IS THIS THE END OF IT?
ARE LADY SPIDER AND I THE LAST OF THE SPIDERS? AND NOW WE JUST KILL TIME UNTIL MORLUN AND HIS PALS TRACK US DOWN AND--
MAY?
BLAAUGHH
SORRY. I'M...I'M SO SORRY. THAT WAS...
...UNPROFESSIONAL.

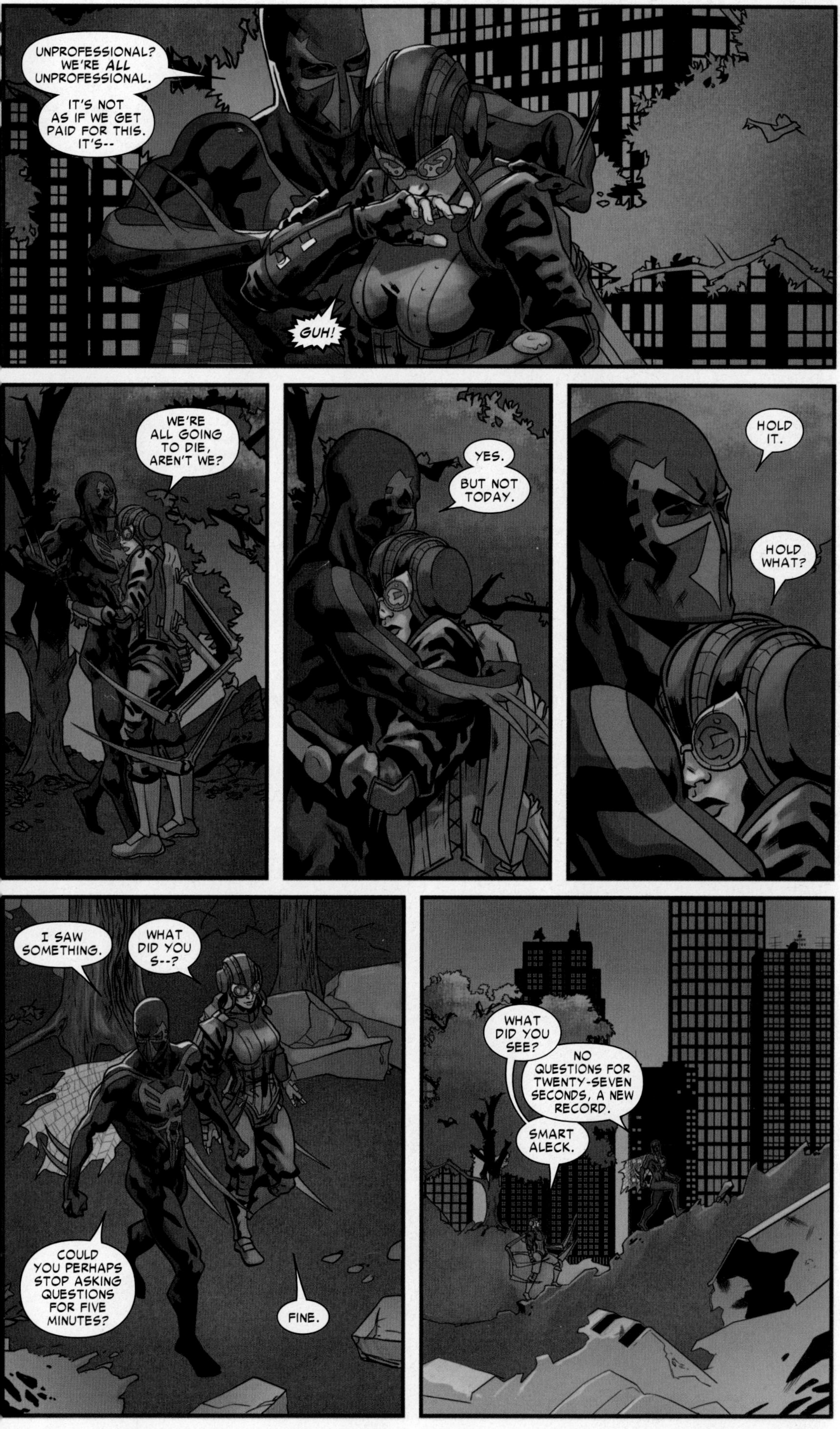
UNPROFESSIONAL? WE'RE ALL UNPROFESSIONAL.
IT'S NOT AS IF WE GET PAID FOR THIS. IT'S--
GUH!
WE'RE ALL GOING TO DIE, AREN'T WE?
YES.
BUT NOT TODAY.
HOLD IT.
HOLD WHAT?
I SAW SOMETHING.
WHAT DID YOU S--?
COULD YOU PERHAPS STOP ASKING QUESTIONS FOR FIVE MINUTES?
FINE.
WHAT DID YOU SEE?
NO QUESTIONS FOR TWENTY-SEVEN SECONDS, A NEW RECORD.
SMART ALECK.

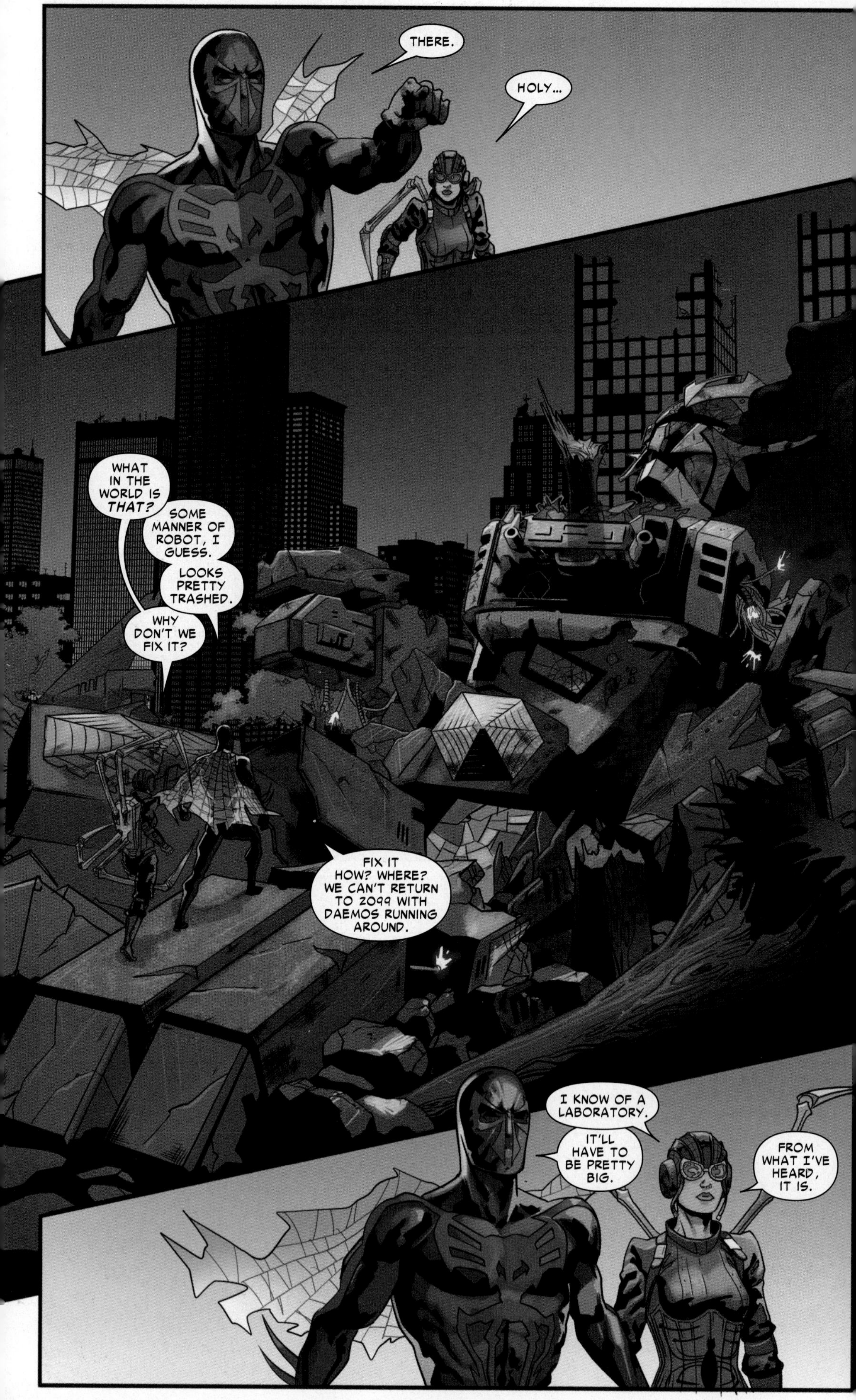
THERE.
HOLY...
WHAT IN THE WORLD IS *THAT?*
SOME MANNER OF ROBOT, I GUESS.
LOOKS PRETTY TRASHED.
WHY DON'T WE FIX IT?
FIX IT HOW? WHERE? WE CAN'T RETURN TO 2099 WITH DAEMOS RUNNING AROUND.
I KNOW OF A LABORATORY.
IT'LL HAVE TO BE PRETTY BIG.
FROM WHAT I'VE HEARD, IT IS.

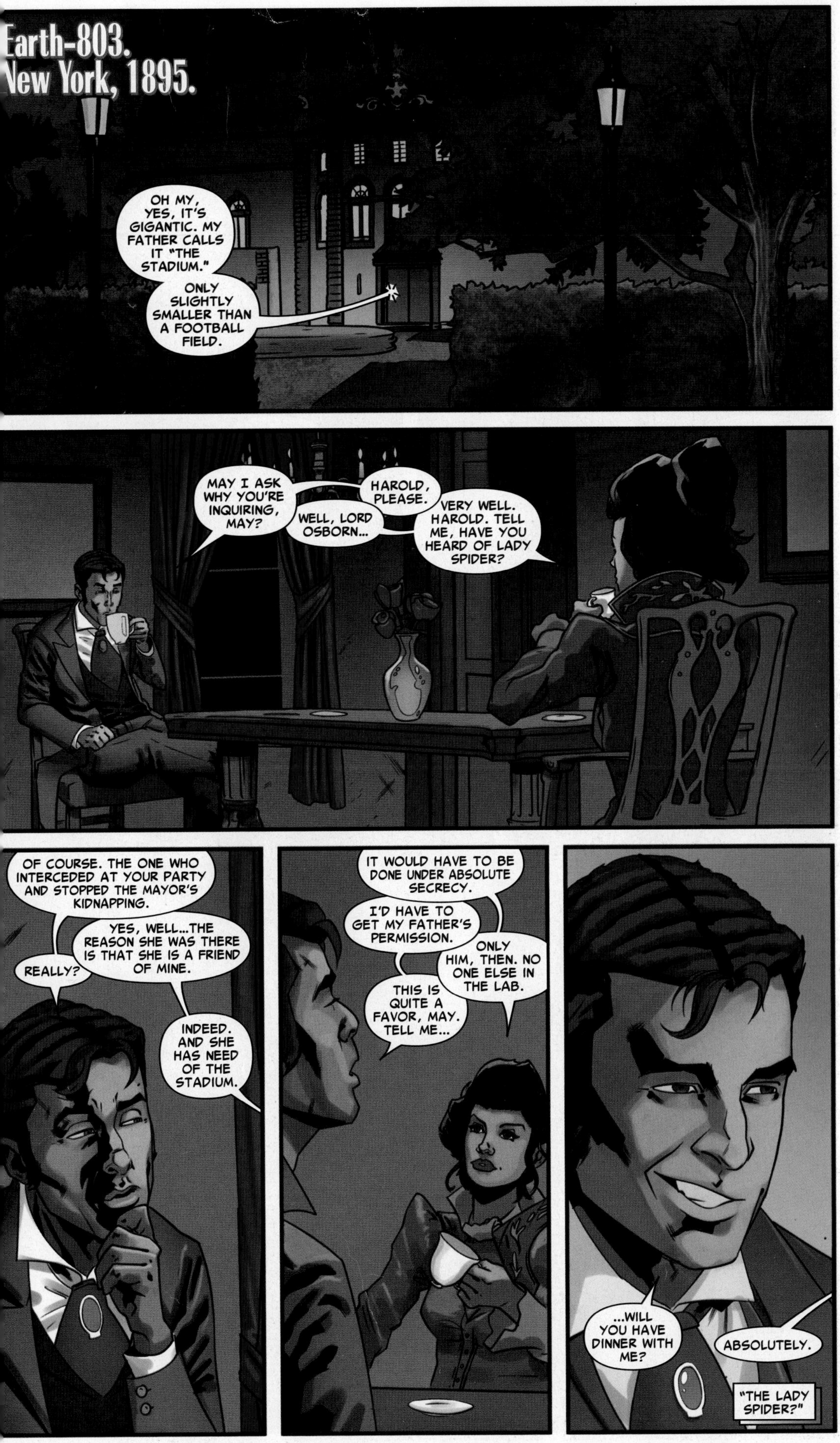
Earth-803.
New York, 1895.
OH MY, YES, IT'S GIGANTIC. MY FATHER CALLS IT "THE STADIUM."
ONLY SLIGHTLY SMALLER THAN A FOOTBALL FIELD.
MAY I ASK WHY YOU'RE INQUIRING, MAY?
WELL, LORD OSBORN...
HAROLD, PLEASE.
VERY WELL. HAROLD. TELL ME, HAVE YOU HEARD OF LADY SPIDER?
OF COURSE. THE ONE WHO INTERCEDED AT YOUR PARTY AND STOPPED THE MAYOR'S KIDNAPPING.
YES, WELL...THE REASON SHE WAS THERE IS THAT SHE IS A FRIEND OF MINE.
REALLY?
INDEED. AND SHE HAS NEED OF THE STADIUM.
IT WOULD HAVE TO BE DONE UNDER ABSOLUTE SECRECY.
I'D HAVE TO GET MY FATHER'S PERMISSION.
ONLY HIM, THEN. NO ONE ELSE IN THE LAB.
THIS IS QUITE A FAVOR, MAY. TELL ME...
...WILL YOU HAVE DINNER WITH ME?
ABSOLUTELY.
"THE LADY SPIDER?"

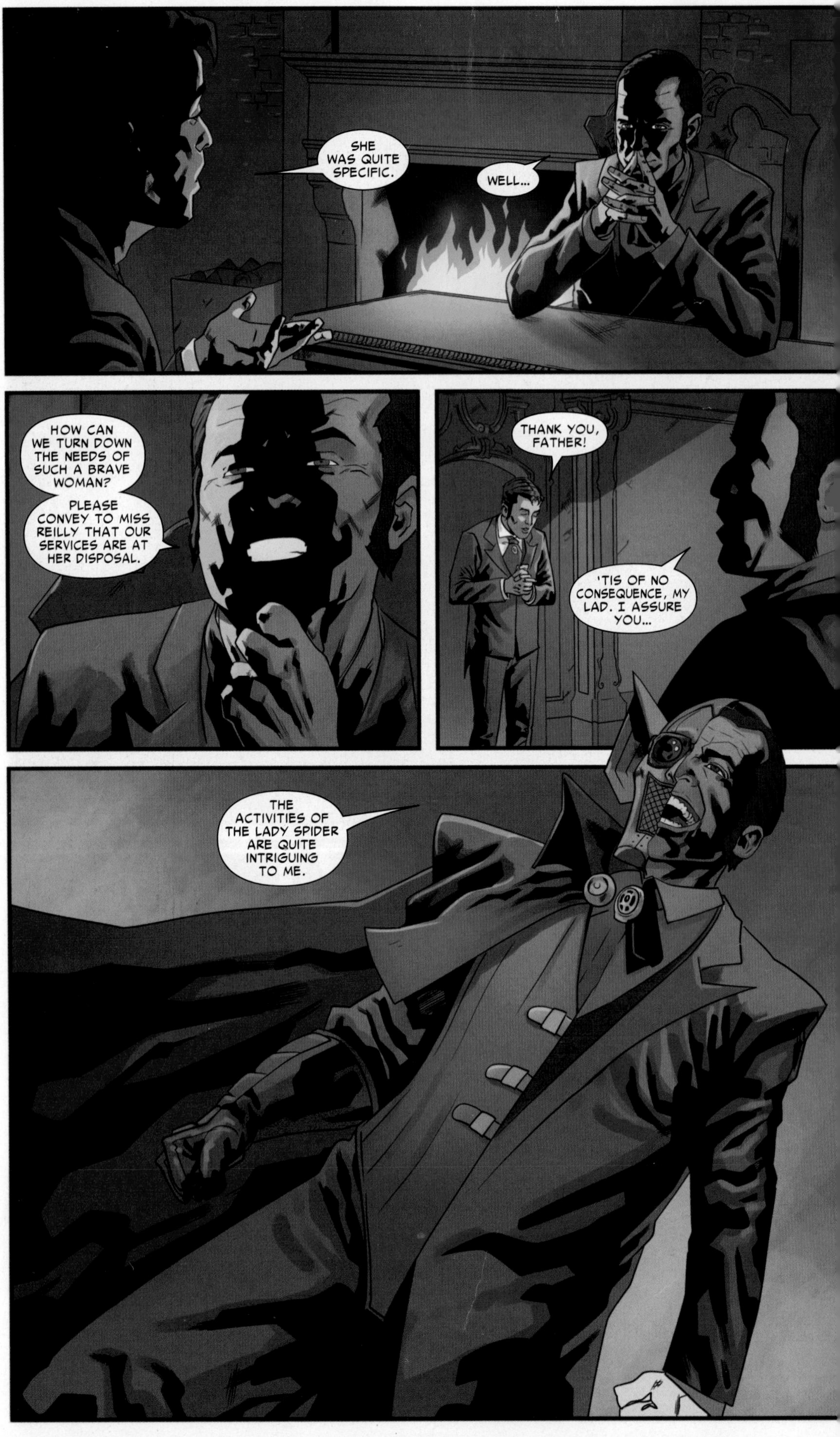
SHE WAS QUITE SPECIFIC.
WELL...
HOW CAN WE TURN DOWN THE NEEDS OF SUCH A BRAVE WOMAN?
PLEASE CONVEY TO MISS REILLY THAT OUR SERVICES ARE AT HER DISPOSAL.
THANK YOU, FATHER!
'TIS OF NO CONSEQUENCE, MY LAD. I ASSURE YOU...
THE ACTIVITIES OF THE LADY SPIDER ARE QUITE INTRIGUING TO ME.

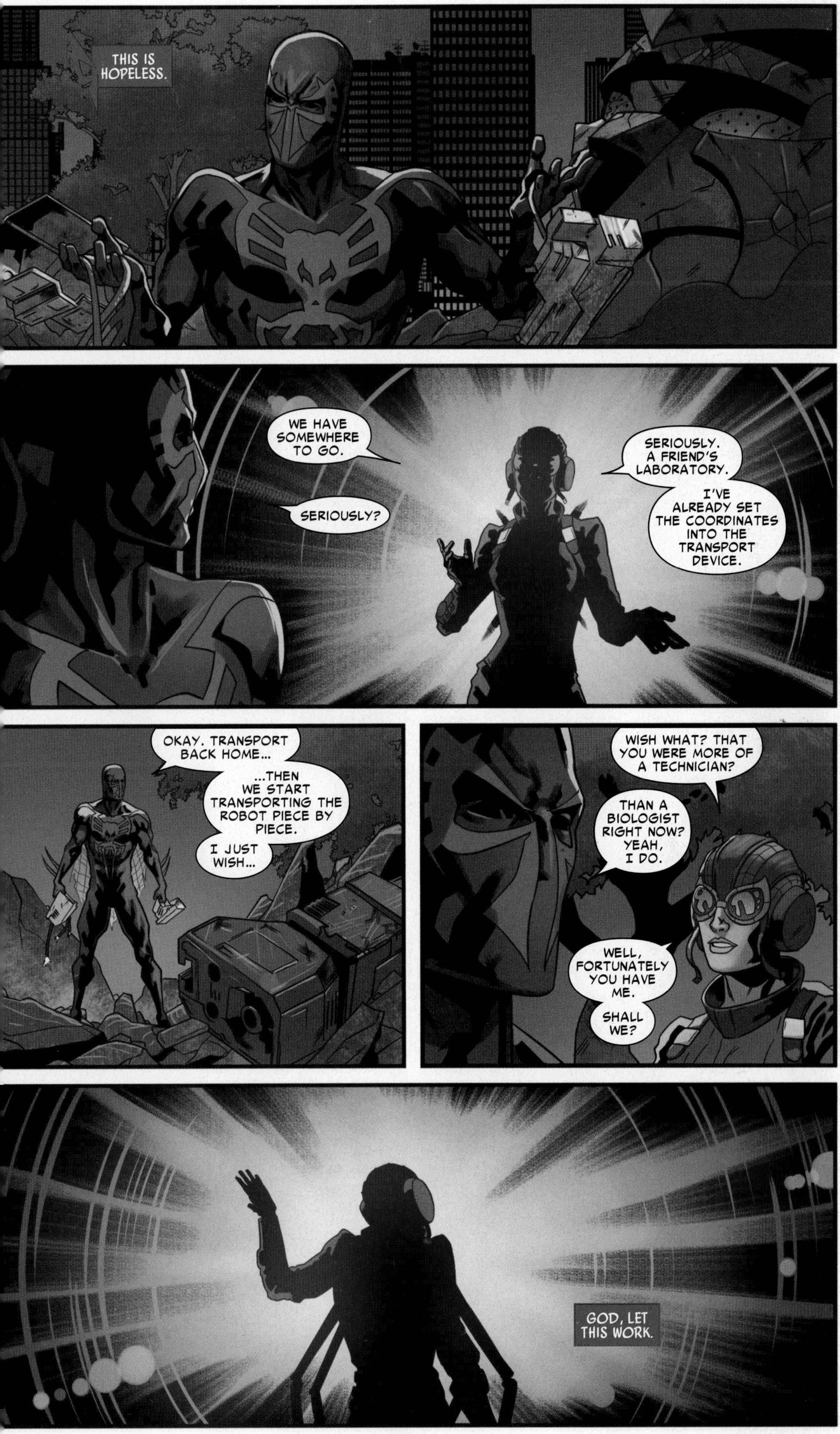
THIS IS HOPELESS.
WE HAVE SOMEWHERE TO GO.
SERIOUSLY?
SERIOUSLY. A FRIEND'S LABORATORY.
I'VE ALREADY SET THE COORDINATES INTO THE TRANSPORT DEVICE.
OKAY. TRANSPORT BACK HOME...
...THEN WE START TRANSPORTING THE ROBOT PIECE BY PIECE.
I JUST WISH...
WISH WHAT? THAT YOU WERE MORE OF A TECHNICIAN?
THAN A BIOLOGIST RIGHT NOW? YEAH, I DO.
WELL, FORTUNATELY YOU HAVE ME.
SHALL WE?
GOD, LET THIS WORK.

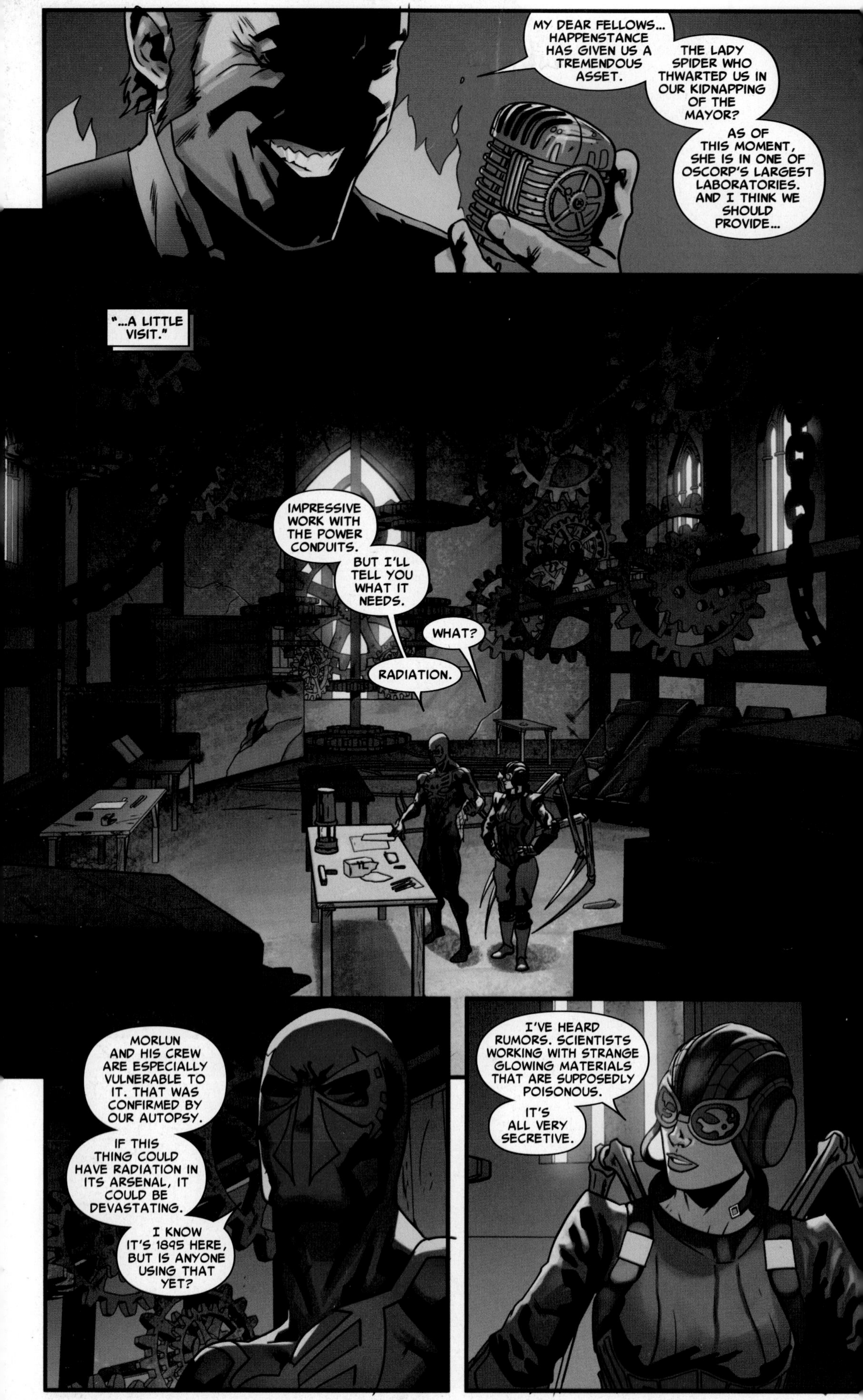

MY DEAR FELLOWS... HAPPENSTANCE HAS GIVEN US A TREMENDOUS ASSET.
THE LADY SPIDER WHO THWARTED US IN OUR KIDNAPPING OF THE MAYOR?
AS OF THIS MOMENT, SHE IS IN ONE OF OSCORP'S LARGEST LABORATORIES. AND I THINK WE SHOULD PROVIDE...
"...A LITTLE VISIT."
IMPRESSIVE WORK WITH THE POWER CONDUITS.
BUT I'LL TELL YOU WHAT IT NEEDS.
WHAT?
RADIATION.
MORLUN AND HIS CREW ARE ESPECIALLY VULNERABLE TO IT. THAT WAS CONFIRMED BY OUR AUTOPSY.
IF THIS THING COULD HAVE RADIATION IN ITS ARSENAL, IT COULD BE DEVASTATING.
I KNOW IT'S 1895 HERE, BUT IS ANYONE USING THAT YET?
I'VE HEARD RUMORS. SCIENTISTS WORKING WITH STRANGE GLOWING MATERIALS THAT ARE SUPPOSEDLY POISONOUS.
IT'S ALL VERY SECRETIVE.

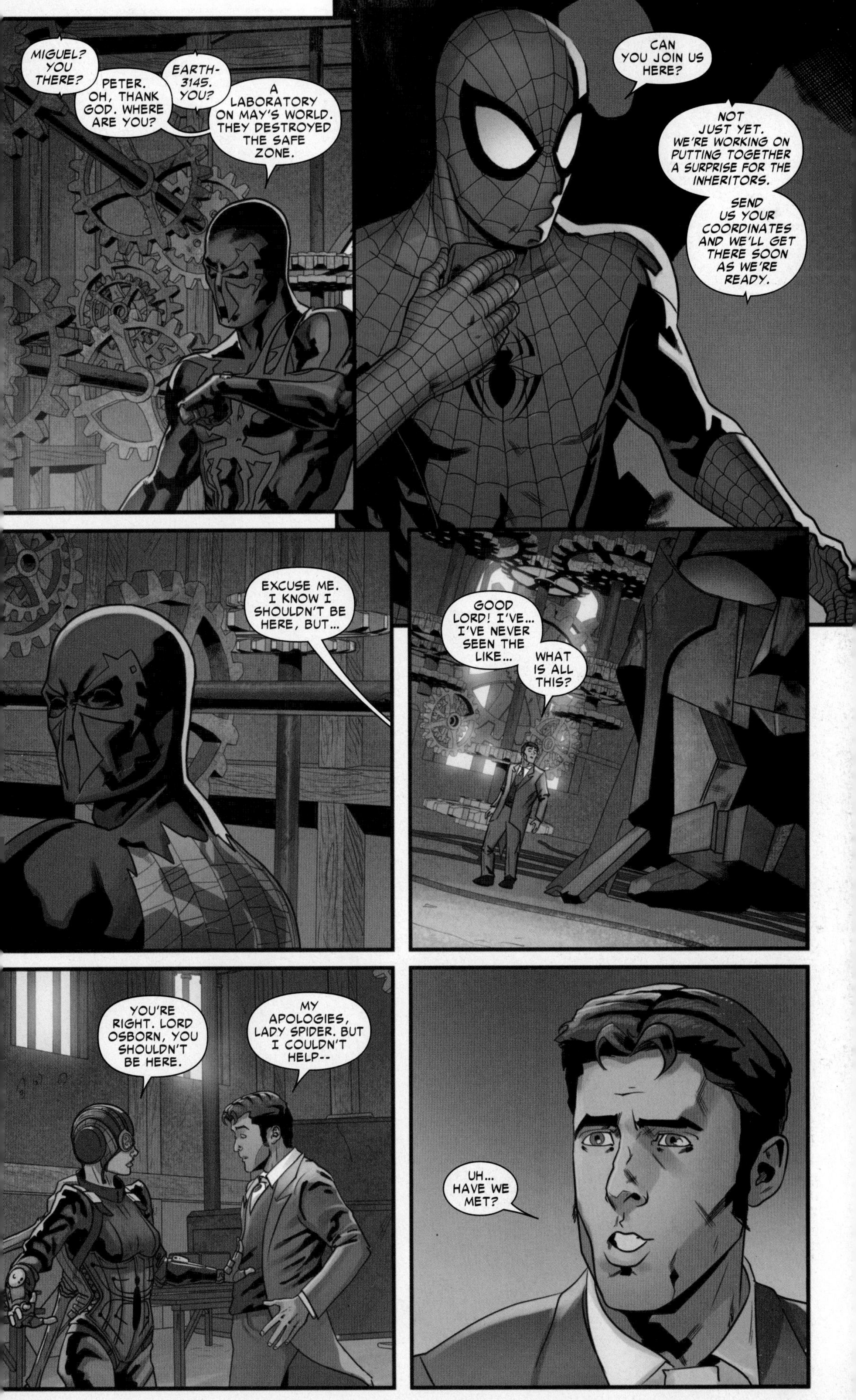
MIGUEL? YOU THERE?
PETER. OH, THANK GOD. WHERE ARE YOU?
EARTH-3145. YOU?
A LABORATORY ON MAY'S WORLD. THEY DESTROYED THE SAFE ZONE.
CAN YOU JOIN US HERE?
NOT JUST YET. WE'RE WORKING ON PUTTING TOGETHER A SURPRISE FOR THE INHERITORS.
SEND US YOUR COORDINATES AND WE'LL GET THERE SOON AS WE'RE READY.
EXCUSE ME. I KNOW I SHOULDN'T BE HERE, BUT...
GOOD LORD! I'VE... I'VE NEVER SEEN THE LIKE...
WHAT IS ALL THIS?
YOU'RE RIGHT. LORD OSBORN, YOU SHOULDN'T BE HERE.
MY APOLOGIES, LADY SPIDER. BUT I COULDN'T HELP--
UH... HAVE WE MET?

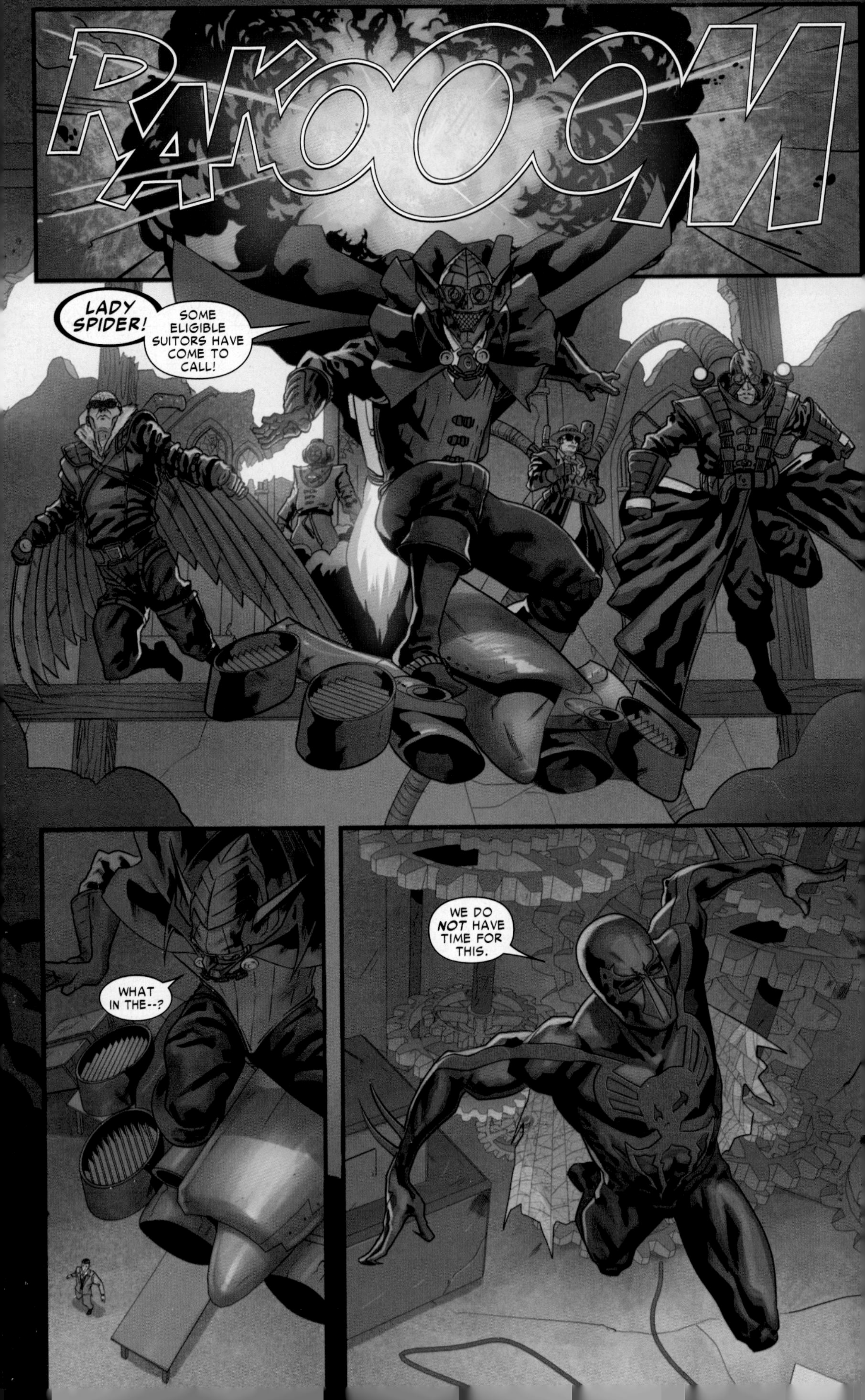
RAKOOOM
LADY SPIDER!
SOME ELIGIBLE SUITORS HAVE COME TO CALL!
WHAT IN THE--?
WE DO NOT HAVE TIME FOR THIS.

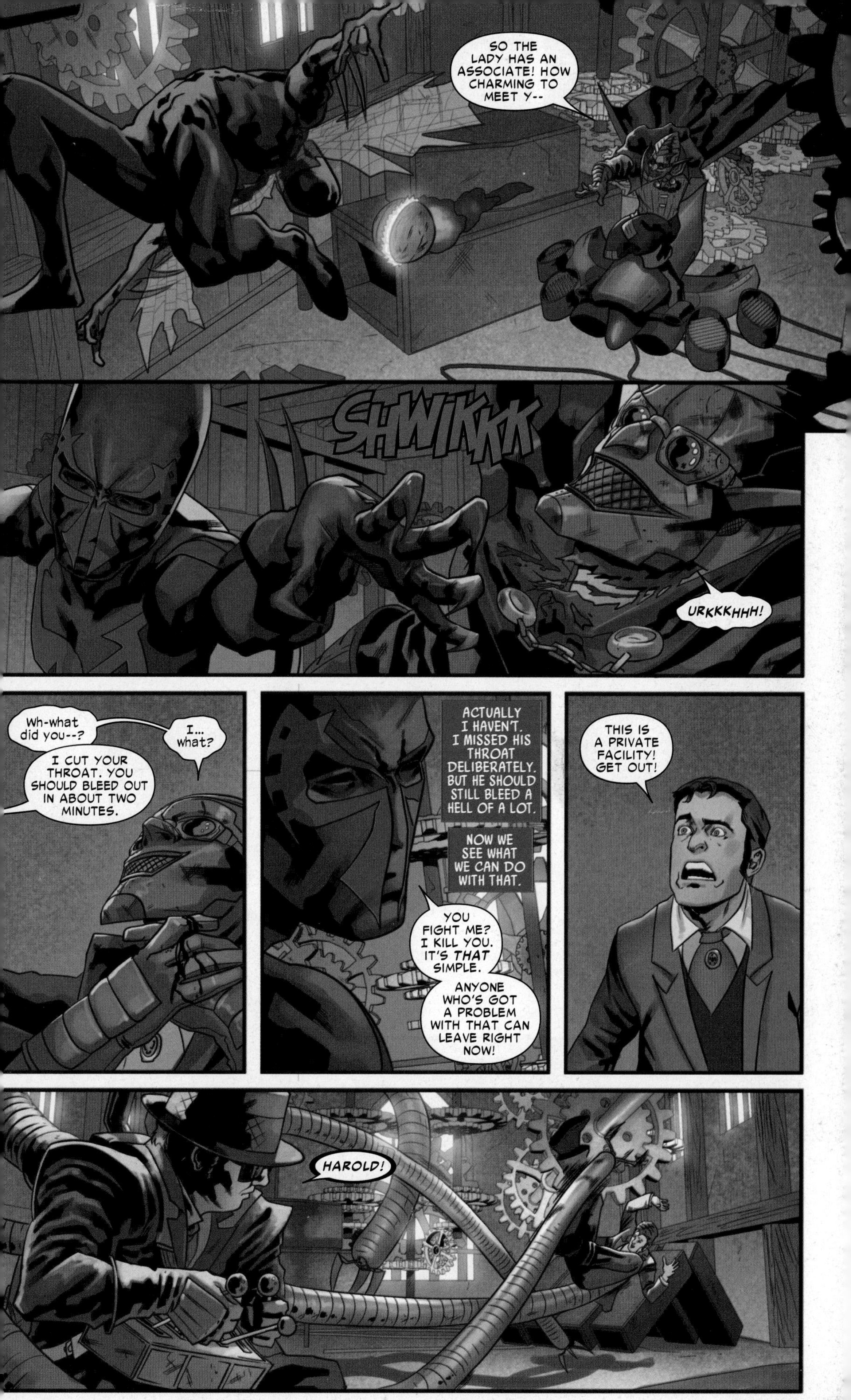
SO THE LADY HAS AN ASSOCIATE! HOW CHARMING TO MEET Y--
SHWIKKK
URKKKHHH!
Wh-what did you--?
I... what?
I CUT YOUR THROAT. YOU SHOULD BLEED OUT IN ABOUT TWO MINUTES.
ACTUALLY I HAVEN'T. I MISSED HIS THROAT DELIBERATELY. BUT HE SHOULD STILL BLEED A HELL OF A LOT.
NOW WE SEE WHAT WE CAN DO WITH THAT.
YOU FIGHT ME? I KILL YOU. IT'S THAT SIMPLE.
ANYONE WHO'S GOT A PROBLEM WITH THAT CAN LEAVE RIGHT NOW!
THIS IS A PRIVATE FACILITY! GET OUT!
HAROLD!

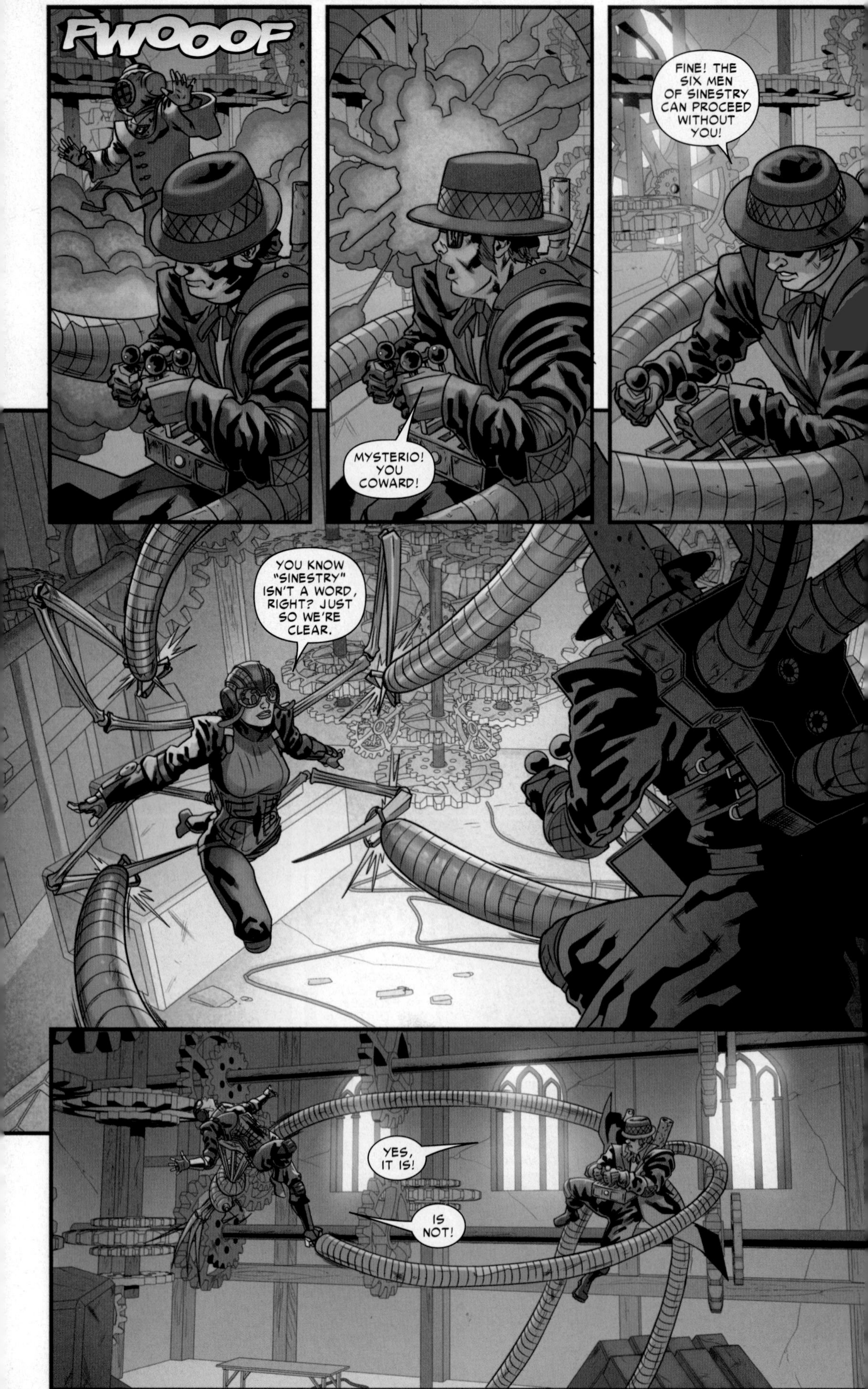
FWOOOF
MYSTERIO! YOU COWARD!
FINE! THE SIX MEN OF SINESTRY CAN PROCEED WITHOUT YOU!
YOU KNOW "SINESTRY" ISN'T A WORD, RIGHT? JUST SO WE'RE CLEAR.
YES, IT IS!
IS NOT!

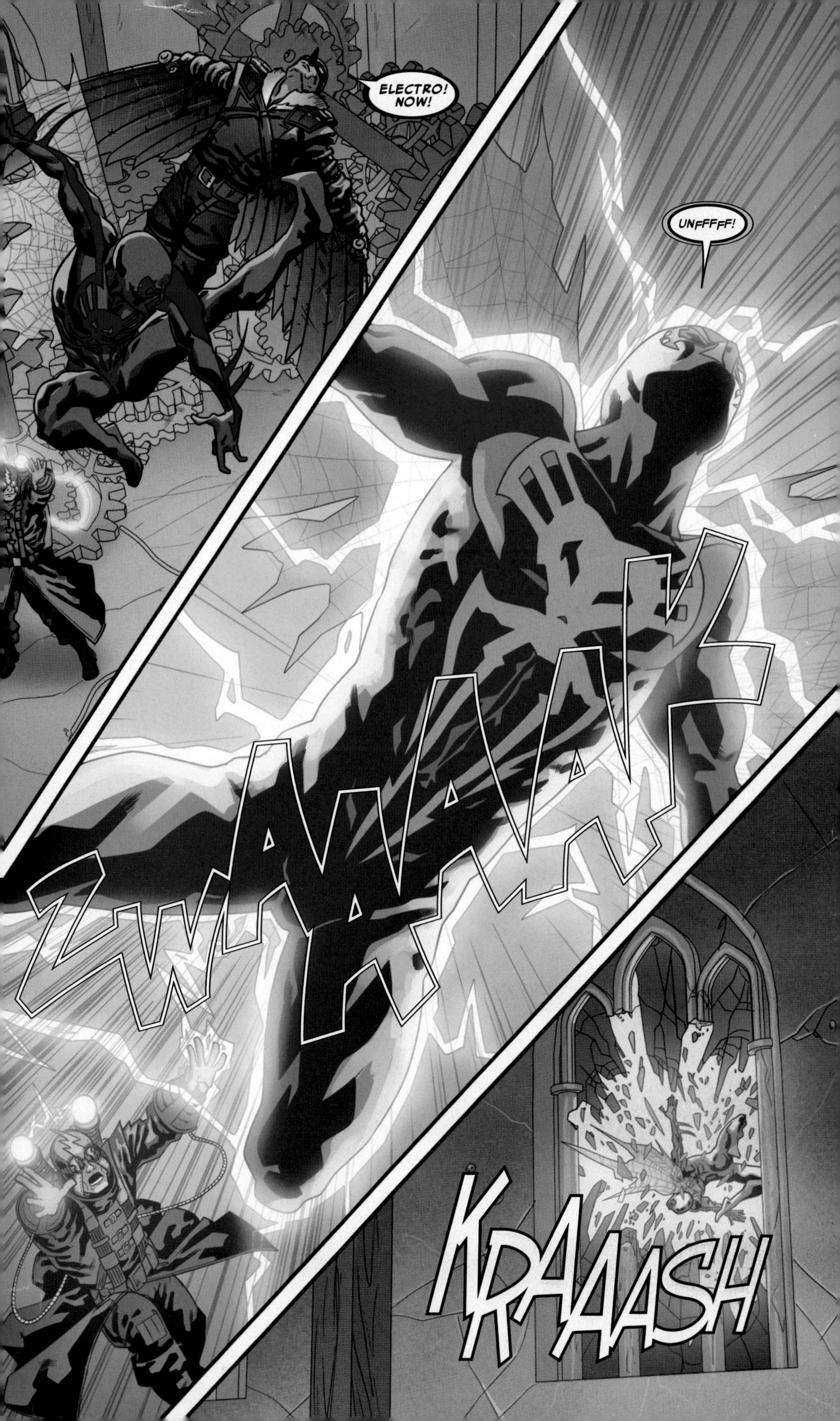
ELECTRO! NOW!
UNFFFFF!
ZWAAAAK
KRAAASH

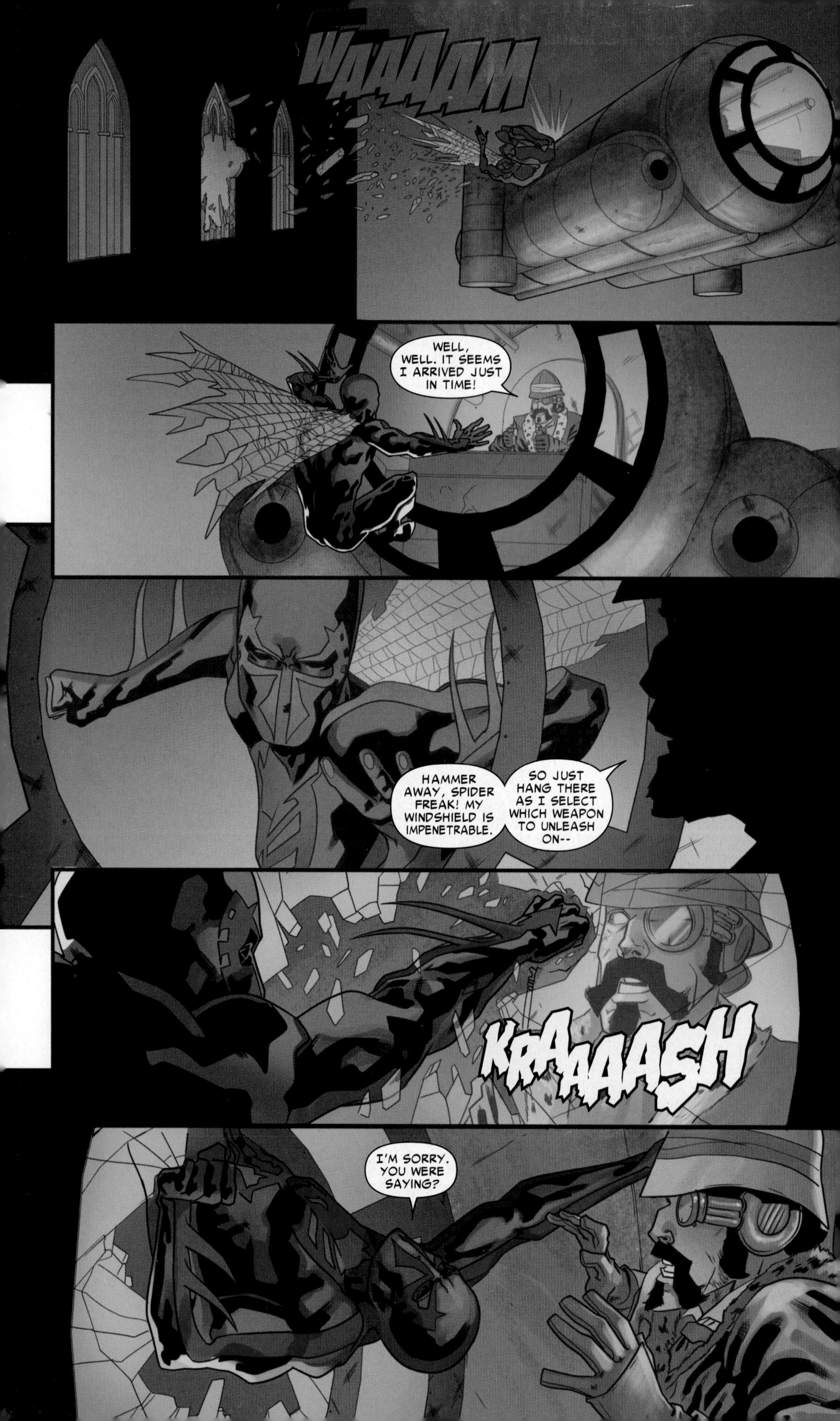
WAAAAM
WELL, WELL. IT SEEMS I ARRIVED JUST IN TIME!
HAMMER AWAY, SPIDER FREAK! MY WINDSHIELD IS IMPENETRABLE.
SO JUST HANG THERE AS I SELECT WHICH WEAPON TO UNLEASH ON--
KRAAAAASH
I'M SORRY. YOU WERE SAYING?

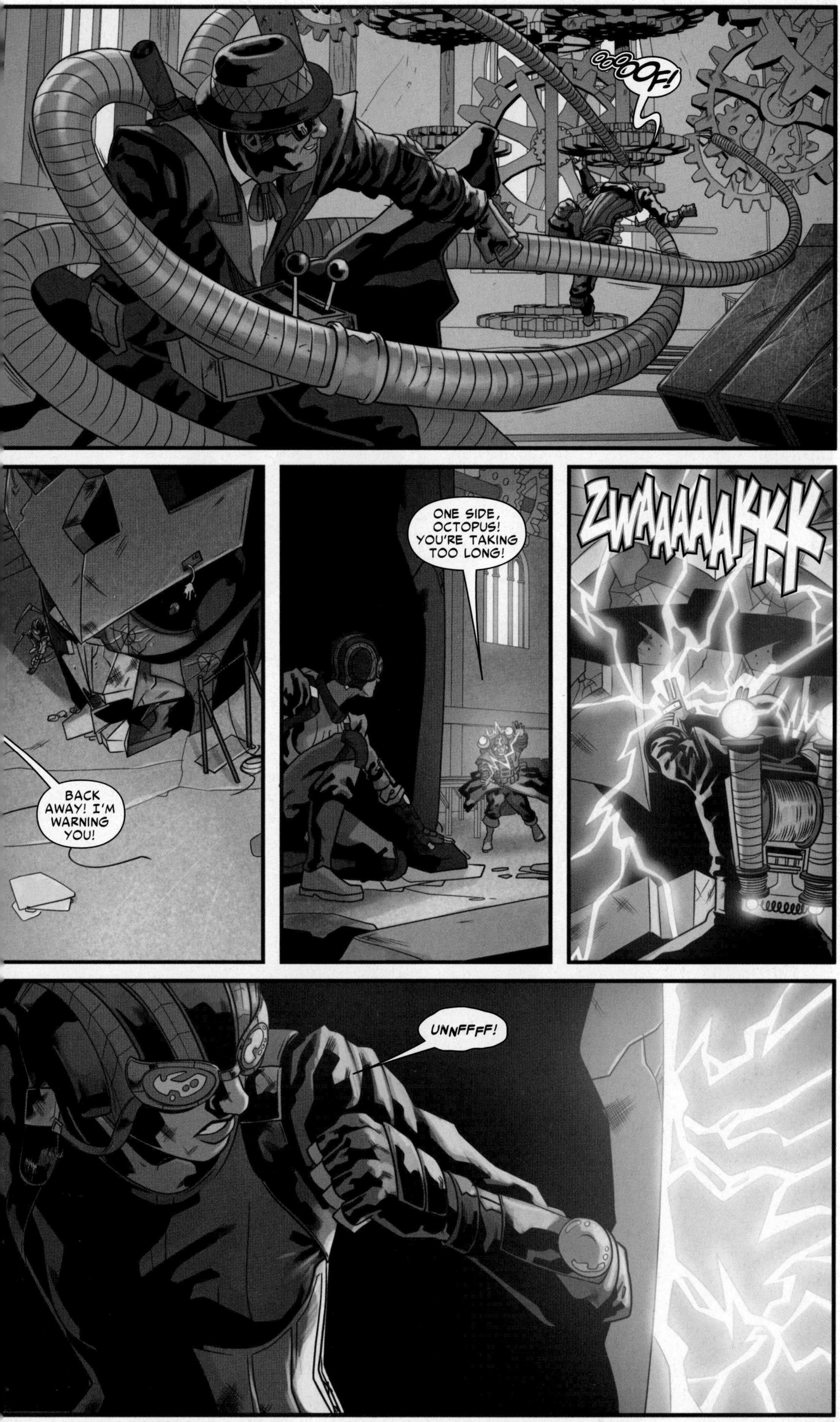

OOOOOF!
BACK AWAY! I'M WARNING YOU!
ONE SIDE, OCTOPUS! YOU'RE TAKING TOO LONG!
ZWAAAAAKKK
UNNFFFF!

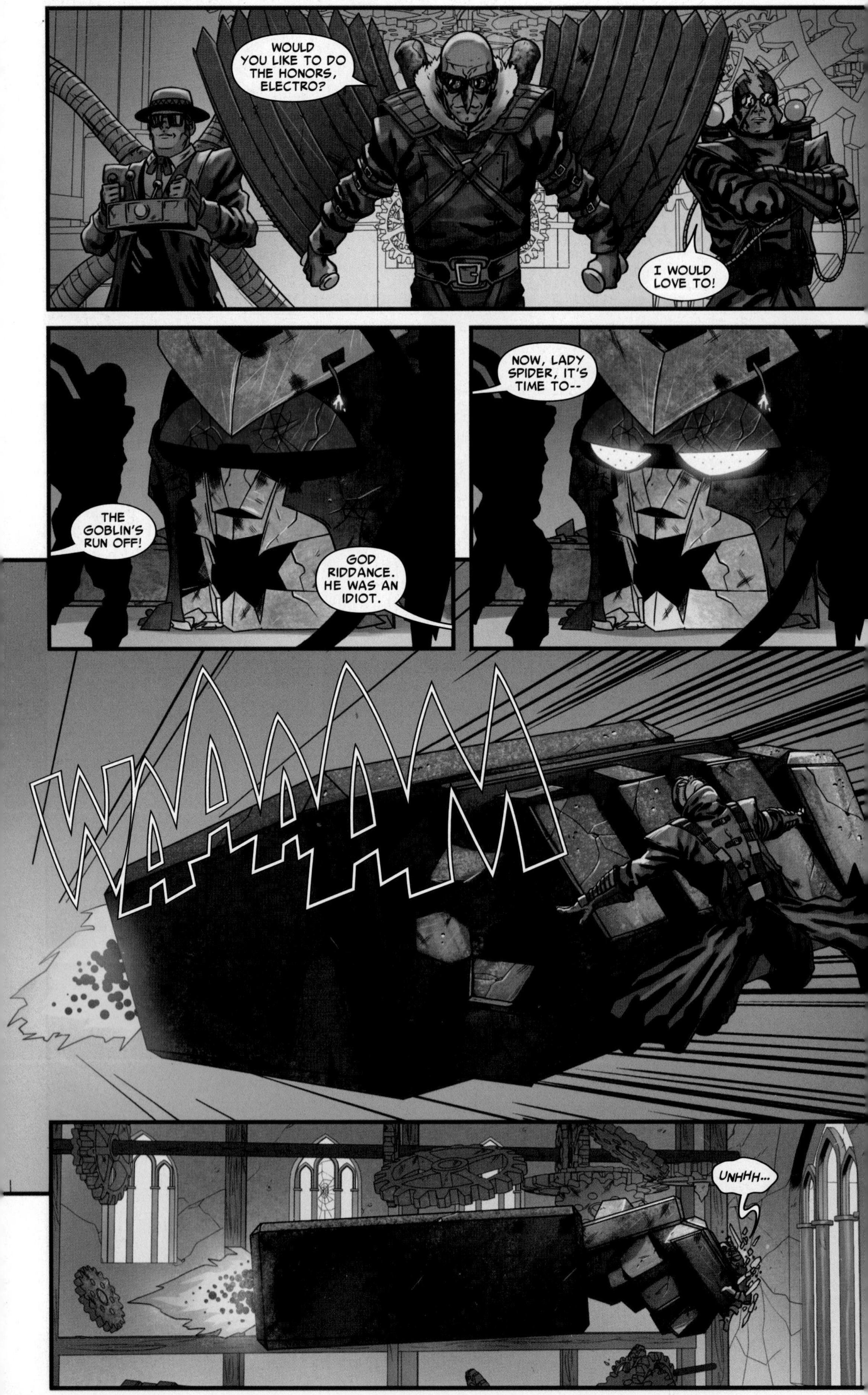
WOULD YOU LIKE TO DO THE HONORS, ELECTRO?
I WOULD LOVE TO!
THE GOBLIN'S RUN OFF!
GOD RIDDANCE. HE WAS AN IDIOT.
NOW, LADY SPIDER, IT'S TIME TO--
WHAAAM
UNHHH...

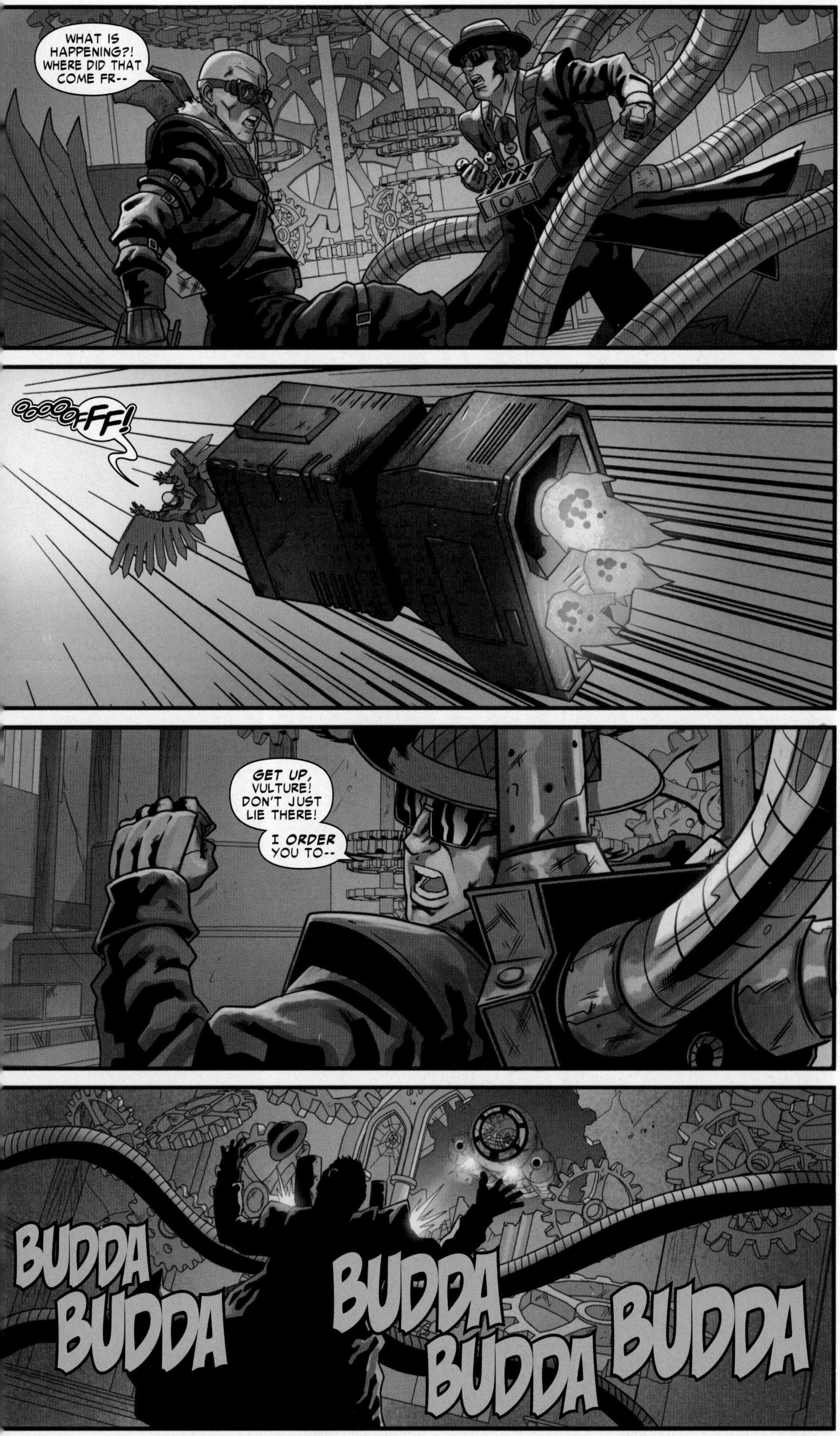
WHAT IS HAPPENING?! WHERE DID THAT COME FR--
OOOOOFFF!
GET UP, VULTURE! DON'T JUST LIE THERE!
I ORDER YOU TO--
BUDDA BUDDA
BUDDA BUDDA
BUDDA

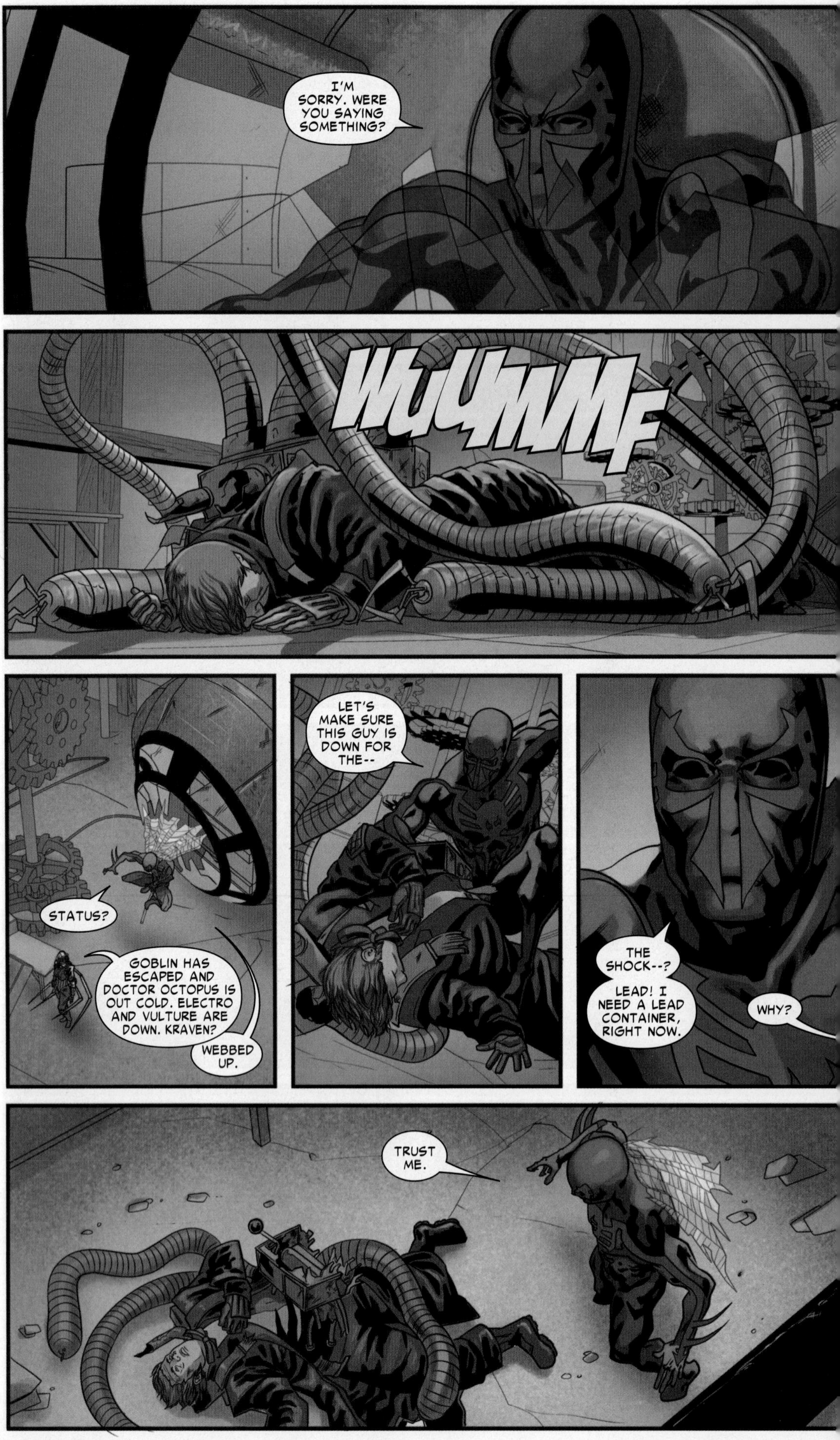
I'M SORRY. WERE YOU SAYING SOMETHING?
WUUMMF
STATUS?
GOBLIN HAS ESCAPED AND DOCTOR OCTOPUS IS OUT COLD. ELECTRO AND VULTURE ARE DOWN. KRAVEN?
WEBBED UP.
LET'S MAKE SURE THIS GUY IS DOWN FOR THE--
THE SHOCK--?
LEAD! I NEED A LEAD CONTAINER, RIGHT NOW.
WHY?
TRUST ME.

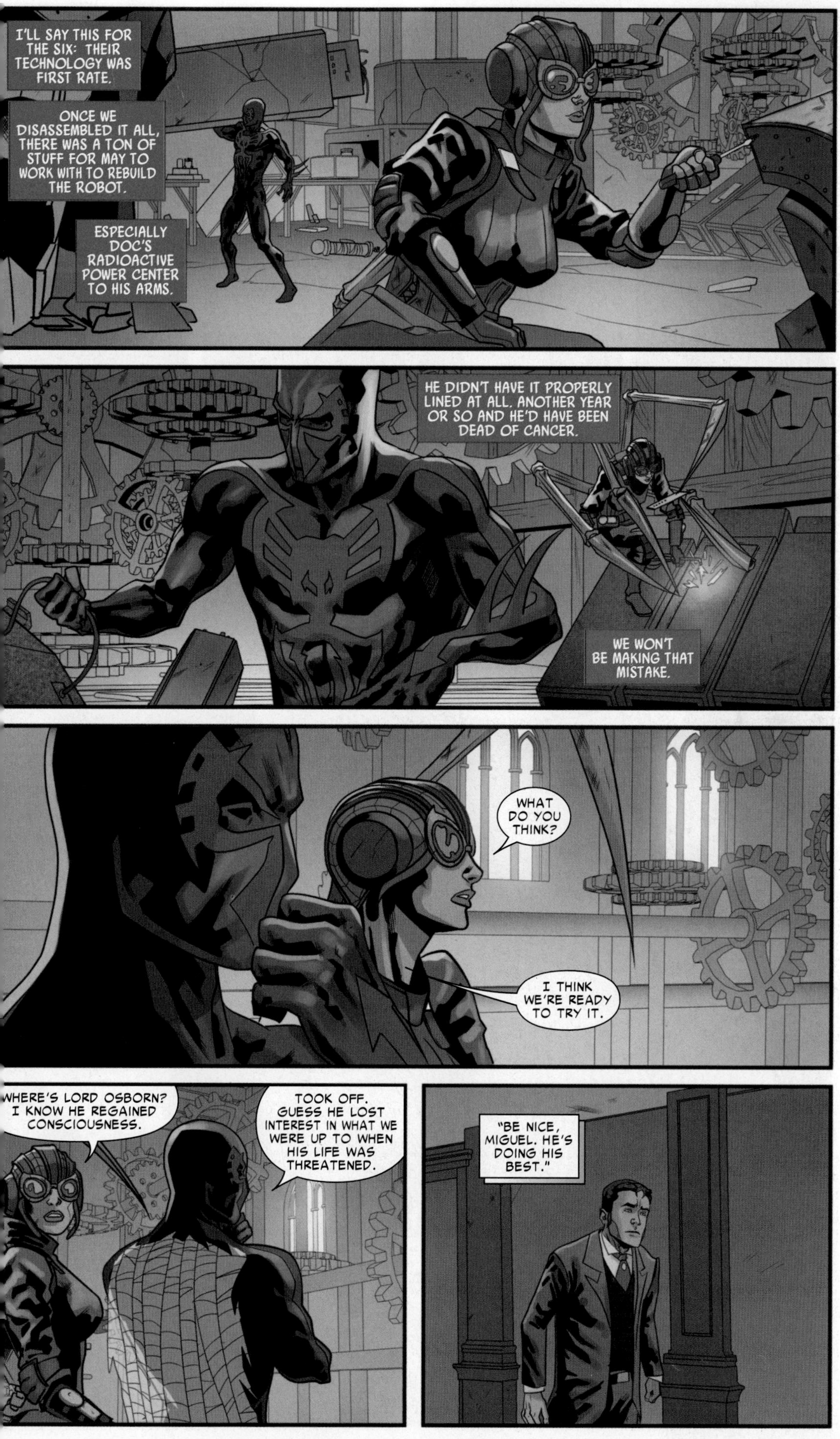
I'LL SAY THIS FOR THE SIX: THEIR TECHNOLOGY WAS FIRST RATE.
ONCE WE DISASSEMBLED IT ALL, THERE WAS A TON OF STUFF FOR MAY TO WORK WITH TO REBUILD THE ROBOT.
ESPECIALLY DOC'S RADIOACTIVE POWER CENTER TO HIS ARMS.
HE DIDN'T HAVE IT PROPERLY LINED AT ALL. ANOTHER YEAR OR SO AND HE'D HAVE BEEN DEAD OF CANCER.
WE WON'T BE MAKING THAT MISTAKE.
WHAT DO YOU THINK?
I THINK WE'RE READY TO TRY IT.
WHERE'S LORD OSBORN? I KNOW HE REGAINED CONSCIOUSNESS.
TOOK OFF. GUESS HE LOST INTEREST IN WHAT WE WERE UP TO WHEN HIS LIFE WAS THREATENED.
"BE NICE, MIGUEL. HE'S DOING HIS BEST."

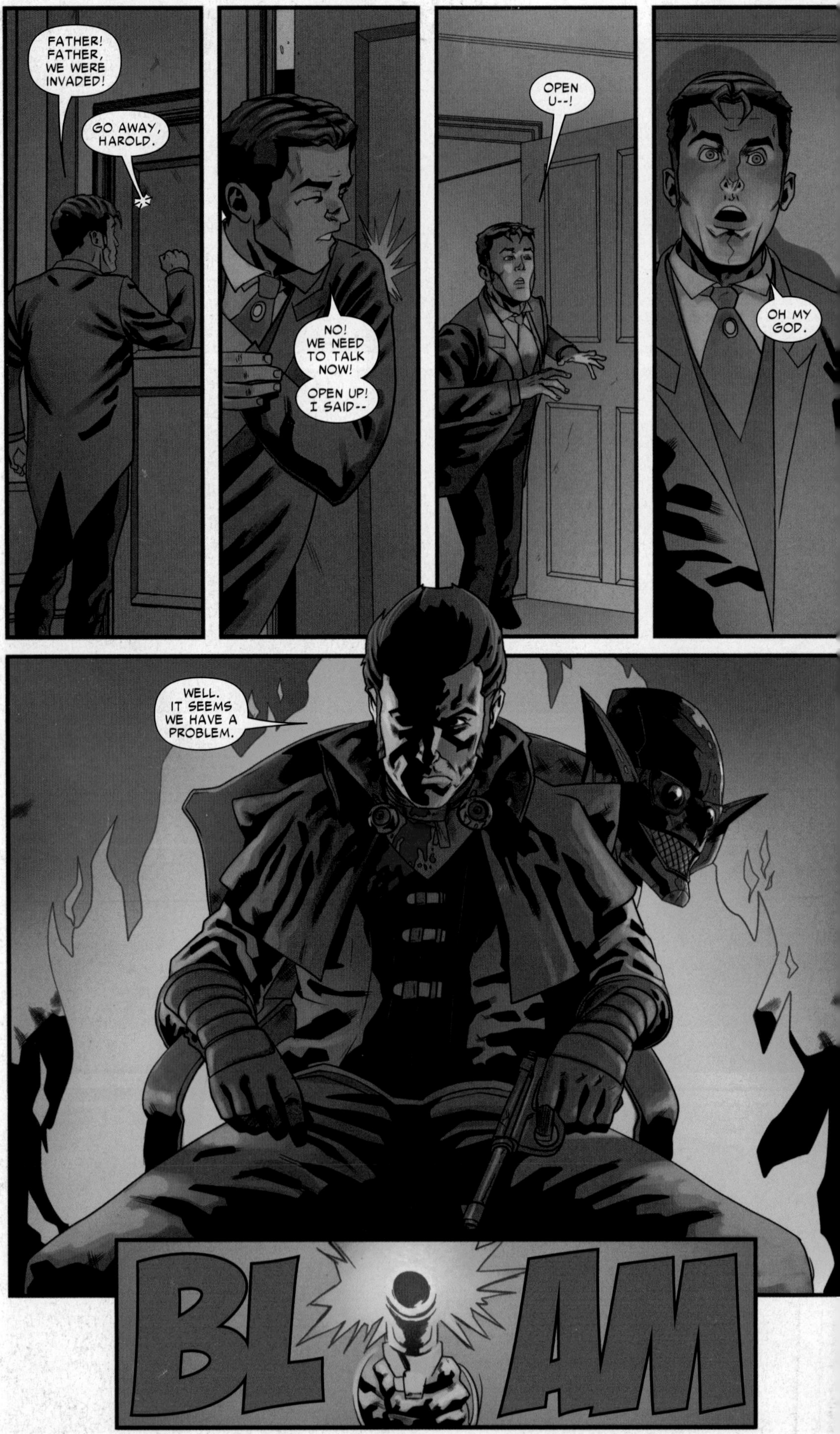
FATHER! FATHER, WE WERE INVADED!
GO AWAY, HAROLD.
NO! WE NEED TO TALK NOW!
OPEN UP! I SAID--
OPEN U--!
OH MY GOD.
WELL. IT SEEMS WE HAVE A PROBLEM.
BLAM

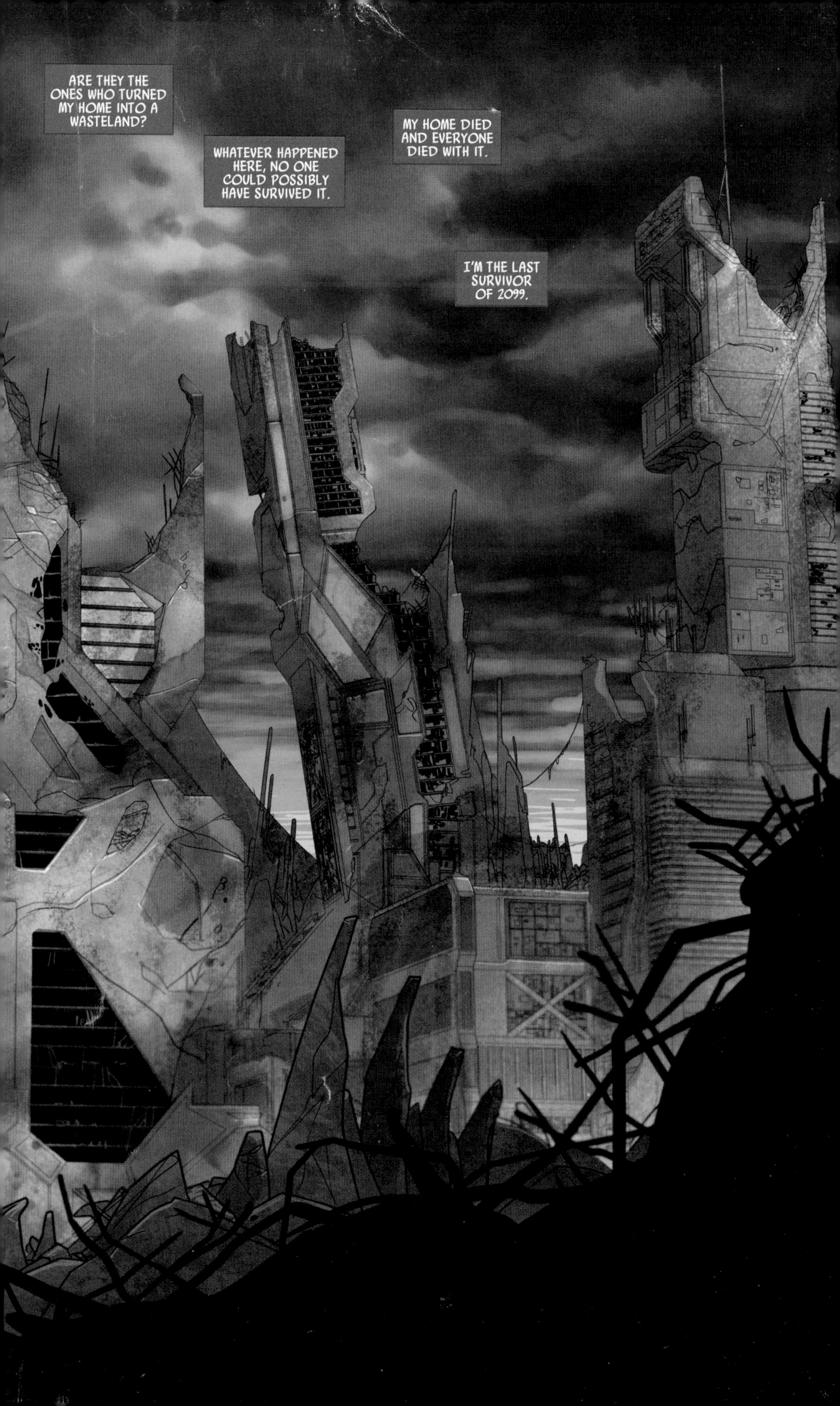
ARE THEY THE ONES WHO TURNED MY HOME INTO A WASTELAND?
WHATEVER HAPPENED HERE, NO ONE COULD POSSIBLY HAVE SURVIVED IT.
MY HOME DIED AND EVERYONE DIED WITH IT.
I'M THE LAST SURVIVOR OF 2099.

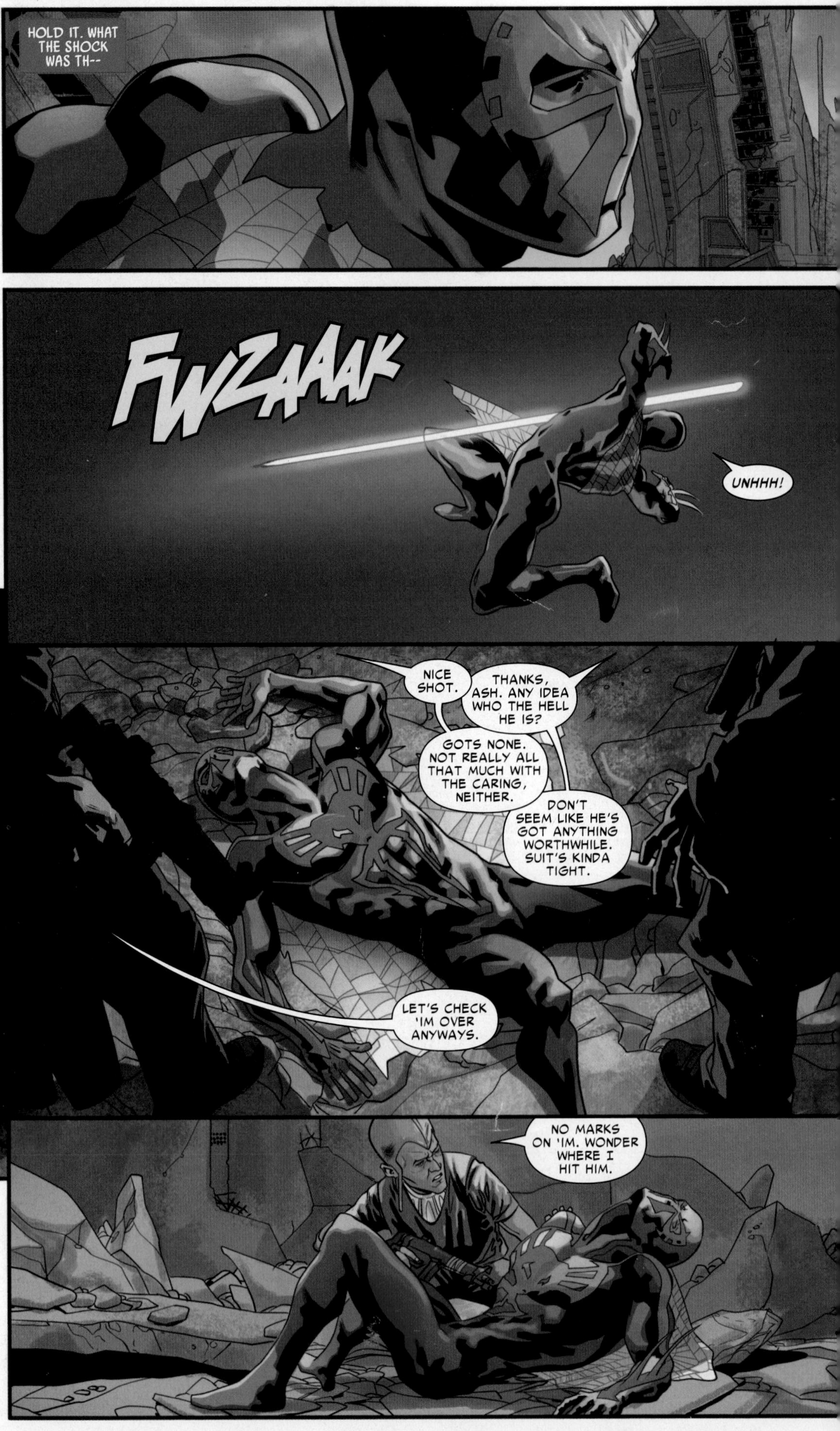
HOLD IT. WHAT THE SHOCK WAS TH--
FWZAAAK
UNHHH!
NICE SHOT.
THANKS, ASH. ANY IDEA WHO THE HELL HE IS?
GOTS NONE. NOT REALLY ALL THAT MUCH WITH THE CARING, NEITHER.
DON'T SEEM LIKE HE'S GOT ANYTHING WORTHWHILE. SUIT'S KINDA TIGHT.
LET'S CHECK 'IM OVER ANYWAYS.
NO MARKS ON 'IM. WONDER WHERE I HIT HIM.

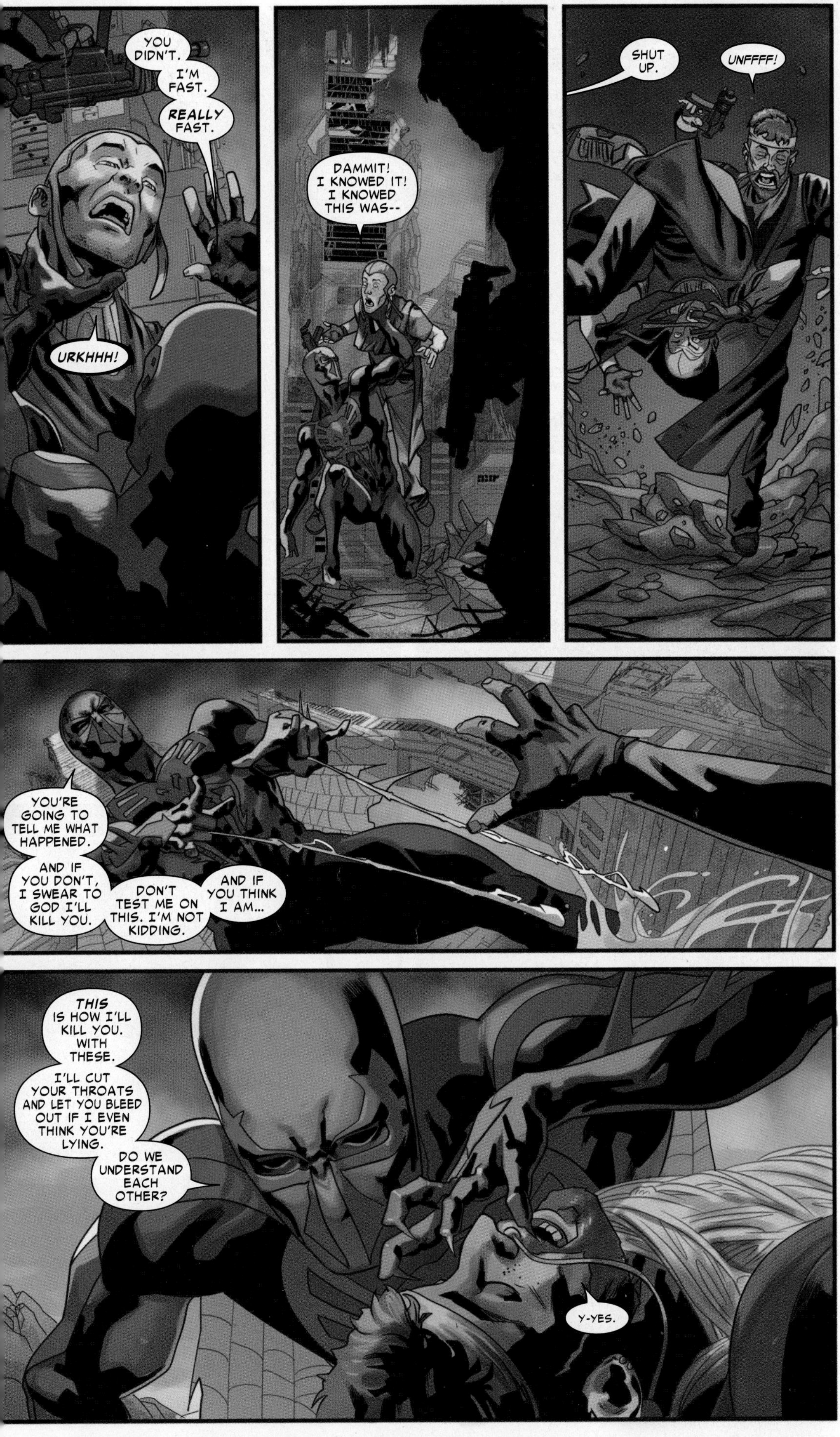
YOU DIDN'T.
I'M FAST.
REALLY FAST.
URKHHH!
DAMMIT! I KNOWED IT! I KNOWED THIS WAS--
SHUT UP.
UNFFFF!
YOU'RE GOING TO TELL ME WHAT HAPPENED.
AND IF YOU DON'T, I SWEAR TO GOD I'LL KILL YOU.
DON'T TEST ME ON THIS. I'M NOT KIDDING.
AND IF YOU THINK I AM...
THIS IS HOW I'LL KILL YOU. WITH THESE.
I'LL CUT YOUR THROATS AND LET YOU BLEED OUT IF I EVEN THINK YOU'RE LYING.
DO WE UNDERSTAND EACH OTHER?
Y-YES.

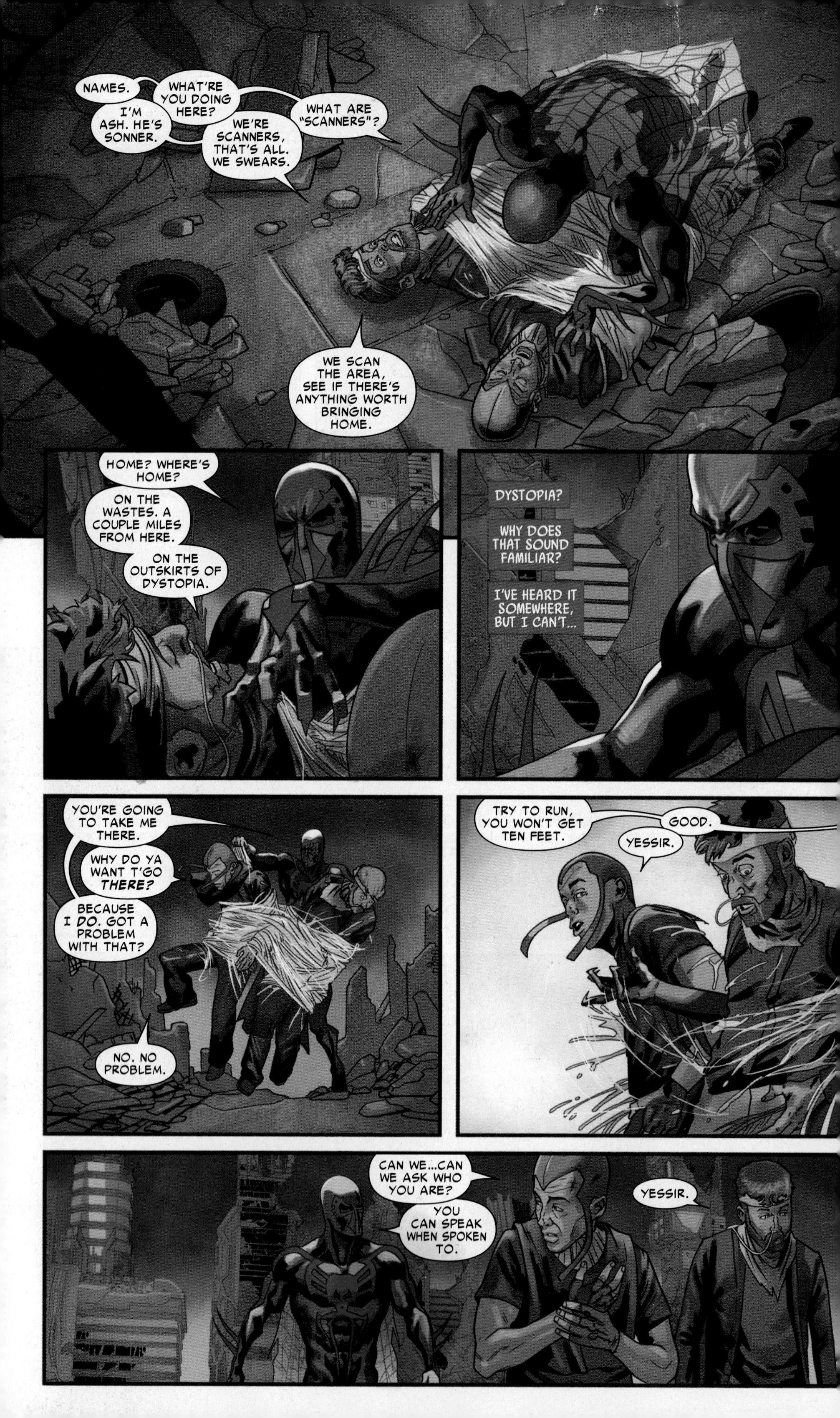
NAMES.
WHAT'RE YOU DOING HERE?
I'M ASH. HE'S SONNER.
WE'RE SCANNERS, THAT'S ALL. WE SWEARS.
WHAT ARE "SCANNERS"?
WE SCAN THE AREA, SEE IF THERE'S ANYTHING WORTH BRINGING HOME.
HOME? WHERE'S HOME?
ON THE WASTES. A COUPLE MILES FROM HERE.
ON THE OUTSKIRTS OF DYSTOPIA.
DYSTOPIA?
WHY DOES THAT SOUND FAMILIAR?
I'VE HEARD IT SOMEWHERE, BUT I CAN'T...
YOU'RE GOING TO TAKE ME THERE.
WHY DO YA WANT T'GO *THERE?*
BECAUSE I *DO.* GOT A PROBLEM WITH THAT?
NO. NO PROBLEM.
TRY TO RUN, YOU WON'T GET TEN FEET.
GOOD.
YESSIR.
CAN WE...CAN WE ASK WHO YOU ARE?
YOU CAN SPEAK WHEN SPOKEN TO.
YESSIR.

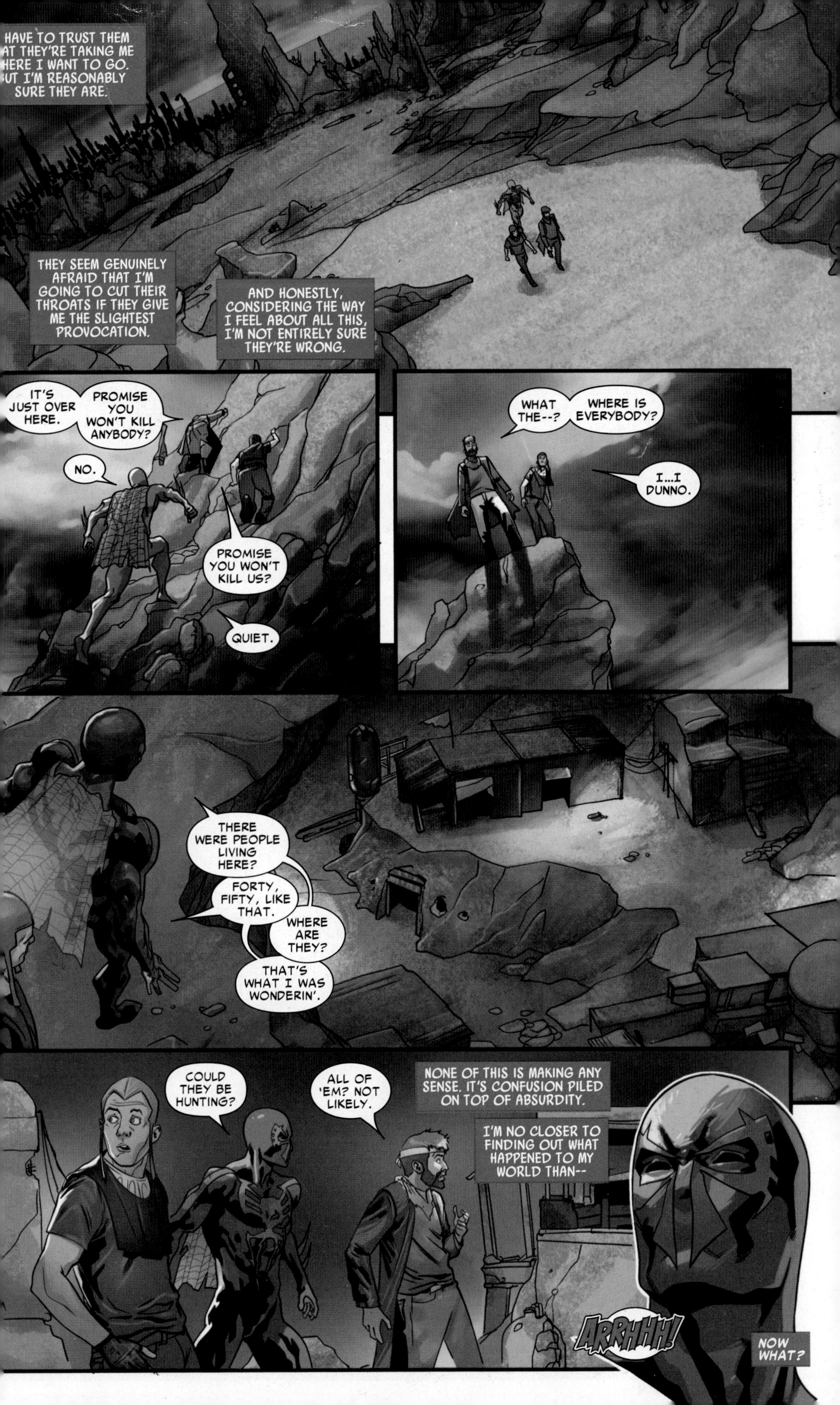
HAVE TO TRUST THEM
AT THEY'RE TAKING ME
HERE I WANT TO GO.
UT I'M REASONABLY
SURE THEY ARE.
THEY SEEM GENUINELY AFRAID THAT I'M GOING TO CUT THEIR THROATS IF THEY GIVE ME THE SLIGHTEST PROVOCATION.
AND HONESTLY, CONSIDERING THE WAY I FEEL ABOUT ALL THIS, I'M NOT ENTIRELY SURE THEY'RE WRONG.
IT'S JUST OVER HERE.
PROMISE YOU WON'T KILL ANYBODY?
NO.
PROMISE YOU WON'T KILL US?
QUIET.
WHAT THE--?
WHERE IS EVERYBODY?
I...I DUNNO.
THERE WERE PEOPLE LIVING HERE?
FORTY, FIFTY, LIKE THAT.
WHERE ARE THEY?
THAT'S WHAT I WAS WONDERIN'.
COULD THEY BE HUNTING?
ALL OF 'EM? NOT LIKELY.
NONE OF THIS IS MAKING ANY SENSE. IT'S CONFUSION PILED ON TOP OF ABSURDITY.
I'M NO CLOSER TO FINDING OUT WHAT HAPPENED TO MY WORLD THAN--
ARRHHH!
NOW WHAT?

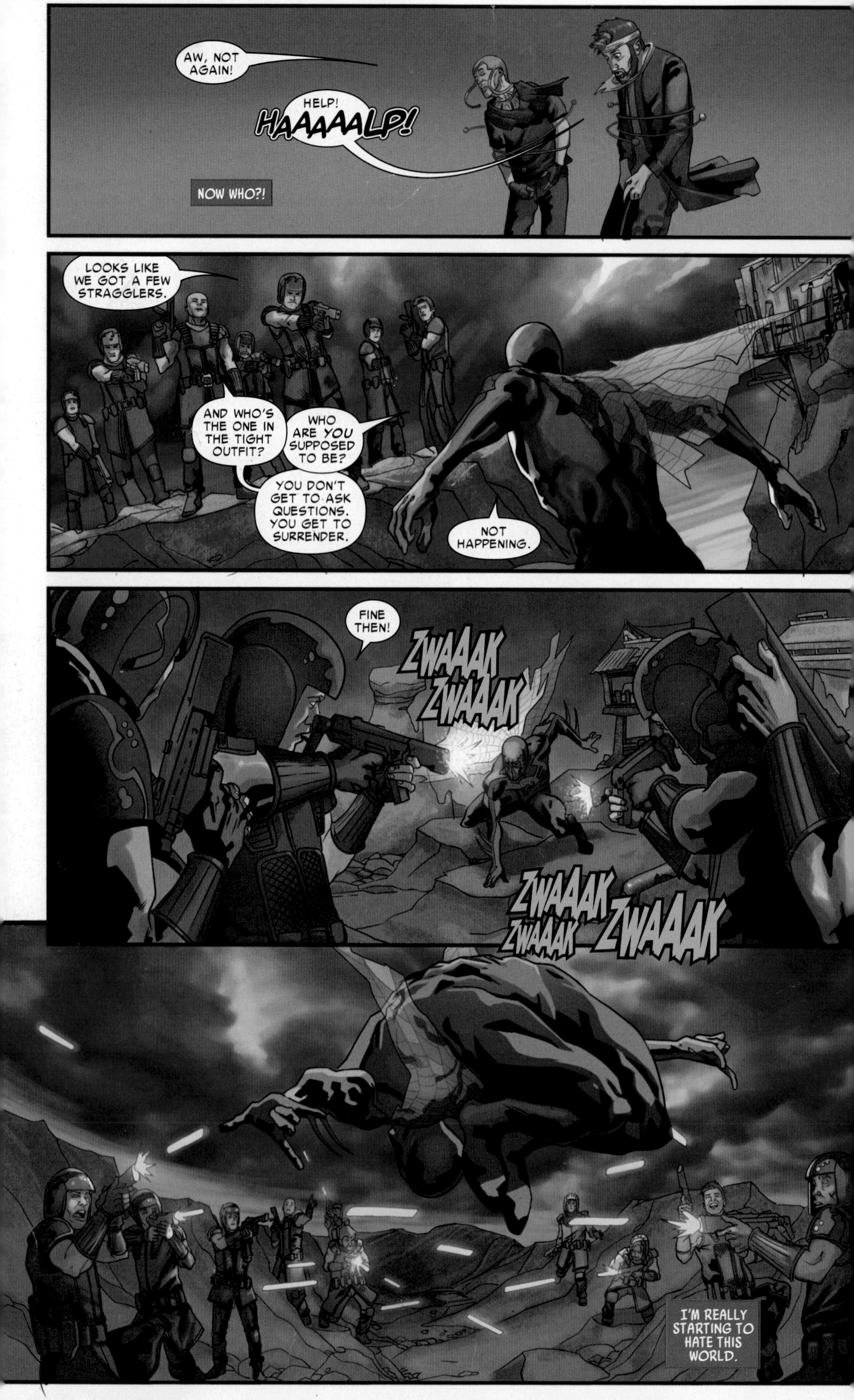
AW, NOT AGAIN!
HELP! HAAAAALP!
NOW WHO?!
LOOKS LIKE WE GOT A FEW STRAGGLERS.
AND WHO'S THE ONE IN THE TIGHT OUTFIT?
WHO ARE *YOU* SUPPOSED TO BE?
YOU DON'T GET TO ASK QUESTIONS. YOU GET TO SURRENDER.
NOT HAPPENING.
FINE THEN!
ZWAAAK ZWAAAK
ZWAAAK ZWAAAK ZWAAAK
I'M REALLY STARTING TO HATE THIS WORLD.

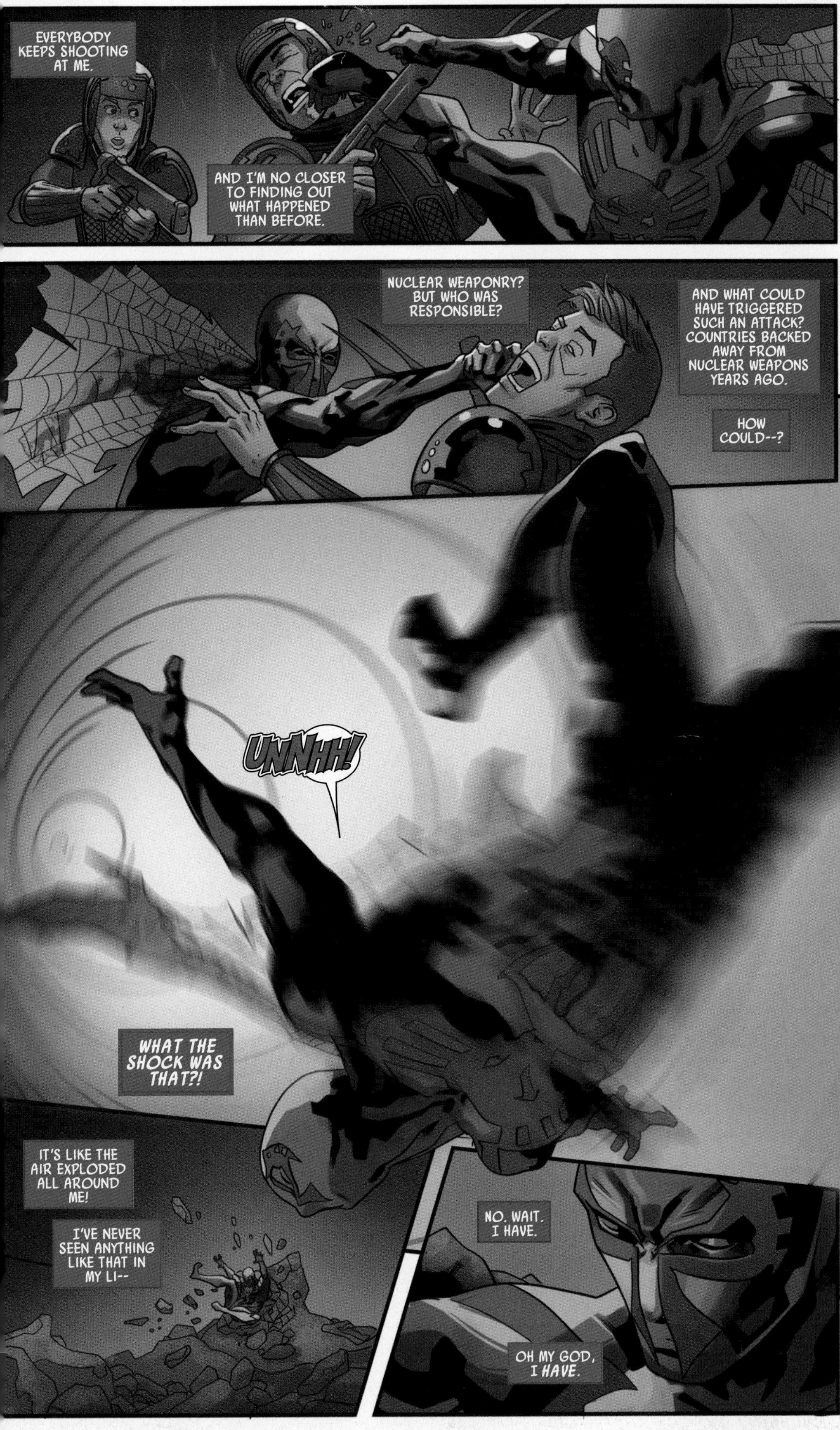
EVERYBODY KEEPS SHOOTING AT ME.
AND I'M NO CLOSER TO FINDING OUT WHAT HAPPENED THAN BEFORE.
NUCLEAR WEAPONRY? BUT WHO WAS RESPONSIBLE?
AND WHAT COULD HAVE TRIGGERED SUCH AN ATTACK? COUNTRIES BACKED AWAY FROM NUCLEAR WEAPONS YEARS AGO.
HOW COULD--?
UNNHH!
WHAT THE SHOCK WAS THAT?!
IT'S LIKE THE AIR EXPLODED ALL AROUND ME!
I'VE NEVER SEEN ANYTHING LIKE THAT IN MY LI--
NO. WAIT. I HAVE.
OH MY GOD, I HAVE.

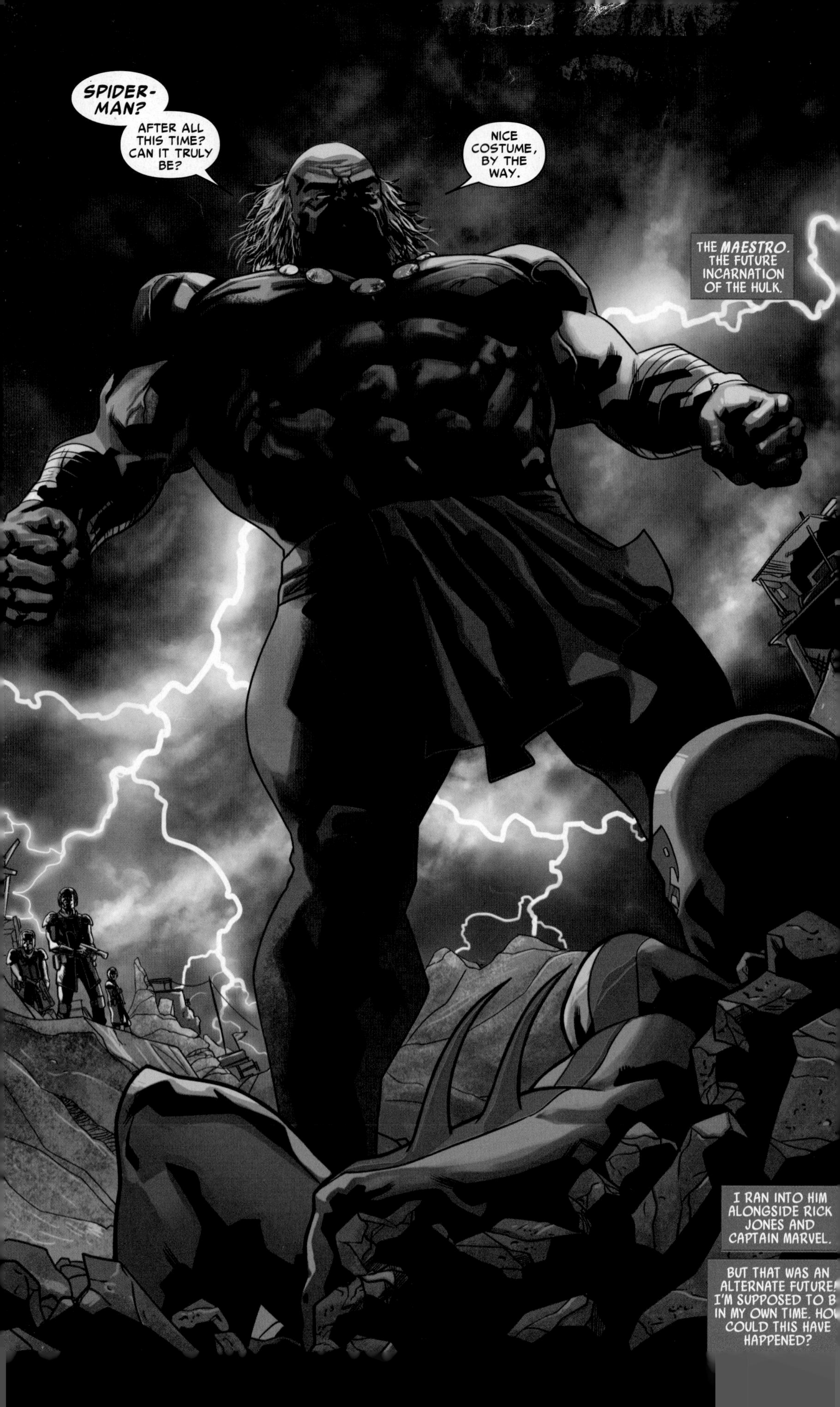
SPIDER-MAN?
AFTER ALL THIS TIME? CAN IT TRULY BE?
NICE COSTUME, BY THE WAY.
THE MAESTRO. THE FUTURE INCARNATION OF THE HULK.
I RAN INTO HIM ALONGSIDE RICK JONES AND CAPTAIN MARVEL.
BUT THAT WAS AN ALTERNATE FUTURE! I'M SUPPOSED TO B IN MY OWN TIME. HO COULD THIS HAVE HAPPENED?

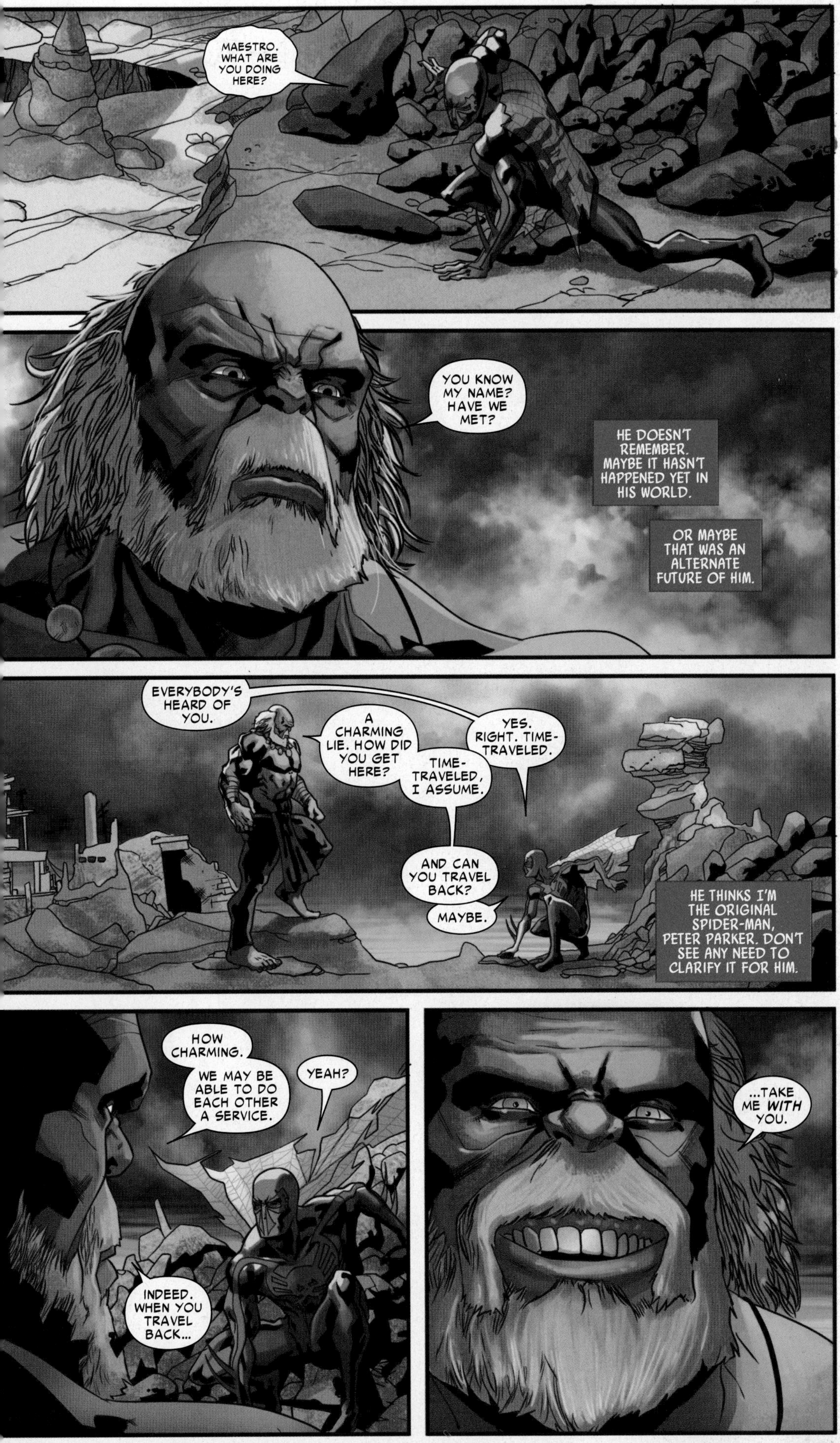
MAESTRO. WHAT ARE YOU DOING HERE?
YOU KNOW MY NAME? HAVE WE MET?
HE DOESN'T REMEMBER. MAYBE IT HASN'T HAPPENED YET IN HIS WORLD.
OR MAYBE THAT WAS AN ALTERNATE FUTURE OF HIM.
EVERYBODY'S HEARD OF YOU.
A CHARMING LIE. HOW DID YOU GET HERE?
TIME-TRAVELED, I ASSUME.
YES. RIGHT. TIME-TRAVELED.
AND CAN YOU TRAVEL BACK?
MAYBE.
HE THINKS I'M THE ORIGINAL SPIDER-MAN, PETER PARKER. DON'T SEE ANY NEED TO CLARIFY IT FOR HIM.
HOW CHARMING.
WE MAY BE ABLE TO DO EACH OTHER A SERVICE.
YEAH?
INDEED. WHEN YOU TRAVEL BACK...
...TAKE ME *WITH* YOU.

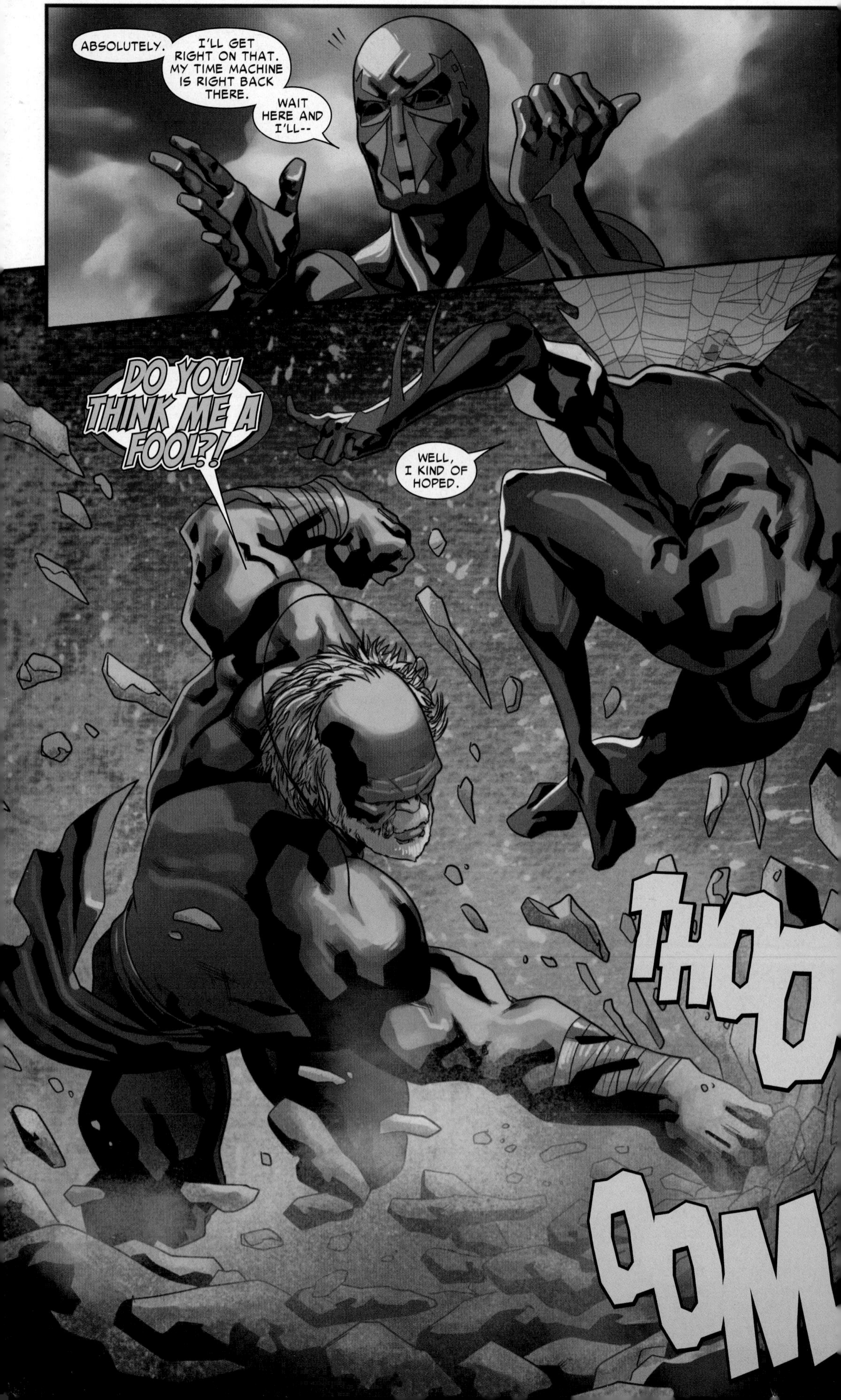
ABSOLUTELY.
I'LL GET RIGHT ON THAT. MY TIME MACHINE IS RIGHT BACK THERE.
WAIT HERE AND I'LL--
DO YOU THINK ME A FOOL?!
WELL, I KIND OF HOPED.
THOOOOM

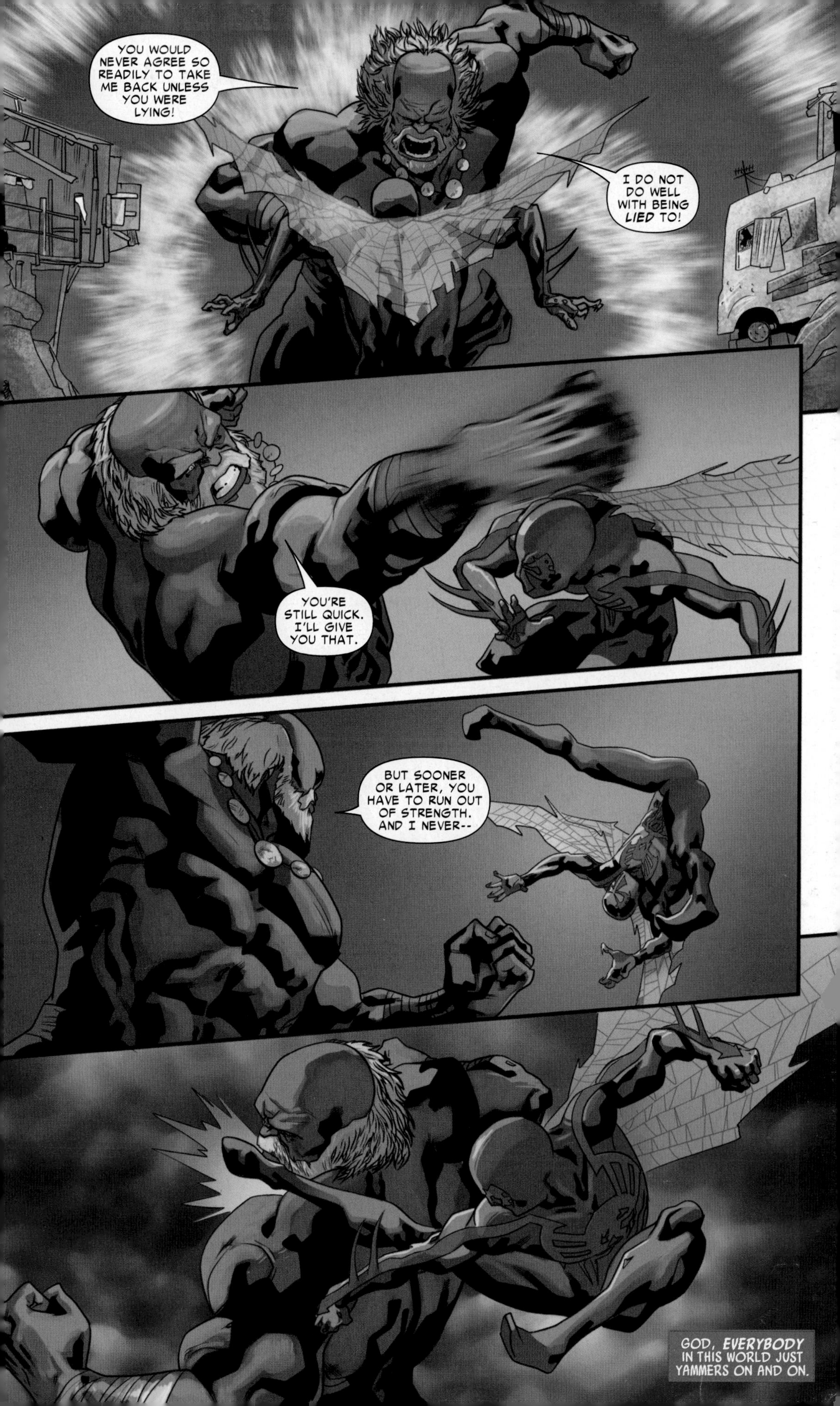
YOU WOULD NEVER AGREE SO READILY TO TAKE ME BACK UNLESS YOU WERE LYING!
I DO NOT DO WELL WITH BEING LIED TO!
YOU'RE STILL QUICK. I'LL GIVE YOU THAT.
BUT SOONER OR LATER, YOU HAVE TO RUN OUT OF STRENGTH. AND I NEVER--
GOD, EVERYBODY IN THIS WORLD JUST YAMMERS ON AND ON.

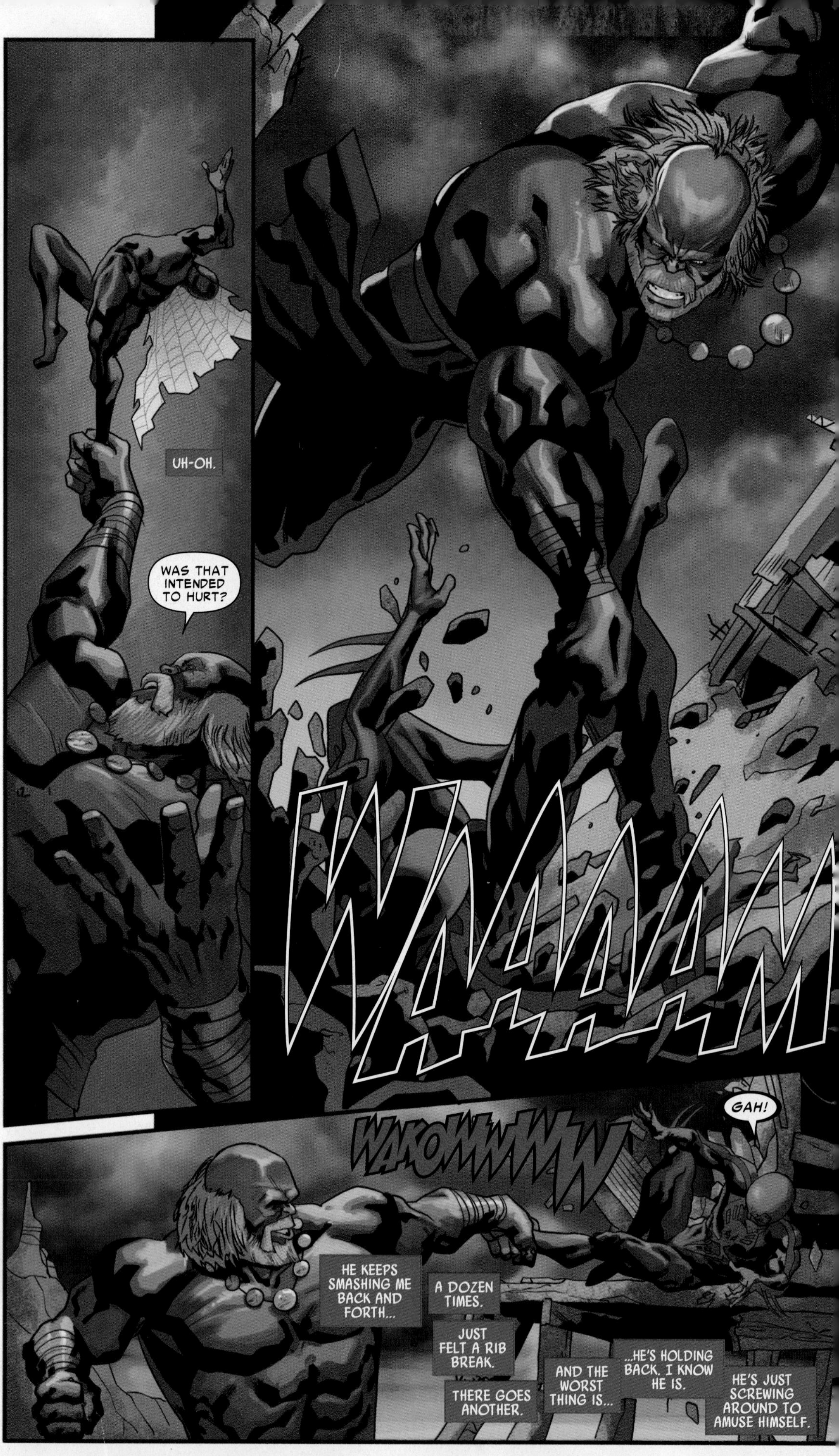
UH-OH.
WAS THAT INTENDED TO HURT?
WHAAAM
GAH!
WAKOWWWW
HE KEEPS SMASHING ME BACK AND FORTH...
A DOZEN TIMES.
JUST FELT A RIB BREAK.
THERE GOES ANOTHER.
AND THE WORST THING IS...
...HE'S HOLDING BACK. I KNOW HE IS.
HE'S JUST SCREWING AROUND TO AMUSE HIMSELF.

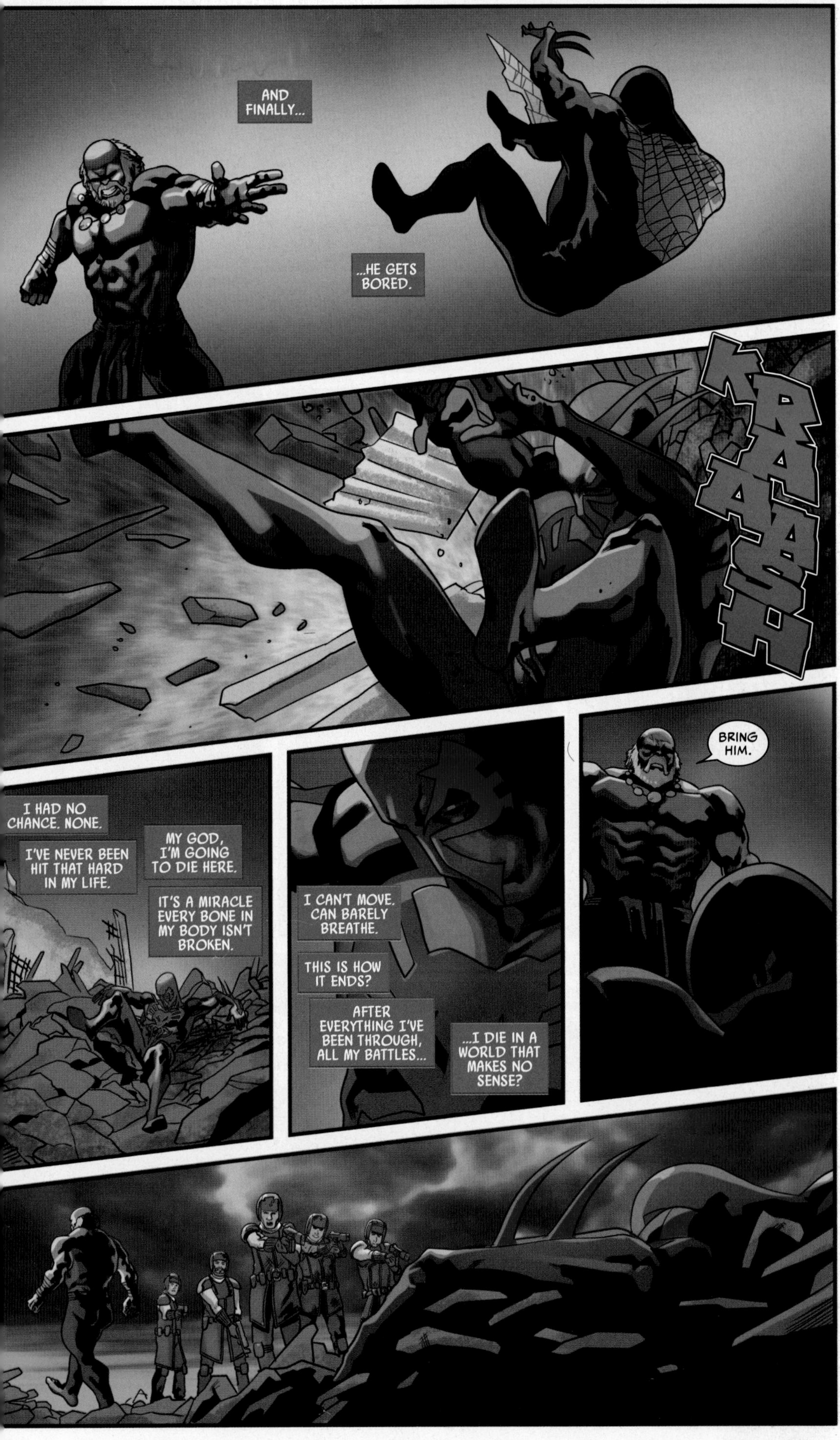
AND FINALLY...
...HE GETS BORED.
KRAAASH
I HAD NO CHANCE. NONE.
I'VE NEVER BEEN HIT THAT HARD IN MY LIFE.
MY GOD, I'M GOING TO DIE HERE.
IT'S A MIRACLE EVERY BONE IN MY BODY ISN'T BROKEN.
I CAN'T MOVE. CAN BARELY BREATHE.
THIS IS HOW IT ENDS?
AFTER EVERYTHING I'VE BEEN THROUGH, ALL MY BATTLES...
...I DIE IN A WORLD THAT MAKES NO SENSE?
BRING HIM.

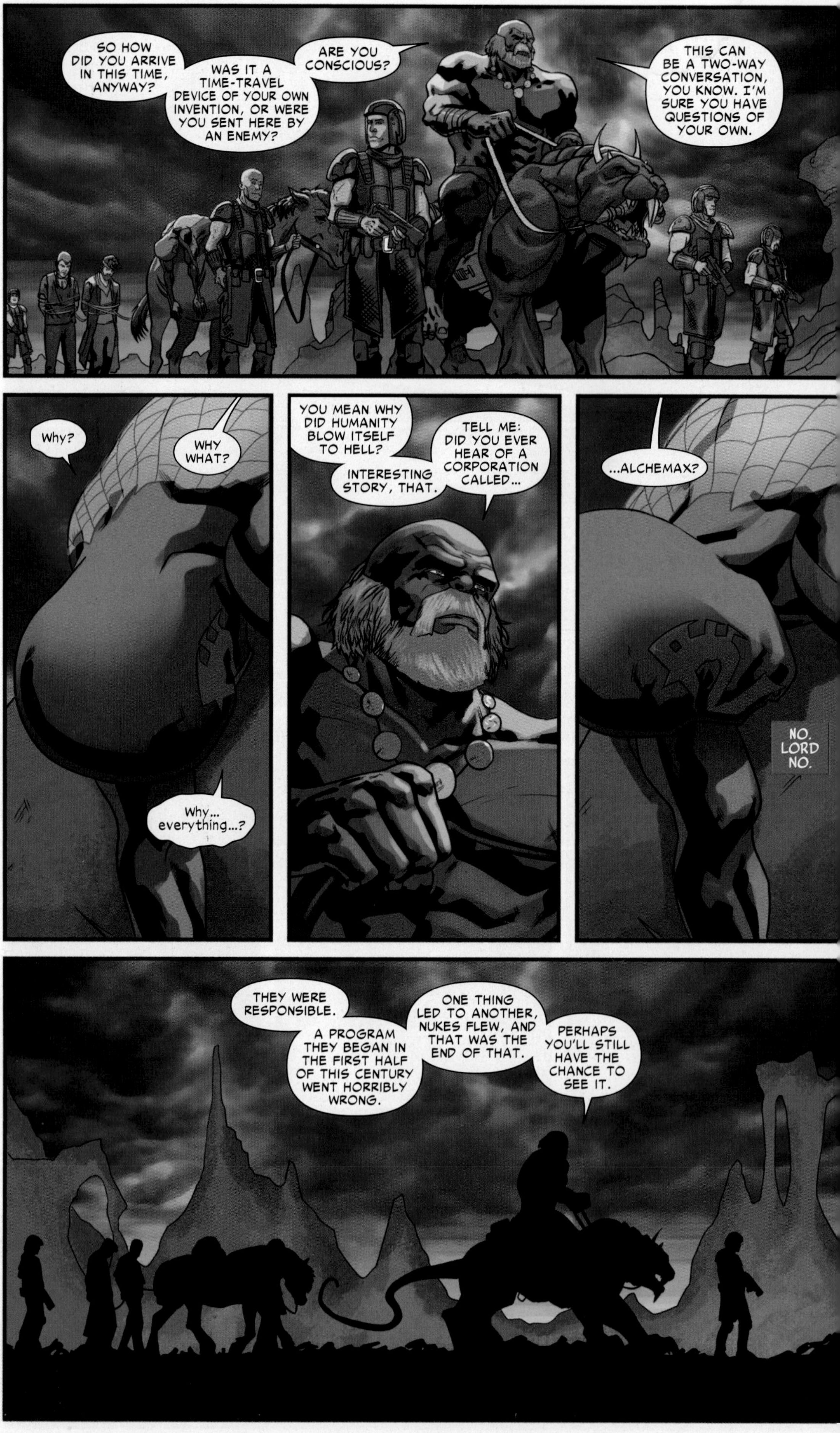
SO HOW DID YOU ARRIVE IN THIS TIME, ANYWAY?
WAS IT A TIME-TRAVEL DEVICE OF YOUR OWN INVENTION, OR WERE YOU SENT HERE BY AN ENEMY?
ARE YOU CONSCIOUS?
THIS CAN BE A TWO-WAY CONVERSATION, YOU KNOW. I'M SURE YOU HAVE QUESTIONS OF YOUR OWN.
Why?
WHY WHAT?
Why... everything...?
YOU MEAN WHY DID HUMANITY BLOW ITSELF TO HELL?
INTERESTING STORY, THAT.
TELL ME: DID YOU EVER HEAR OF A CORPORATION CALLED...
...ALCHEMAX?
NO. LORD NO.
THEY WERE RESPONSIBLE.
A PROGRAM THEY BEGAN IN THE FIRST HALF OF THIS CENTURY WENT HORRIBLY WRONG.
ONE THING LED TO ANOTHER, NUKES FLEW, AND THAT WAS THE END OF THAT.
PERHAPS YOU'LL STILL HAVE THE CHANCE TO SEE IT.

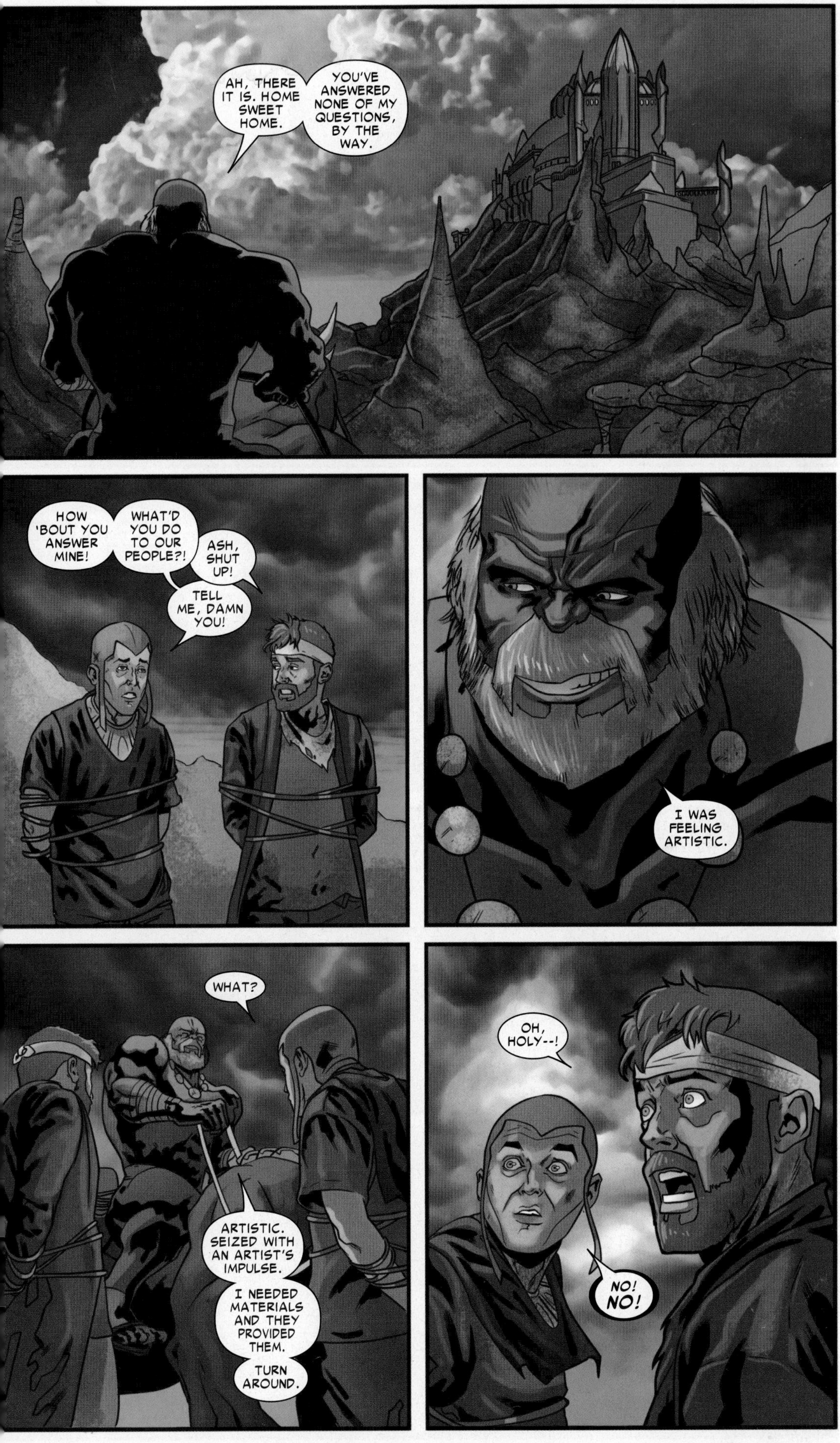
AH, THERE IT IS. HOME SWEET HOME.
YOU'VE ANSWERED NONE OF MY QUESTIONS, BY THE WAY.
HOW 'BOUT YOU ANSWER MINE!
WHAT'D YOU DO TO OUR PEOPLE?!
ASH, SHUT UP!
TELL ME, DAMN YOU!
I WAS FEELING ARTISTIC.
WHAT?
ARTISTIC. SEIZED WITH AN ARTIST'S IMPULSE.
I NEEDED MATERIALS AND THEY PROVIDED THEM.
TURN AROUND.
OH, HOLY--!
NO! NO!

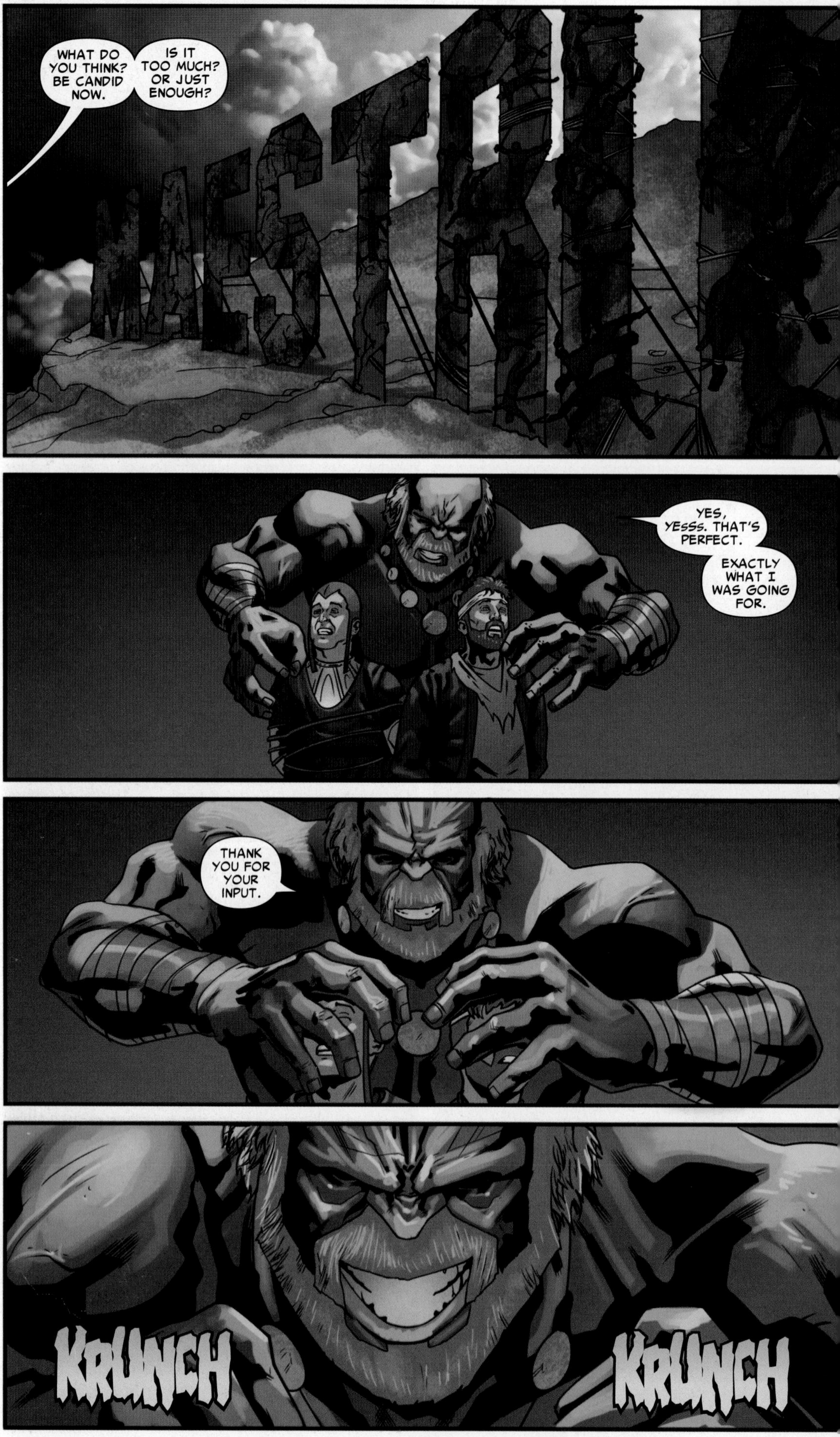
WHAT DO YOU THINK? BE CANDID NOW.
IS IT TOO MUCH? OR JUST ENOUGH?
YES, YESSS. THAT'S PERFECT.
EXACTLY WHAT I WAS GOING FOR.
THANK YOU FOR YOUR INPUT.
KRUNCH
KRUNCH

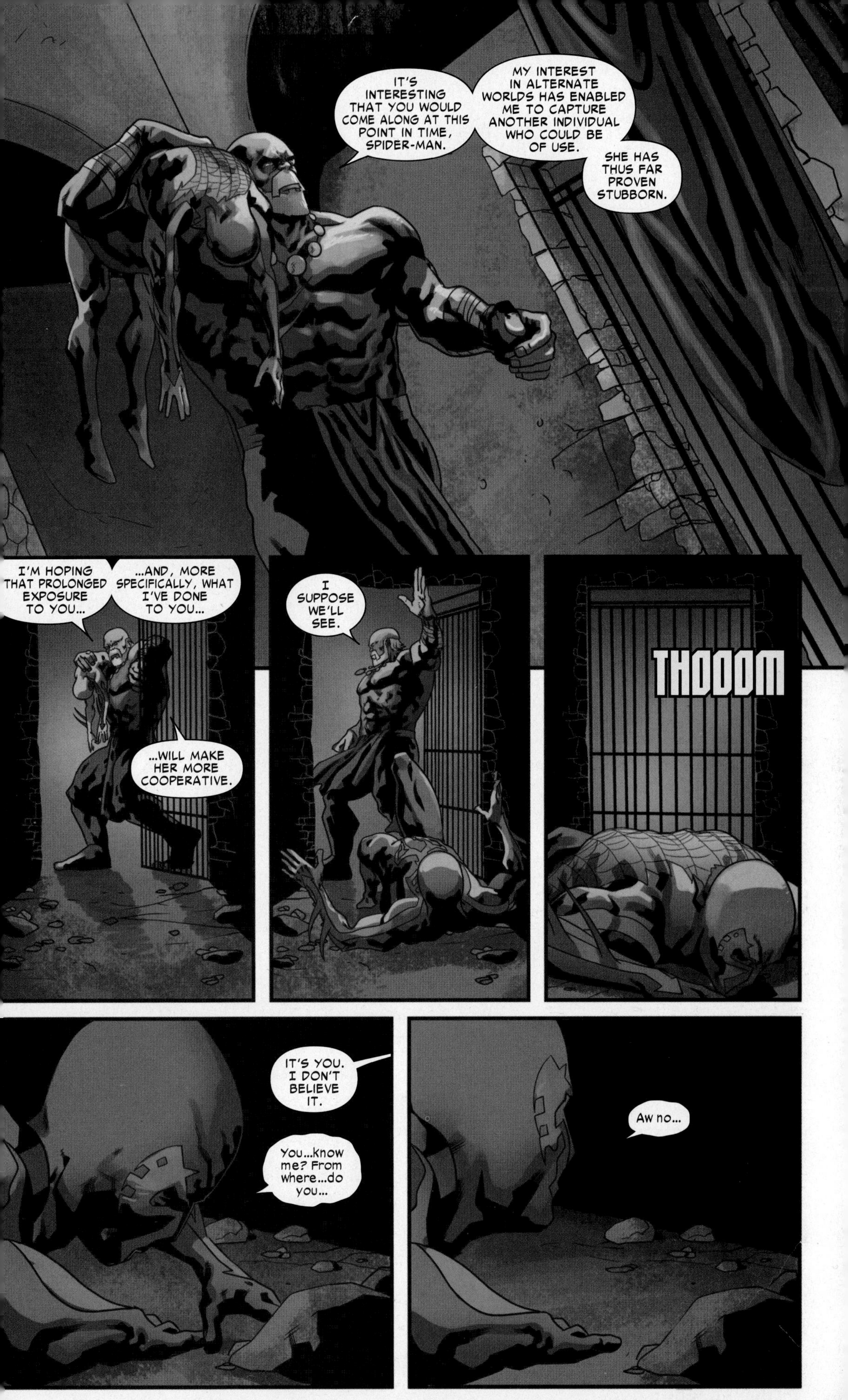

IT'S INTERESTING THAT YOU WOULD COME ALONG AT THIS POINT IN TIME, SPIDER-MAN.
MY INTEREST IN ALTERNATE WORLDS HAS ENABLED ME TO CAPTURE ANOTHER INDIVIDUAL WHO COULD BE OF USE.
SHE HAS THUS FAR PROVEN STUBBORN.
I'M HOPING THAT PROLONGED EXPOSURE TO YOU...
...AND, MORE SPECIFICALLY, WHAT I'VE DONE TO YOU...
...WILL MAKE HER MORE COOPERATIVE.
I SUPPOSE WE'LL SEE.
THOOOM
IT'S YOU. I DON'T BELIEVE IT.
You...know me? From where...do you...
Aw no...

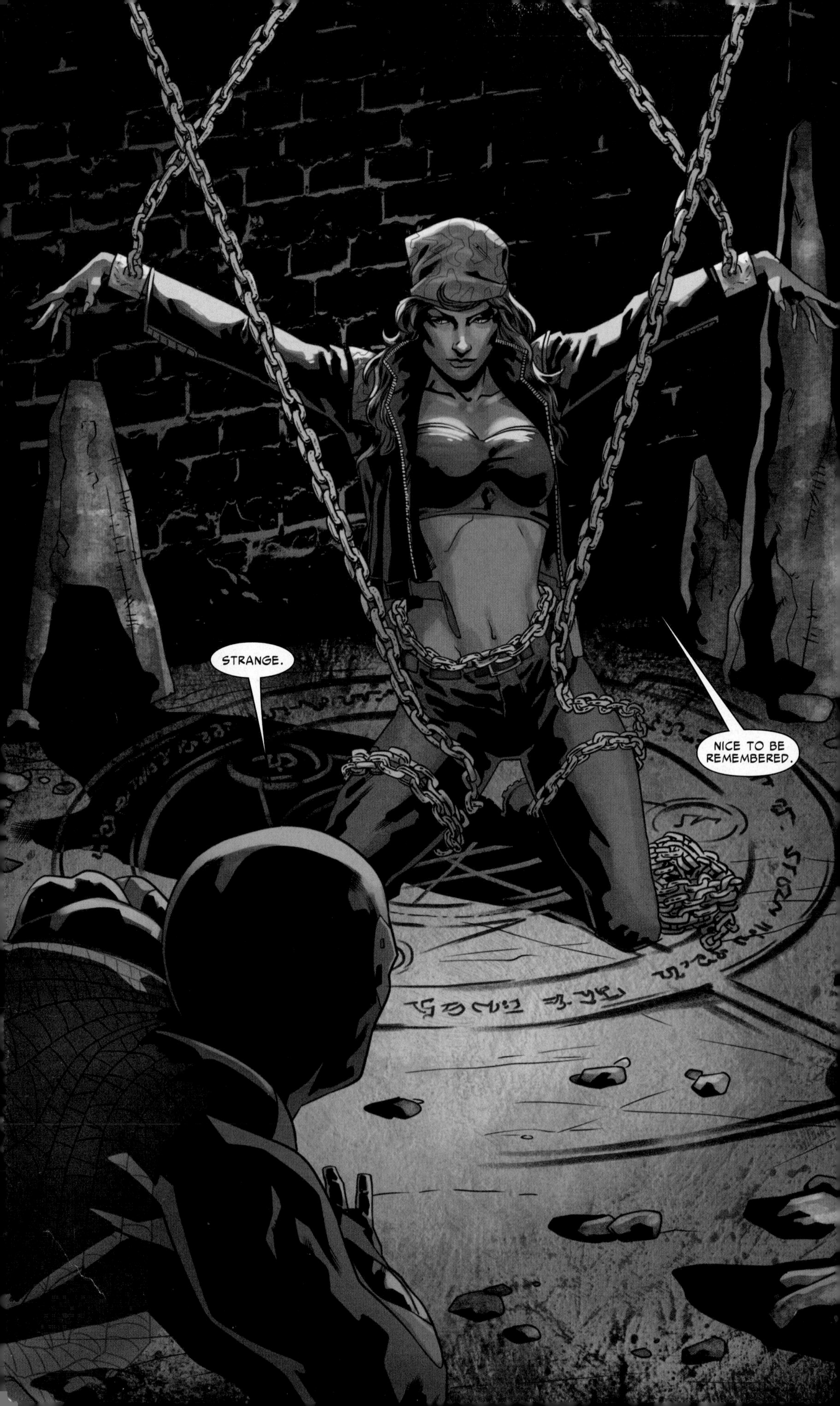
STRANGE.
NICE TO BE REMEMBERED.

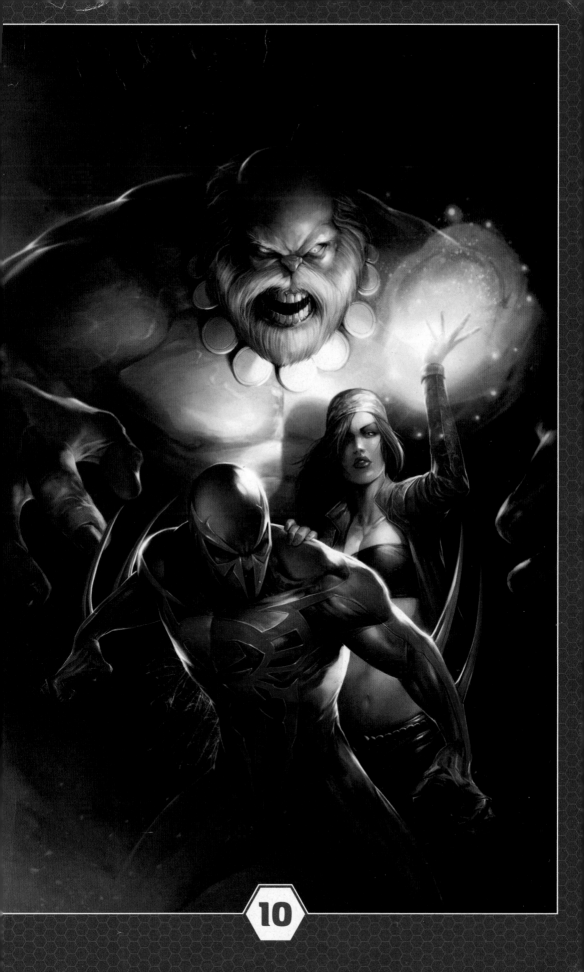

10

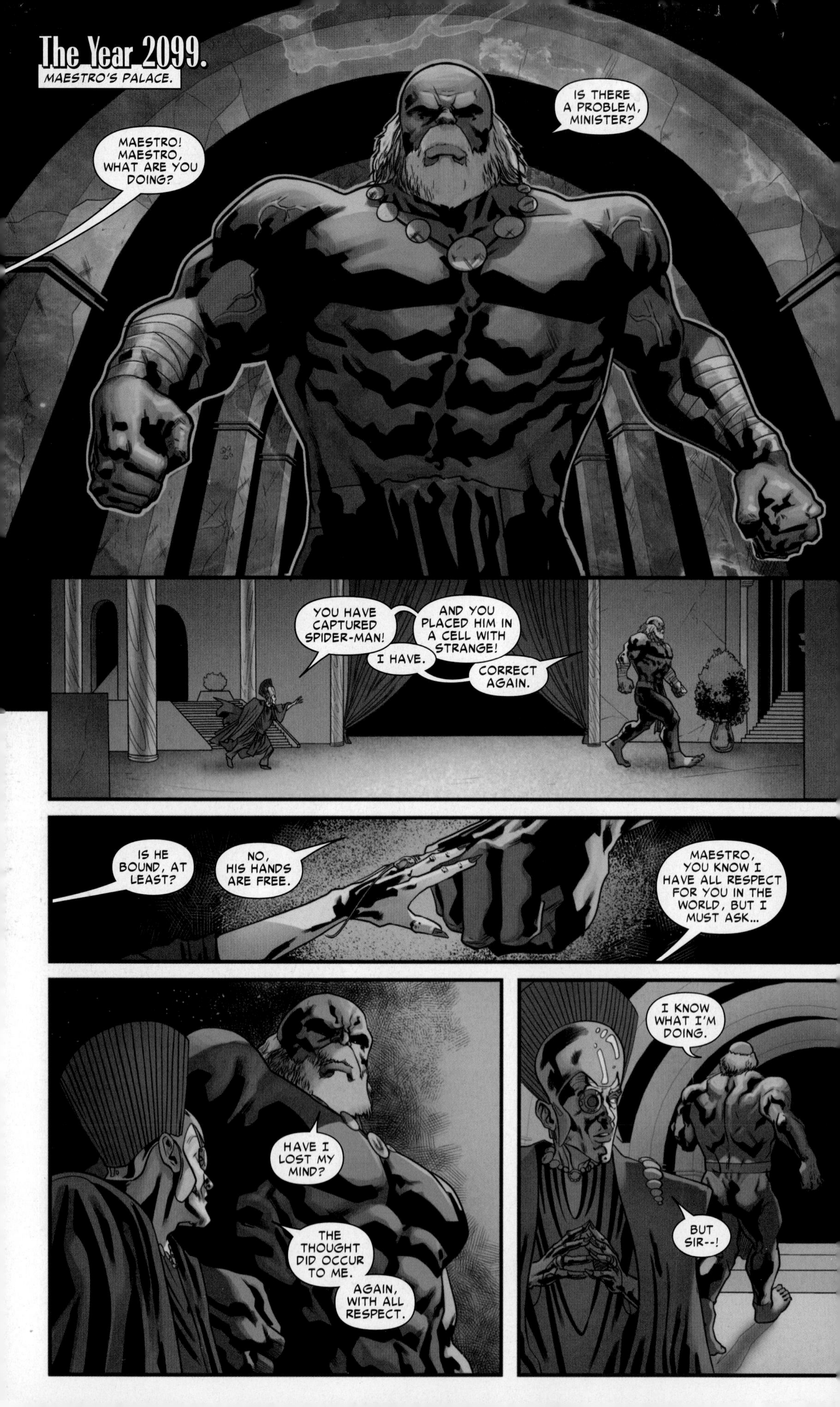
The Year 2099.
MAESTRO'S PALACE.
MAESTRO! MAESTRO, WHAT ARE YOU DOING?
IS THERE A PROBLEM, MINISTER?
YOU HAVE CAPTURED SPIDER-MAN!
I HAVE.
AND YOU PLACED HIM IN A CELL WITH STRANGE!
CORRECT AGAIN.
IS HE BOUND, AT LEAST?
NO, HIS HANDS ARE FREE.
MAESTRO, YOU KNOW I HAVE ALL RESPECT FOR YOU IN THE WORLD, BUT I MUST ASK...
HAVE I LOST MY MIND?
THE THOUGHT DID OCCUR TO ME.
AGAIN, WITH ALL RESPECT.
I KNOW WHAT I'M DOING.
BUT SIR--!

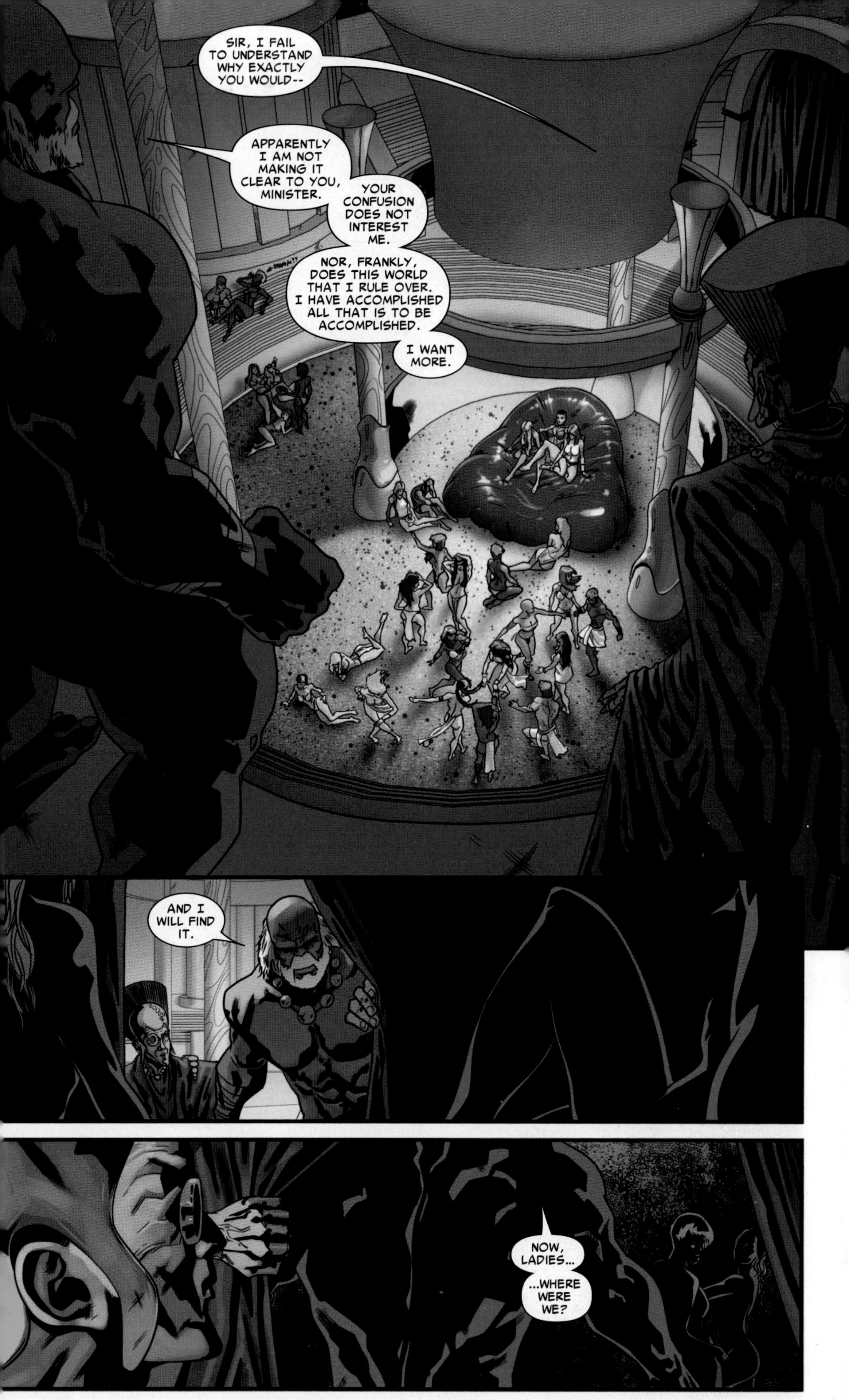
SIR, I FAIL TO UNDERSTAND WHY EXACTLY YOU WOULD--
APPARENTLY I AM NOT MAKING IT CLEAR TO YOU, MINISTER.
YOUR CONFUSION DOES NOT INTEREST ME.
NOR, FRANKLY, DOES THIS WORLD THAT I RULE OVER. I HAVE ACCOMPLISHED ALL THAT IS TO BE ACCOMPLISHED.
I WANT MORE.
AND I WILL FIND IT.
NOW, LADIES...
...WHERE WERE WE?

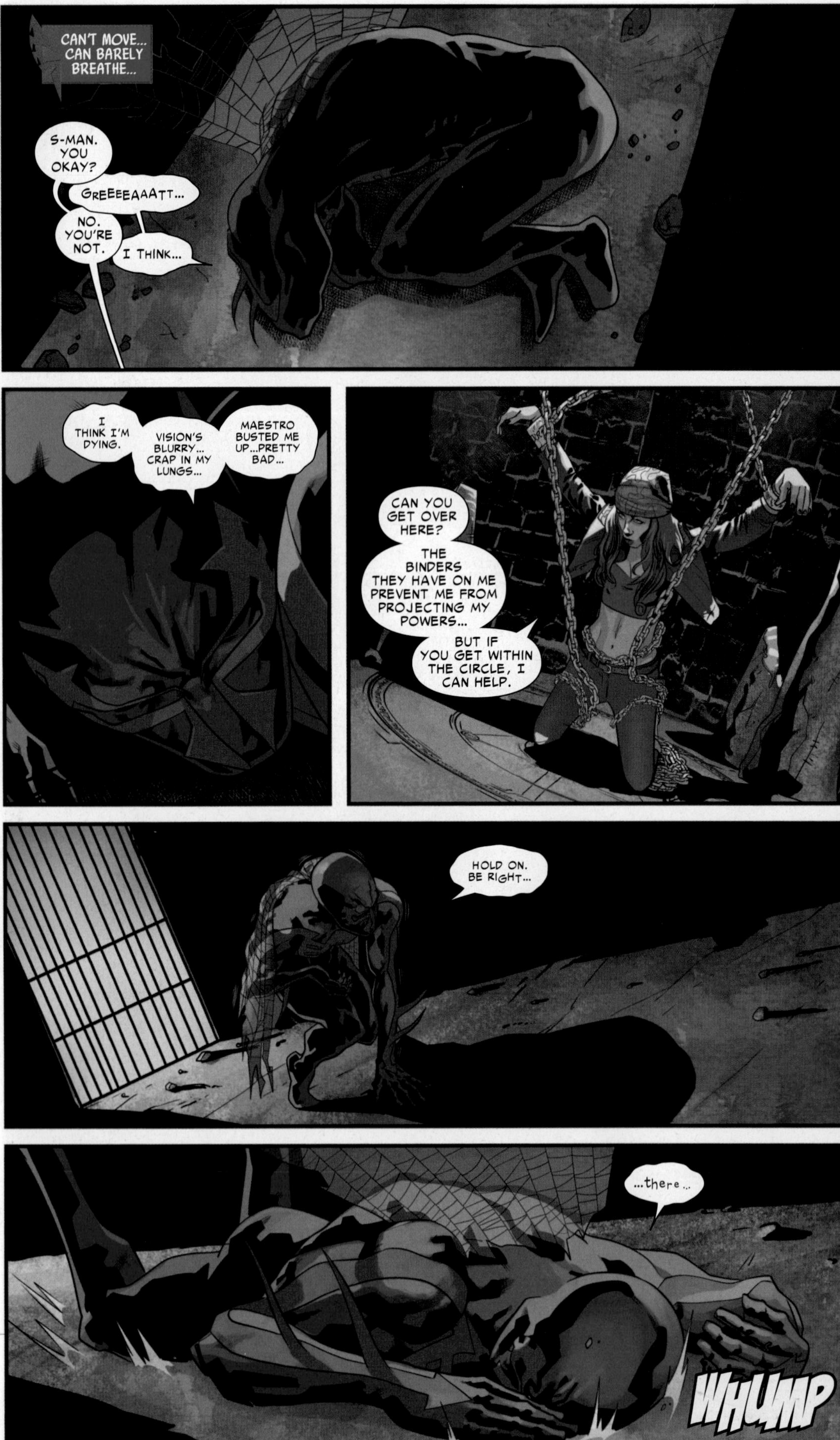
CAN'T MOVE... CAN BARELY BREATHE...
S-MAN. YOU OKAY?
GREEEEAAATT...
NO. YOU'RE NOT.
I THINK...
I THINK I'M DYING.
VISION'S BLURRY... CRAP IN MY LUNGS...
MAESTRO BUSTED ME UP...PRETTY BAD...
CAN YOU GET OVER HERE?
THE BINDERS THEY HAVE ON ME PREVENT ME FROM PROJECTING MY POWERS...
BUT IF YOU GET WITHIN THE CIRCLE, I CAN HELP.
HOLD ON. BE RIGHT...
...there...
WHUMP

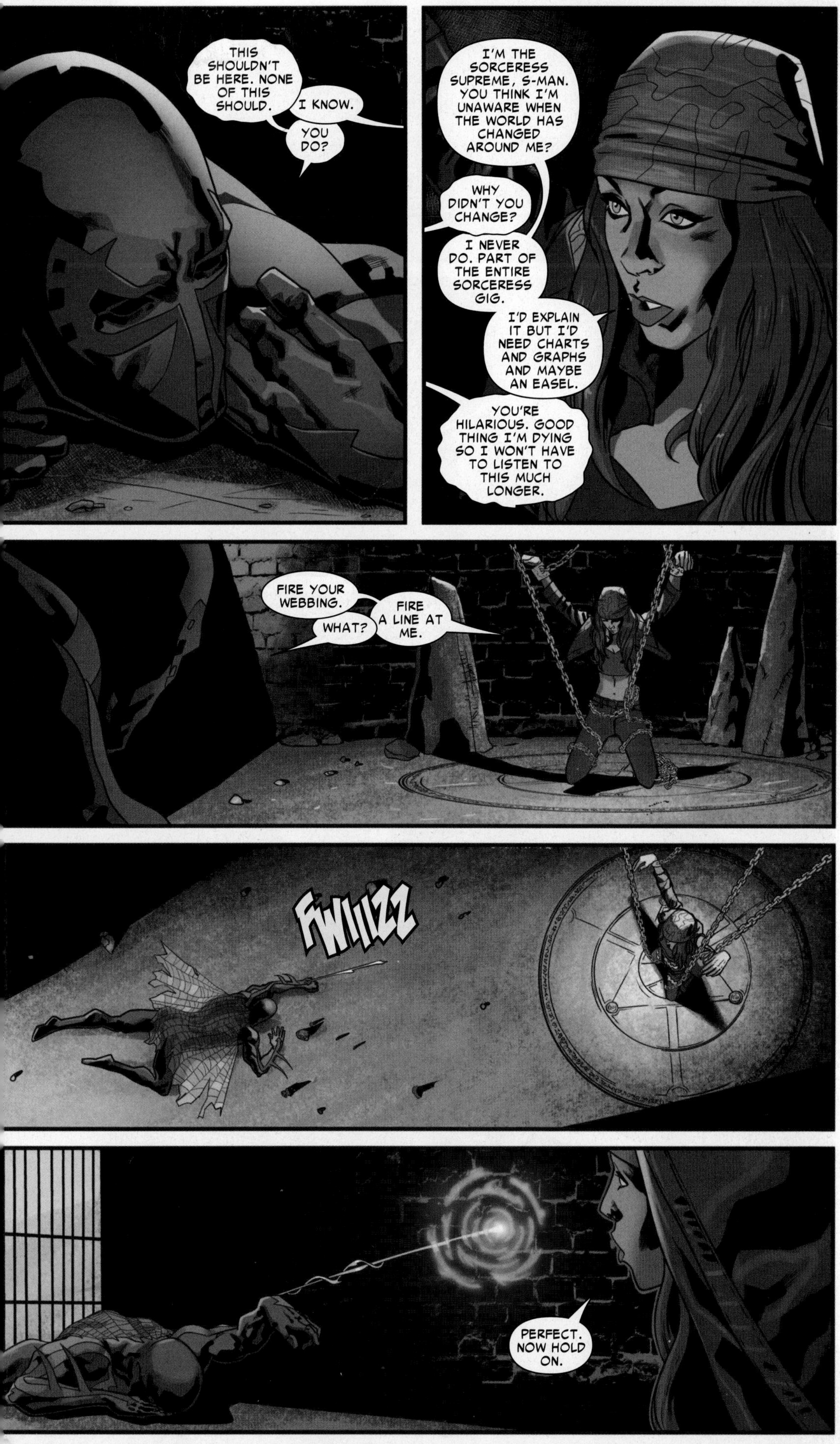

THIS SHOULDN'T BE HERE. NONE OF THIS SHOULD.
I KNOW.
YOU DO?
I'M THE SORCERESS SUPREME, S-MAN. YOU THINK I'M UNAWARE WHEN THE WORLD HAS CHANGED AROUND ME?
WHY DIDN'T YOU CHANGE?
I NEVER DO. PART OF THE ENTIRE SORCERESS GIG.
I'D EXPLAIN IT BUT I'D NEED CHARTS AND GRAPHS AND MAYBE AN EASEL.
YOU'RE HILARIOUS. GOOD THING I'M DYING SO I WON'T HAVE TO LISTEN TO THIS MUCH LONGER.
FIRE YOUR WEBBING.
WHAT?
FIRE A LINE AT ME.
FWIIIZZ
PERFECT. NOW HOLD ON.

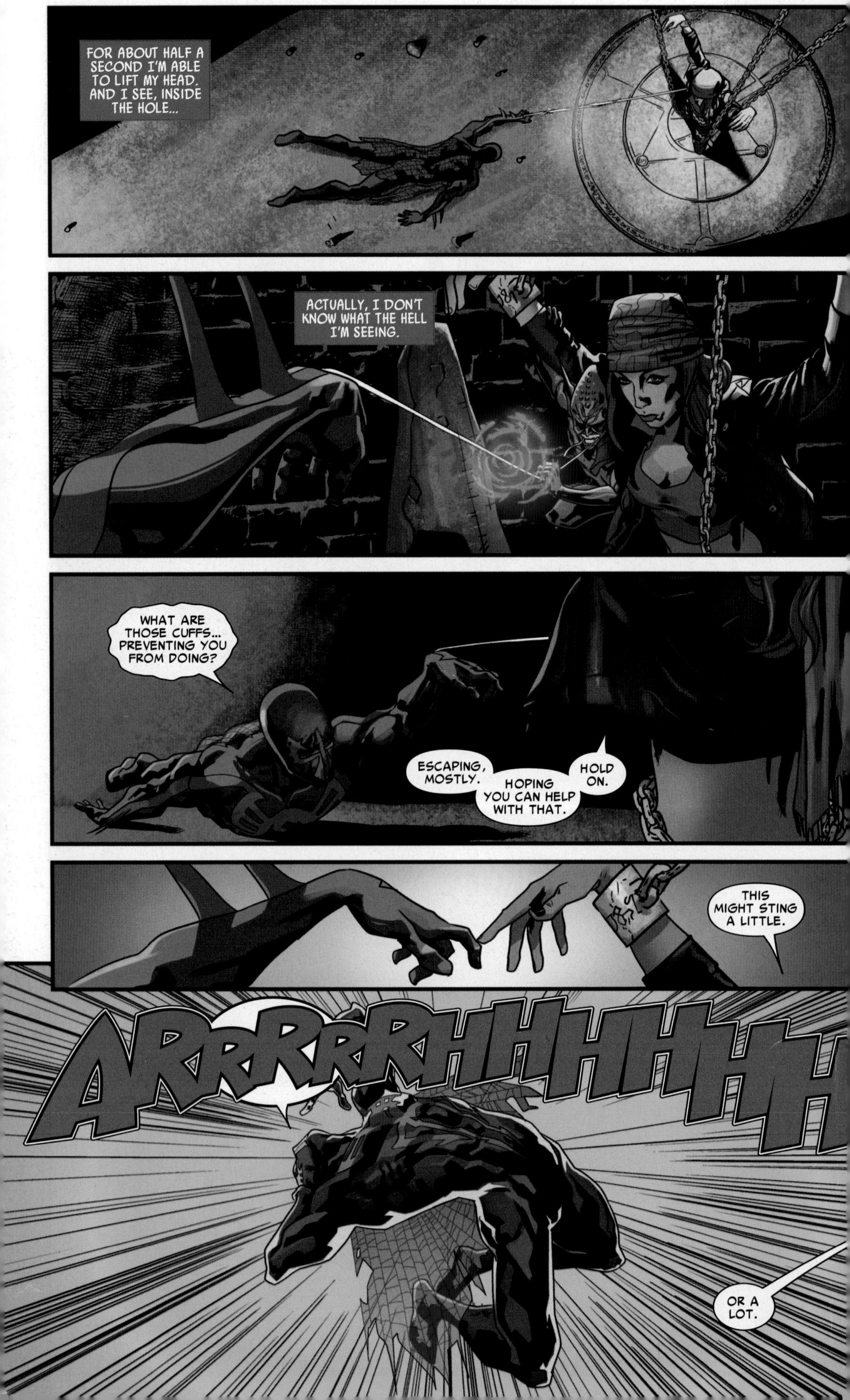

FOR ABOUT HALF A SECOND I'M ABLE TO LIFT MY HEAD. AND I SEE, INSIDE THE HOLE...
ACTUALLY, I DON'T KNOW WHAT THE HELL I'M SEEING.
WHAT ARE THOSE CUFFS... PREVENTING YOU FROM DOING?
ESCAPING, MOSTLY.
HOPING YOU CAN HELP WITH THAT.
HOLD ON.
THIS MIGHT STING A LITTLE.
ARRRRRRHHHHHHHH
OR A LOT.

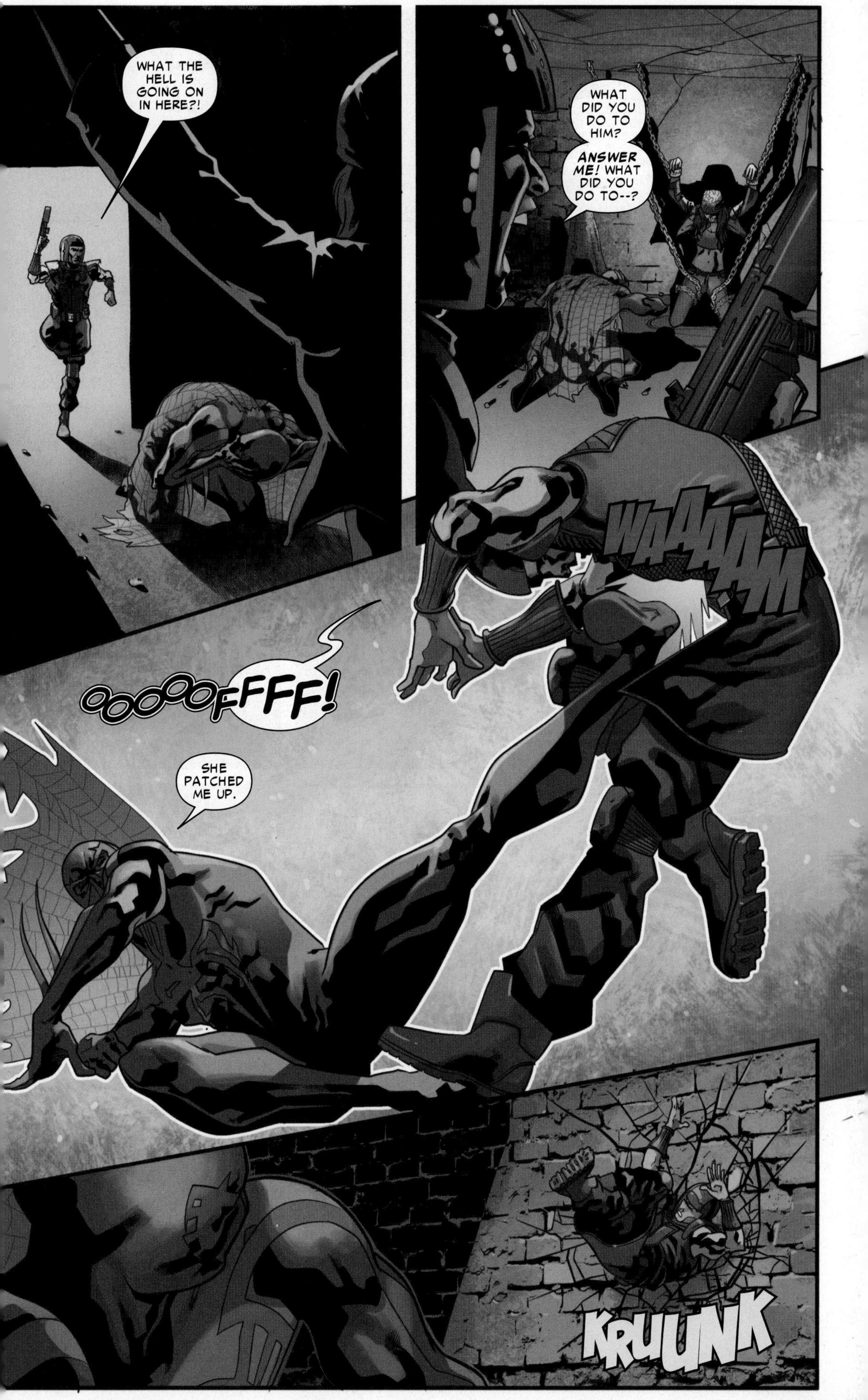
WHAT THE HELL IS GOING ON IN HERE?!
WHAT DID YOU DO TO HIM?
ANSWER ME! WHAT DID YOU DO TO--?
WAAAAAM
OOOOOOFFFF!
SHE PATCHED ME UP.
KRUUNK

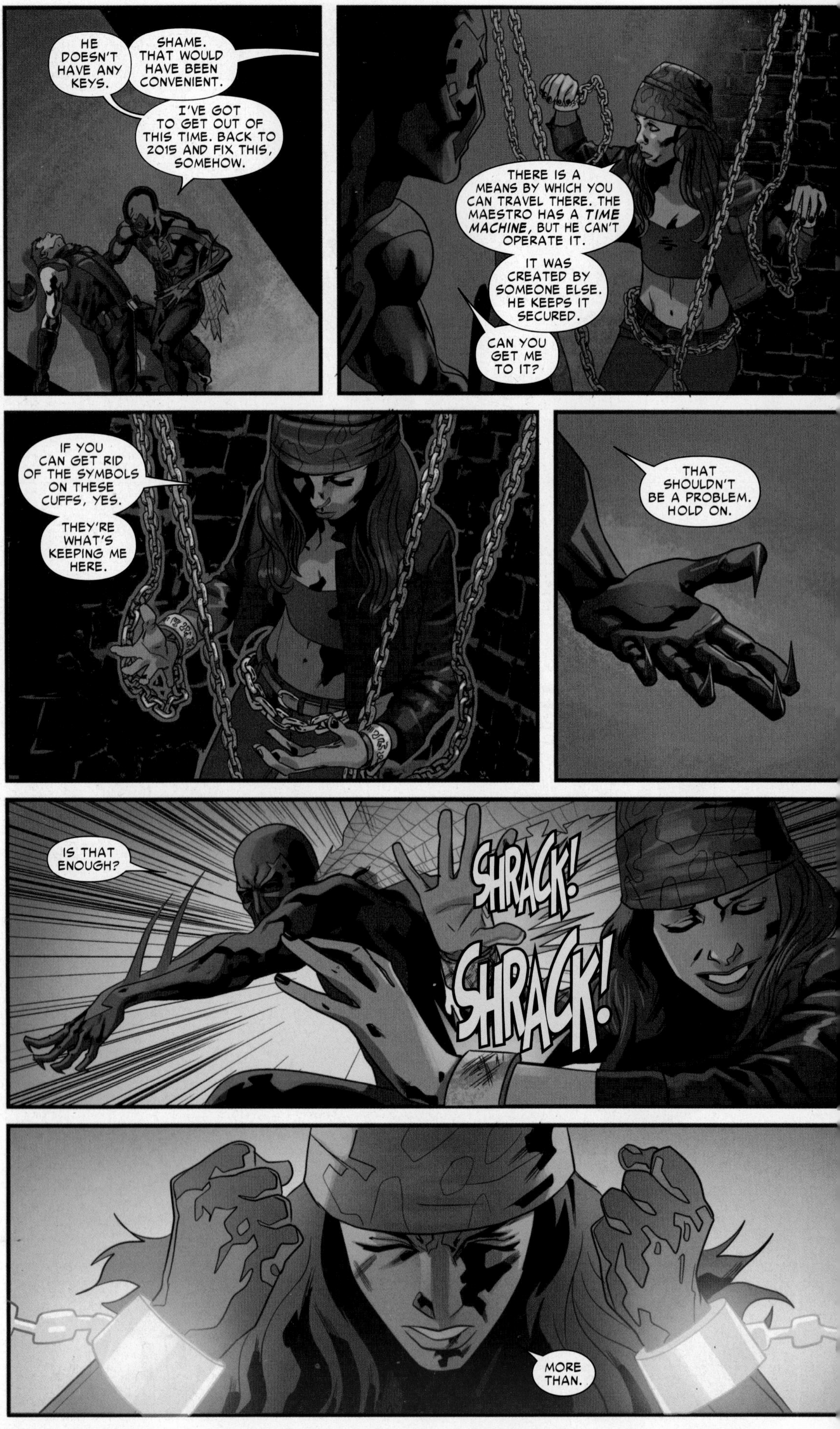
HE DOESN'T HAVE ANY KEYS.
SHAME. THAT WOULD HAVE BEEN CONVENIENT.
I'VE GOT TO GET OUT OF THIS TIME. BACK TO 2015 AND FIX THIS, SOMEHOW.
THERE IS A MEANS BY WHICH YOU CAN TRAVEL THERE. THE MAESTRO HAS A *TIME MACHINE*, BUT HE CAN'T OPERATE IT.
IT WAS CREATED BY SOMEONE ELSE. HE KEEPS IT SECURED.
CAN YOU GET ME TO IT?
IF YOU CAN GET RID OF THE SYMBOLS ON THESE CUFFS, YES.
THEY'RE WHAT'S KEEPING ME HERE.
THAT SHOULDN'T BE A PROBLEM. HOLD ON.
IS THAT ENOUGH?
SHRACK!
SHRACK!
MORE THAN.

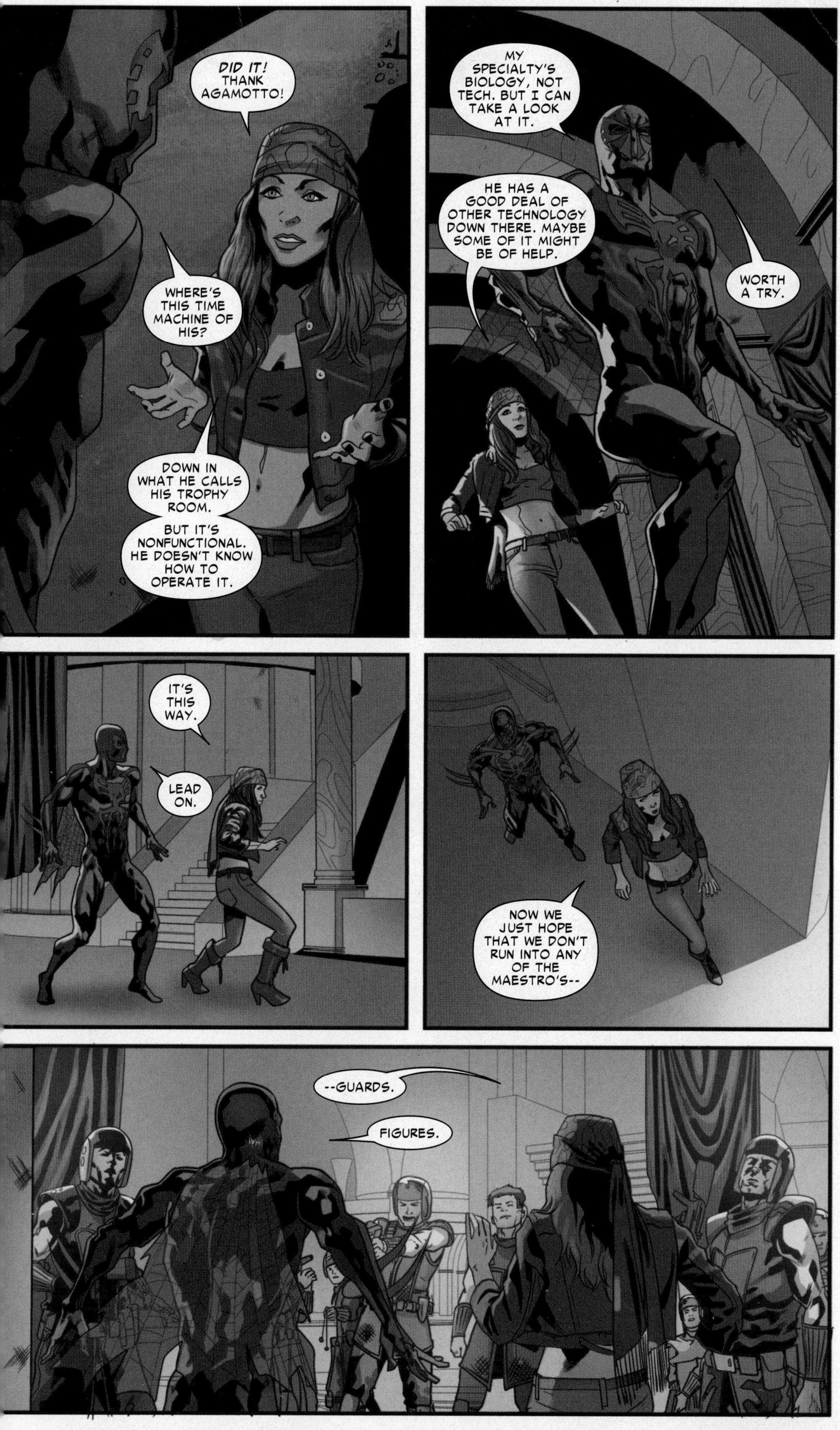
DID IT! THANK AGAMOTTO!
WHERE'S THIS TIME MACHINE OF HIS?
DOWN IN WHAT HE CALLS HIS TROPHY ROOM.
BUT IT'S NONFUNCTIONAL. HE DOESN'T KNOW HOW TO OPERATE IT.
MY SPECIALTY'S BIOLOGY, NOT TECH. BUT I CAN TAKE A LOOK AT IT.
HE HAS A GOOD DEAL OF OTHER TECHNOLOGY DOWN THERE. MAYBE SOME OF IT MIGHT BE OF HELP.
WORTH A TRY.
IT'S THIS WAY.
LEAD ON.
NOW WE JUST HOPE THAT WE DON'T RUN INTO ANY OF THE MAESTRO'S--
--GUARDS.
FIGURES.

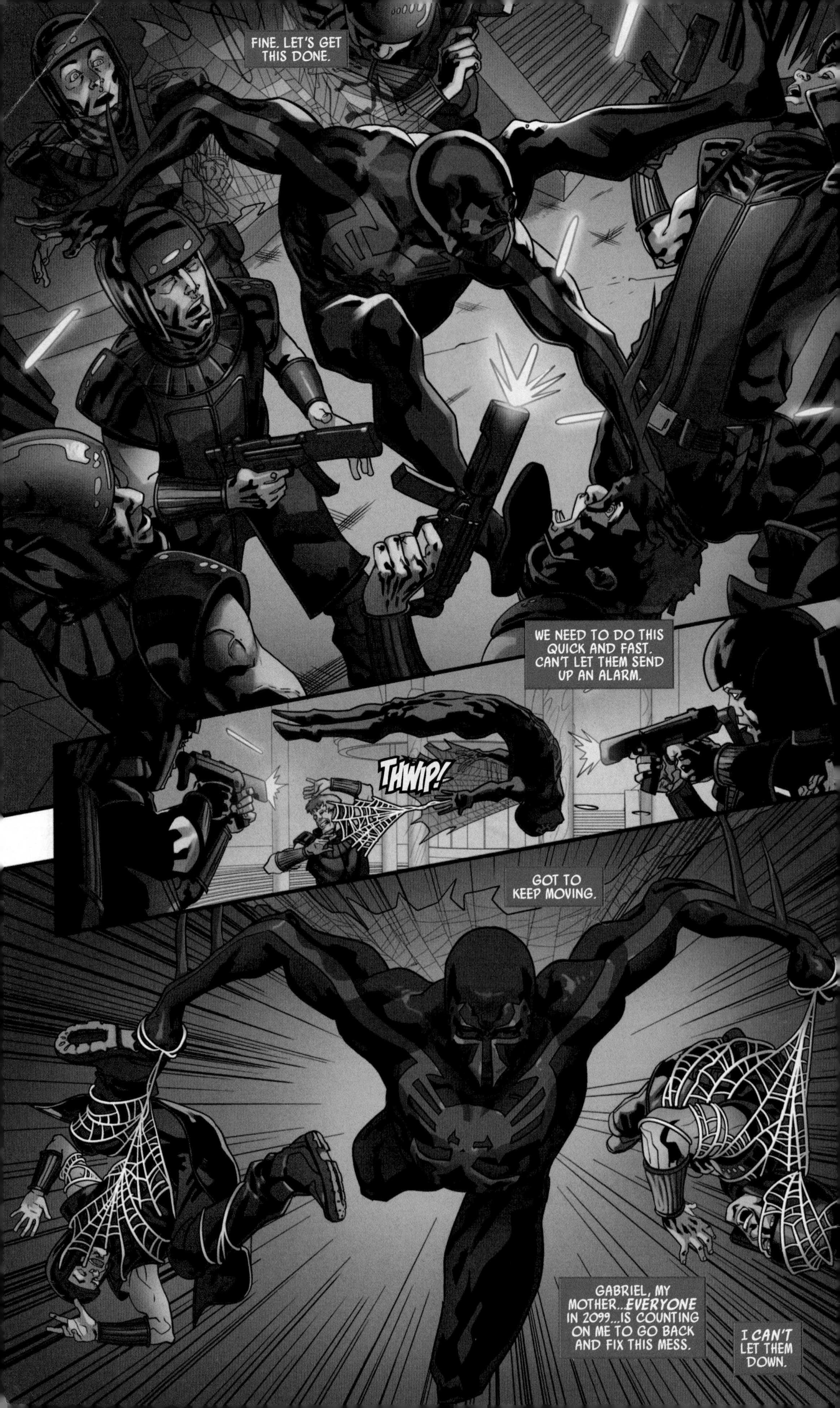
FINE. LET'S GET THIS DONE.
WE NEED TO DO THIS QUICK AND FAST. CAN'T LET THEM SEND UP AN ALARM.
THWIP!
GOT TO KEEP MOVING.
GABRIEL, MY MOTHER...EVERYONE IN 2099...IS COUNTING ON ME TO GO BACK AND FIX THIS MESS.
I CAN'T LET THEM DOWN.

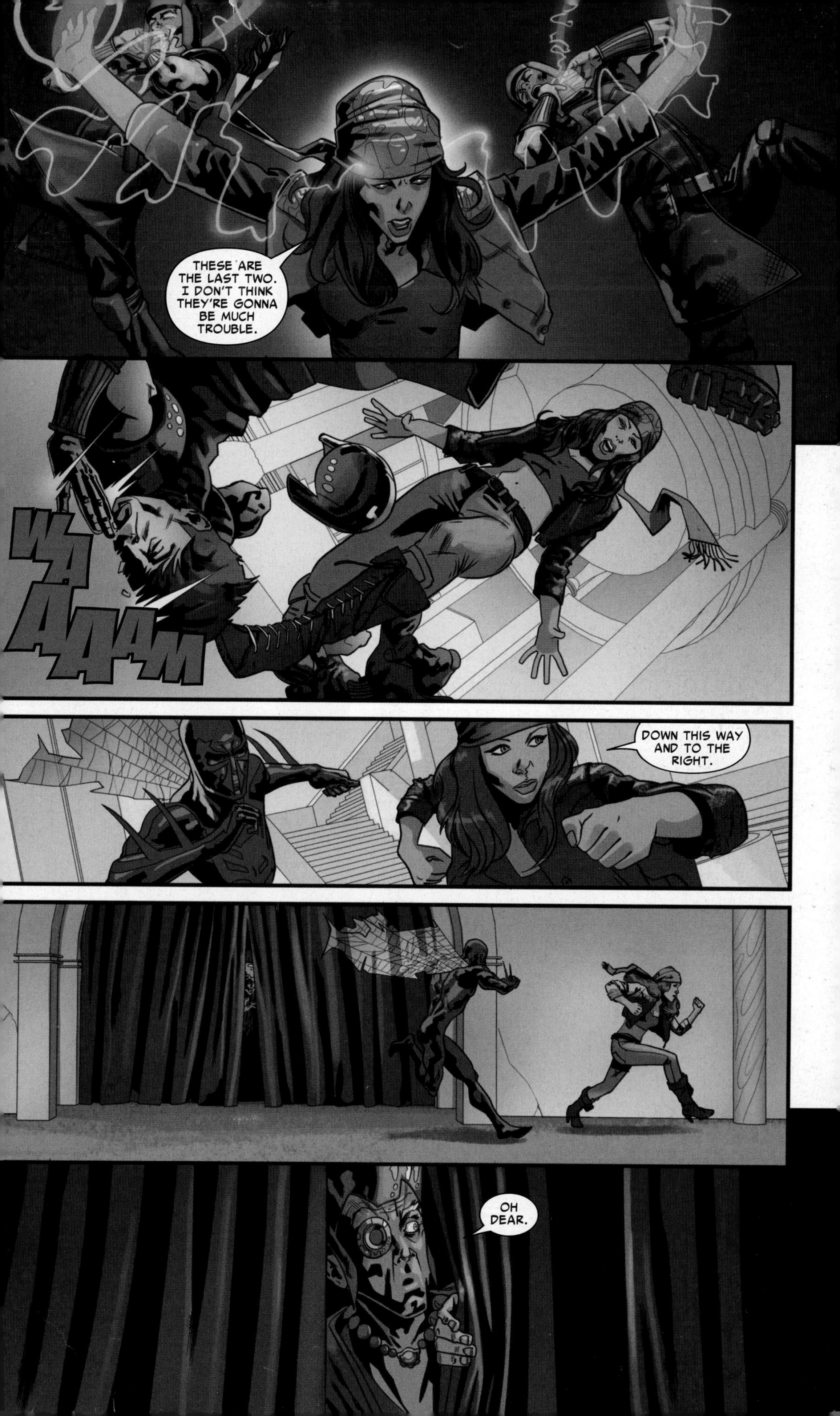
THESE ARE THE LAST TWO. I DON'T THINK THEY'RE GONNA BE MUCH TROUBLE.
WAAAAAM
DOWN THIS WAY AND TO THE RIGHT.
OH DEAR.

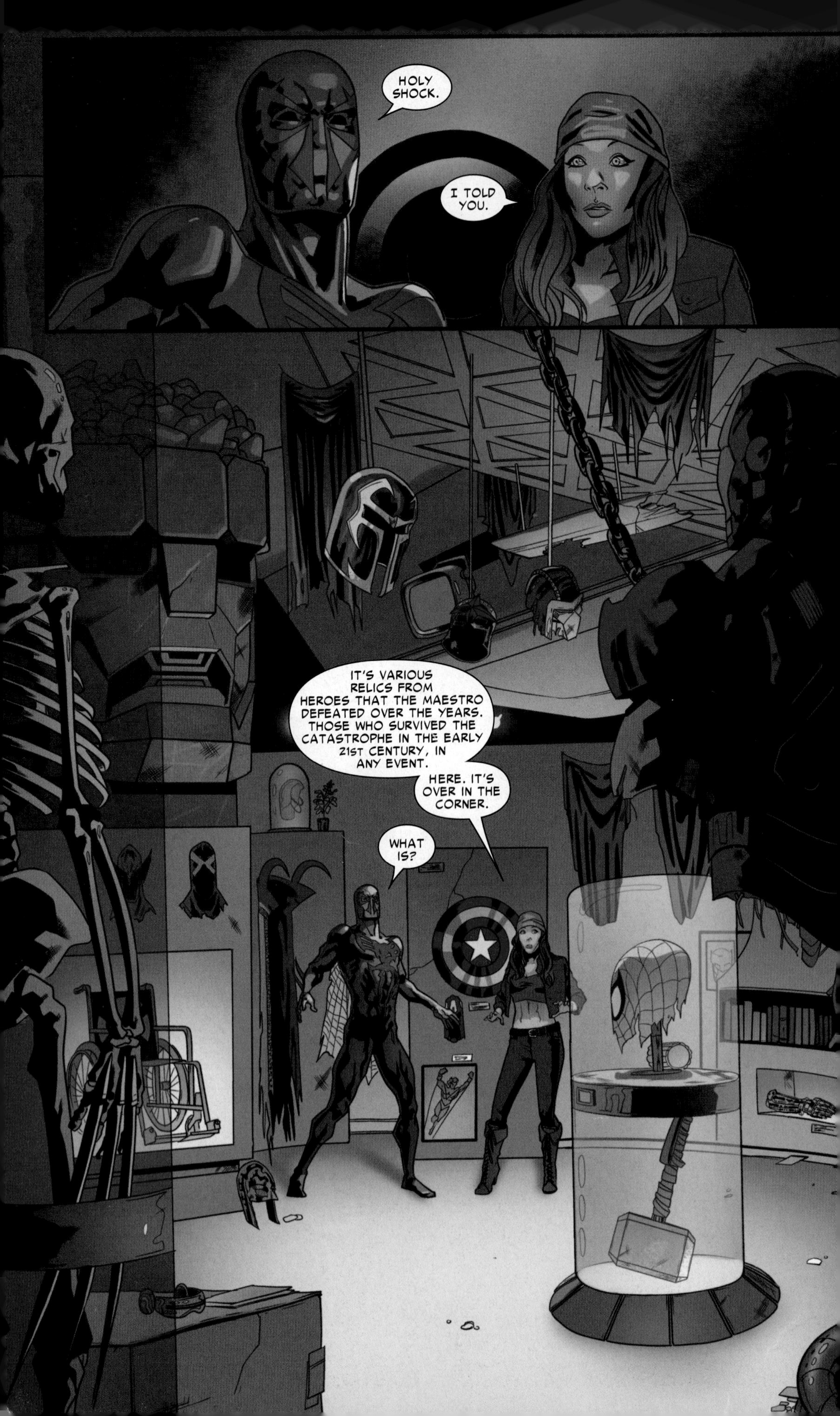
HOLY SHOCK.
I TOLD YOU.
IT'S VARIOUS RELICS FROM HEROES THAT THE MAESTRO DEFEATED OVER THE YEARS. THOSE WHO SURVIVED THE CATASTROPHE IN THE EARLY 21ST CENTURY, IN ANY EVENT.
HERE. IT'S OVER IN THE CORNER.
WHAT IS?

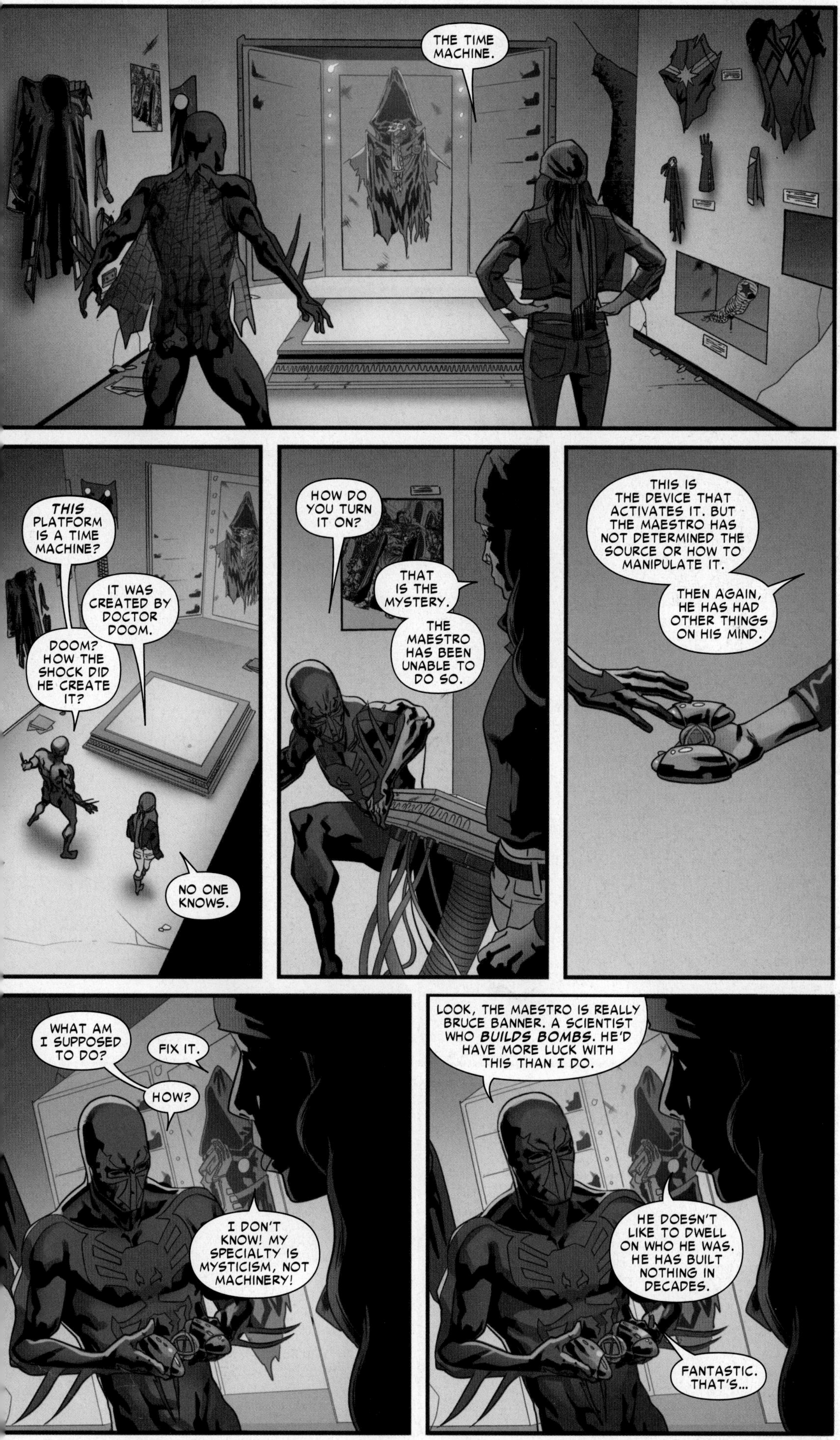
THE TIME MACHINE.
THIS PLATFORM IS A TIME MACHINE?
IT WAS CREATED BY DOCTOR DOOM.
DOOM? HOW THE SHOCK DID HE CREATE IT?
NO ONE KNOWS.
HOW DO YOU TURN IT ON?
THAT IS THE MYSTERY.
THE MAESTRO HAS BEEN UNABLE TO DO SO.
THIS IS THE DEVICE THAT ACTIVATES IT. BUT THE MAESTRO HAS NOT DETERMINED THE SOURCE OR HOW TO MANIPULATE IT.
THEN AGAIN, HE HAS HAD OTHER THINGS ON HIS MIND.
WHAT AM I SUPPOSED TO DO?
FIX IT.
HOW?
I DON'T KNOW! MY SPECIALTY IS MYSTICISM, NOT MACHINERY!
LOOK, THE MAESTRO IS REALLY BRUCE BANNER. A SCIENTIST WHO BUILDS BOMBS. HE'D HAVE MORE LUCK WITH THIS THAN I DO.
HE DOESN'T LIKE TO DWELL ON WHO HE WAS. HE HAS BUILT NOTHING IN DECADES.
FANTASTIC. THAT'S...

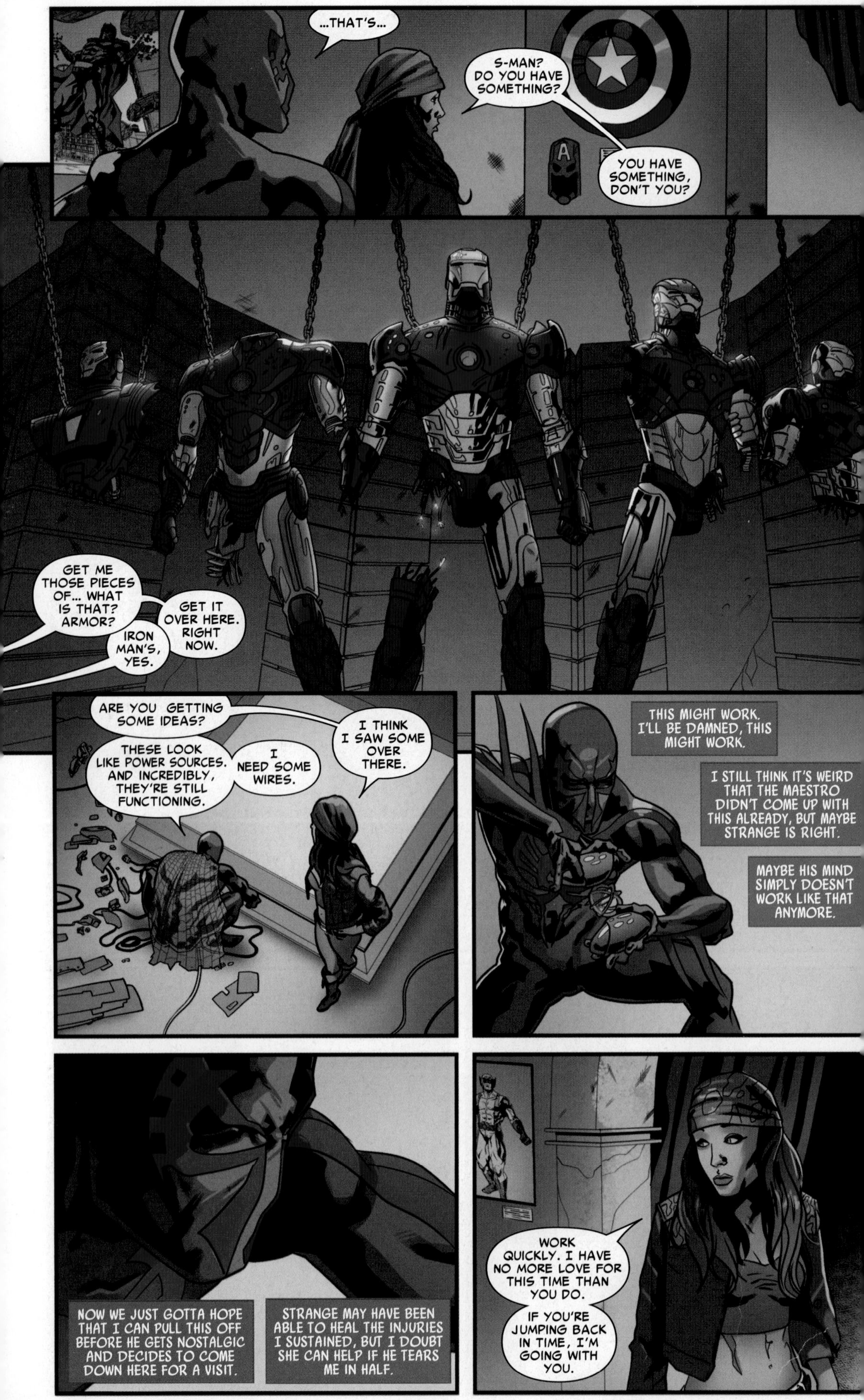
...THAT'S...
S-MAN? DO YOU HAVE SOMETHING?
YOU HAVE SOMETHING, DON'T YOU?
GET ME THOSE PIECES OF... WHAT IS THAT? ARMOR?
IRON MAN'S, YES.
GET IT OVER HERE. RIGHT NOW.
ARE YOU GETTING SOME IDEAS?
THESE LOOK LIKE POWER SOURCES. AND INCREDIBLY, THEY'RE STILL FUNCTIONING.
I NEED SOME WIRES.
I THINK I SAW SOME OVER THERE.
THIS MIGHT WORK. I'LL BE DAMNED, THIS MIGHT WORK.
I STILL THINK IT'S WEIRD THAT THE MAESTRO DIDN'T COME UP WITH THIS ALREADY, BUT MAYBE STRANGE IS RIGHT.
MAYBE HIS MIND SIMPLY DOESN'T WORK LIKE THAT ANYMORE.
NOW WE JUST GOTTA HOPE THAT I CAN PULL THIS OFF BEFORE HE GETS NOSTALGIC AND DECIDES TO COME DOWN HERE FOR A VISIT.
STRANGE MAY HAVE BEEN ABLE TO HEAL THE INJURIES I SUSTAINED, BUT I DOUBT SHE CAN HELP IF HE TEARS ME IN HALF.
WORK QUICKLY. I HAVE NO MORE LOVE FOR THIS TIME THAN YOU DO.
IF YOU'RE JUMPING BACK IN TIME, I'M GOING WITH YOU.

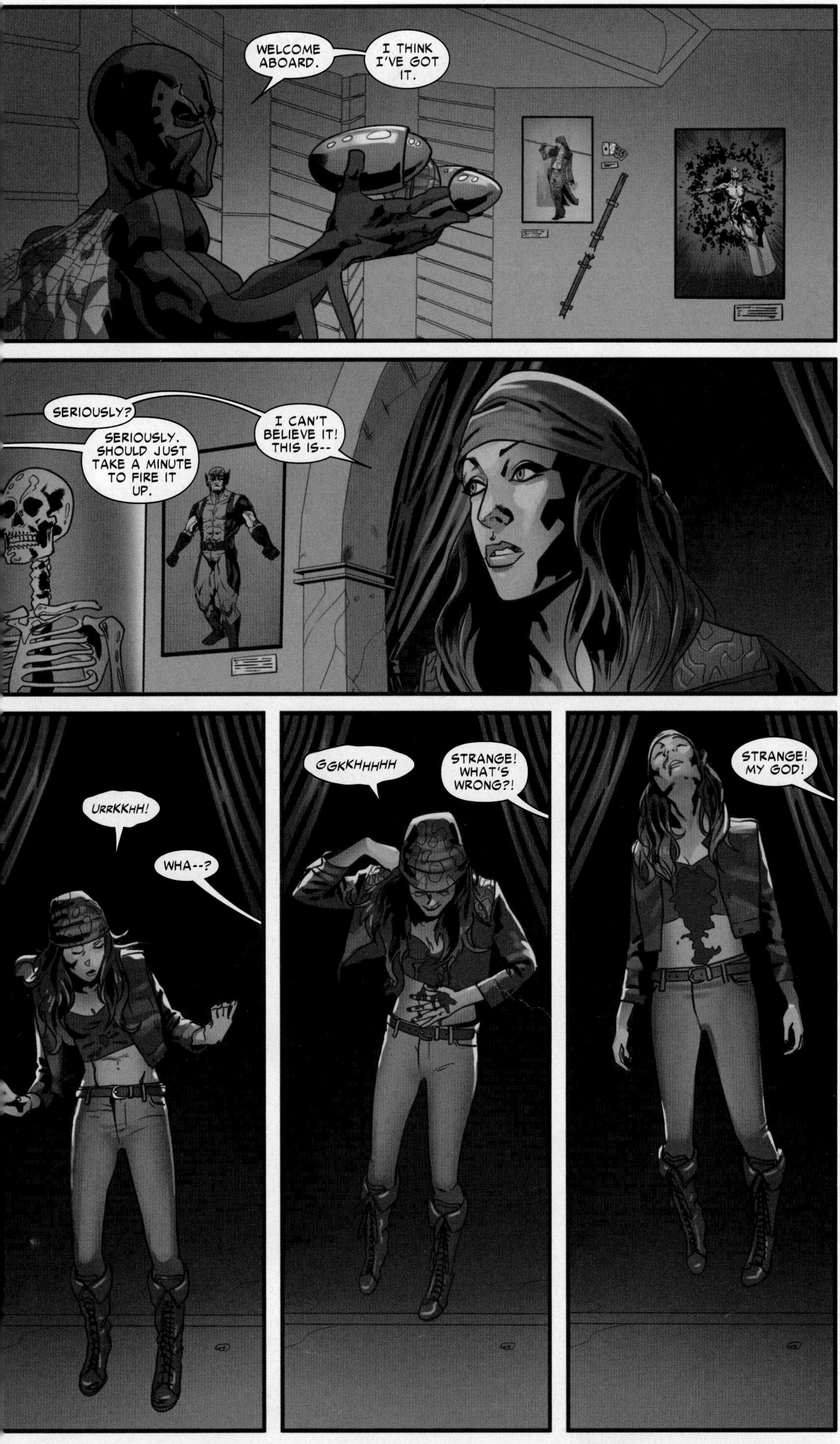
WELCOME ABOARD.
I THINK I'VE GOT IT.
SERIOUSLY?
SERIOUSLY. SHOULD JUST TAKE A MINUTE TO FIRE IT UP.
I CAN'T BELIEVE IT! THIS IS--
URRKKHH!
WHA--?
GGKKHHHHH
STRANGE! WHAT'S WRONG?!
STRANGE! MY GOD!

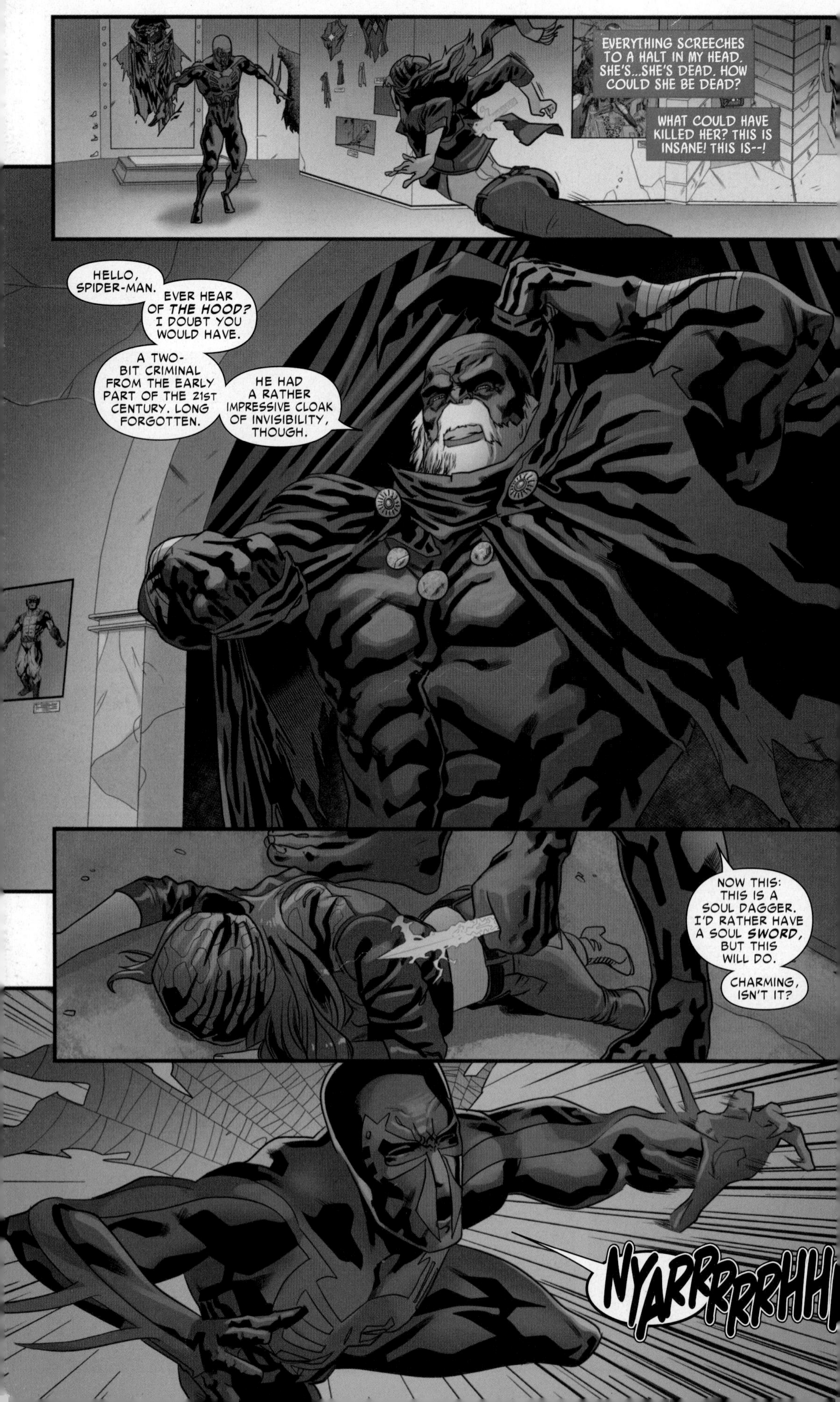
EVERYTHING SCREECHES TO A HALT IN MY HEAD. SHE'S...SHE'S DEAD. HOW COULD SHE BE DEAD?
WHAT COULD HAVE KILLED HER? THIS IS INSANE! THIS IS--!
HELLO, SPIDER-MAN.
EVER HEAR OF *THE HOOD?* I DOUBT YOU WOULD HAVE.
A TWO-BIT CRIMINAL FROM THE EARLY PART OF THE 21ST CENTURY. LONG FORGOTTEN.
HE HAD A RATHER IMPRESSIVE CLOAK OF INVISIBILITY, THOUGH.
NOW THIS: THIS IS A SOUL DAGGER. I'D RATHER HAVE A SOUL **SWORD**, BUT THIS WILL DO.
CHARMING, ISN'T IT?
NYARRRRRRHH

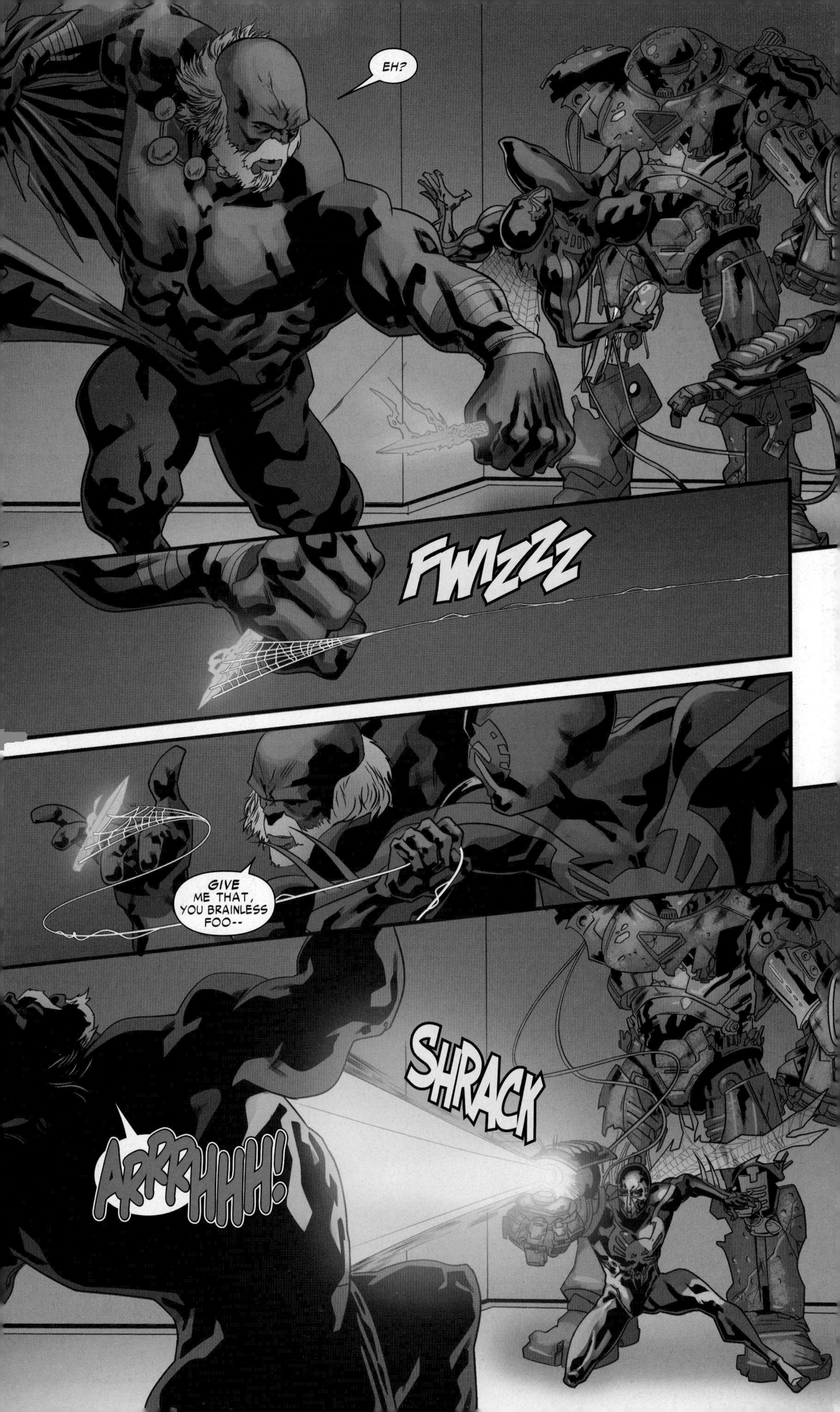

EH?
FWIZZZ
GIVE ME THAT, YOU BRAINLESS FOO--
SHRACK
ARRRHHH!

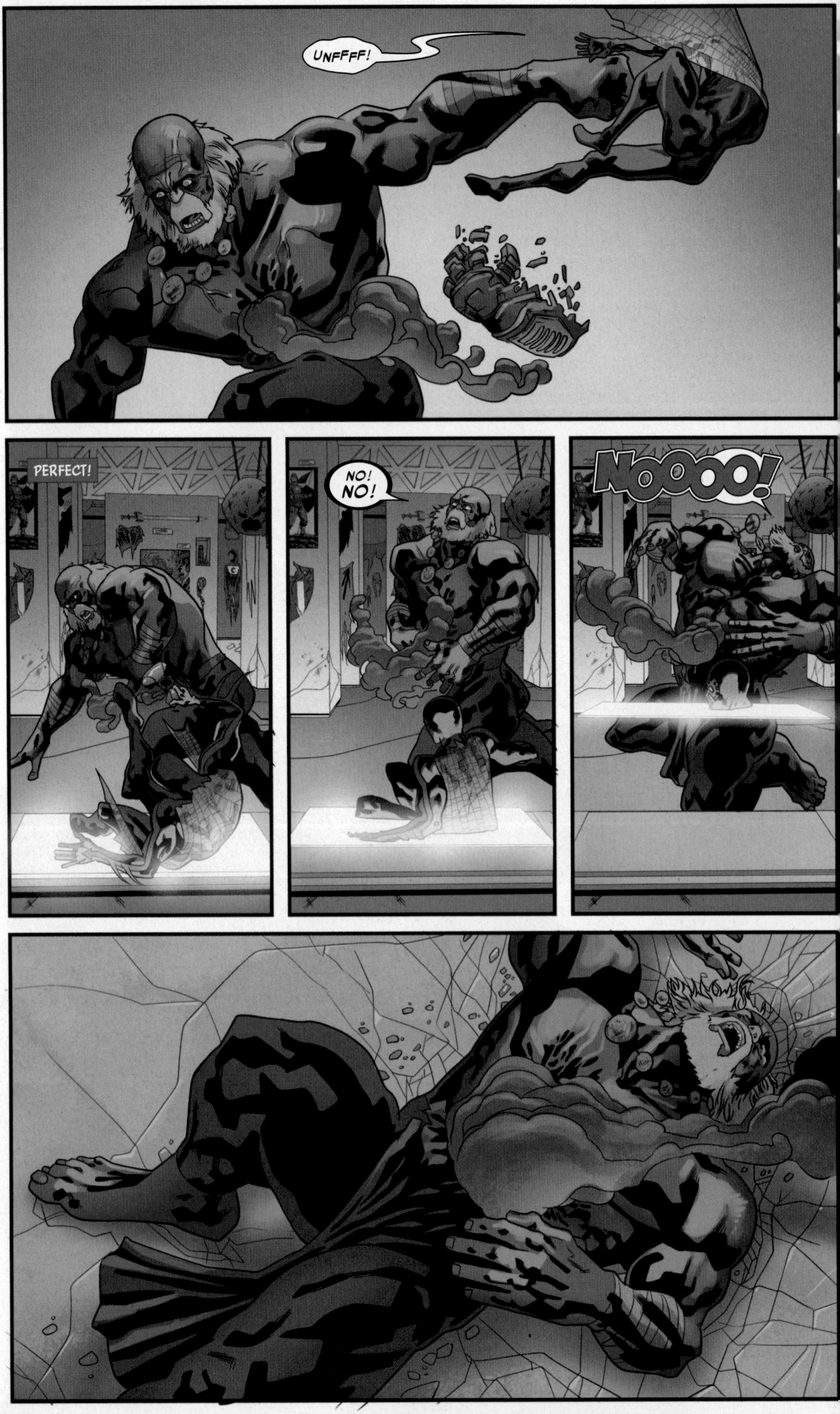

UNFFFF!
PERFECT!
NO! NO!
NOOOO!

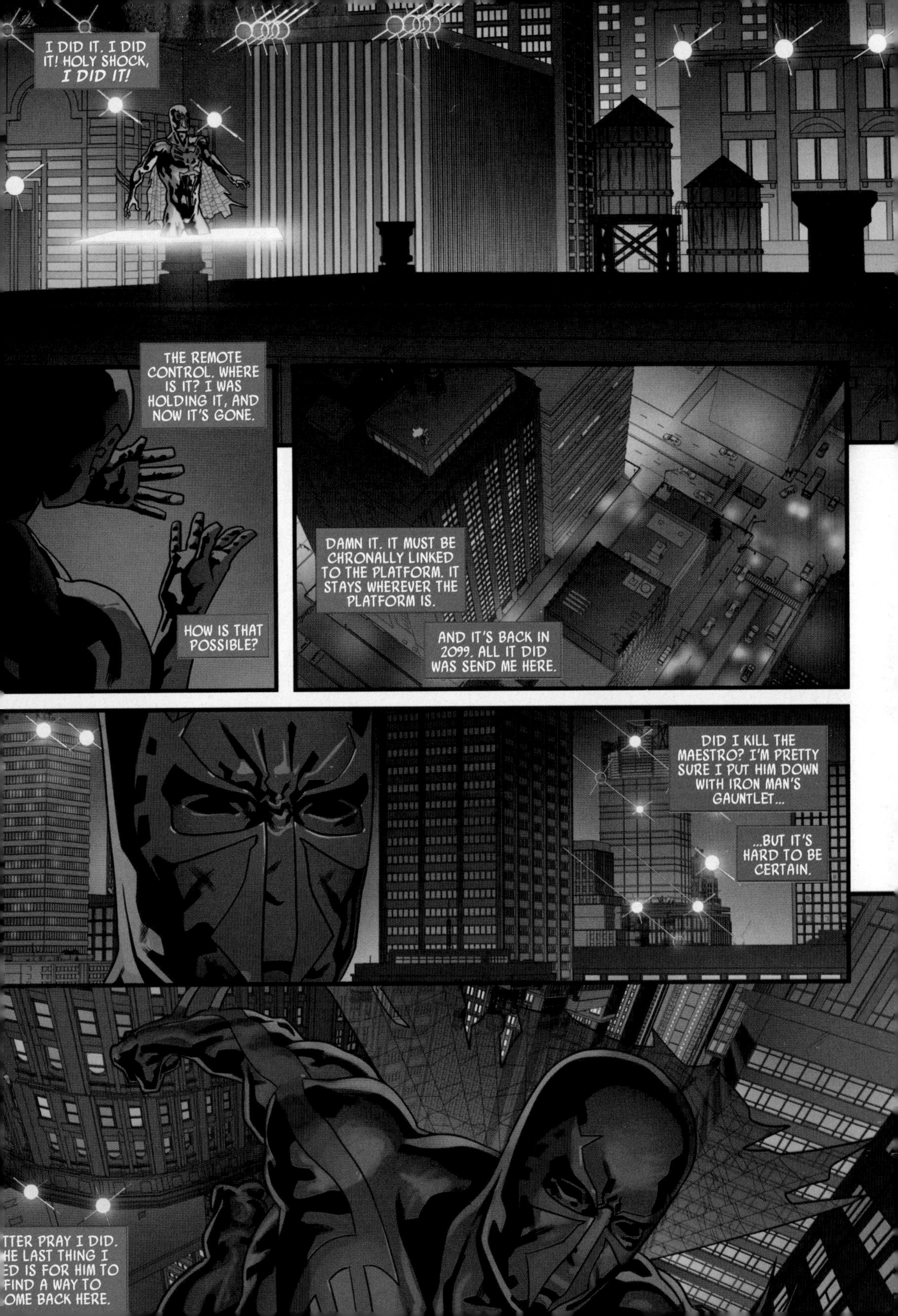
I DID IT. I DID IT! HOLY SHOCK, *I DID IT!*
THE REMOTE CONTROL. WHERE IS IT? I WAS HOLDING IT, AND NOW IT'S GONE.
HOW IS THAT POSSIBLE?
DAMN IT. IT MUST BE CHRONALLY LINKED TO THE PLATFORM. IT STAYS WHEREVER THE PLATFORM IS.
AND IT'S BACK IN 2099. ALL IT DID WAS SEND ME HERE.
DID I KILL THE MAESTRO? I'M PRETTY SURE I PUT HIM DOWN WITH IRON MAN'S GAUNTLET...
...BUT IT'S HARD TO BE CERTAIN.
TTER PRAY I DID. HE LAST THING I ED IS FOR HIM TO FIND A WAY TO OME BACK HERE.

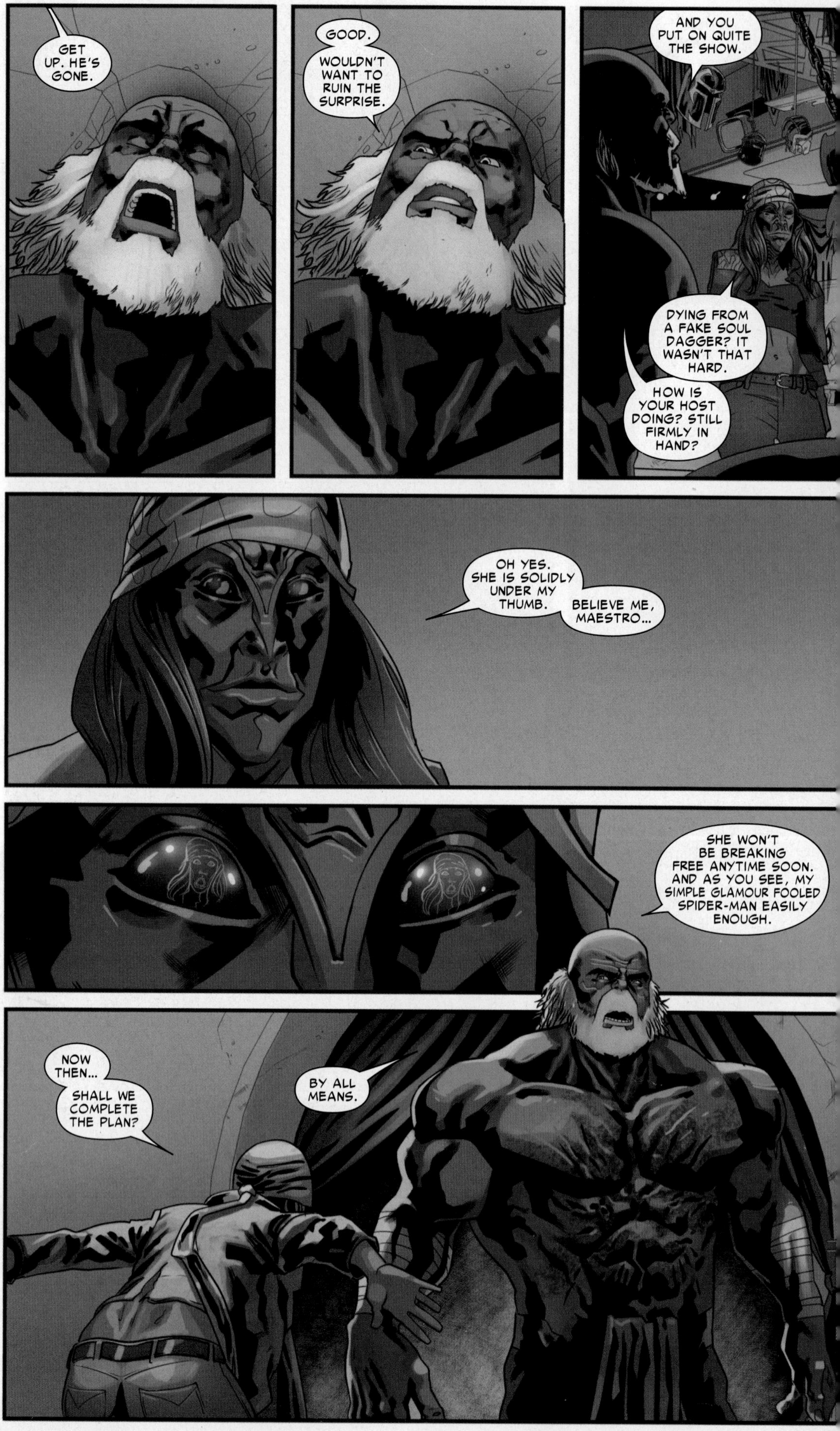
GET UP. HE'S GONE.
GOOD.
WOULDN'T WANT TO RUIN THE SURPRISE.
AND YOU PUT ON QUITE THE SHOW.
DYING FROM A FAKE SOUL DAGGER? IT WASN'T THAT HARD.
HOW IS YOUR HOST DOING? STILL FIRMLY IN HAND?
OH YES. SHE IS SOLIDLY UNDER MY THUMB.
BELIEVE ME, MAESTRO...
SHE WON'T BE BREAKING FREE ANYTIME SOON. AND AS YOU SEE, MY SIMPLE GLAMOUR FOOLED SPIDER-MAN EASILY ENOUGH.
NOW THEN...
SHALL WE COMPLETE THE PLAN?
BY ALL MEANS.

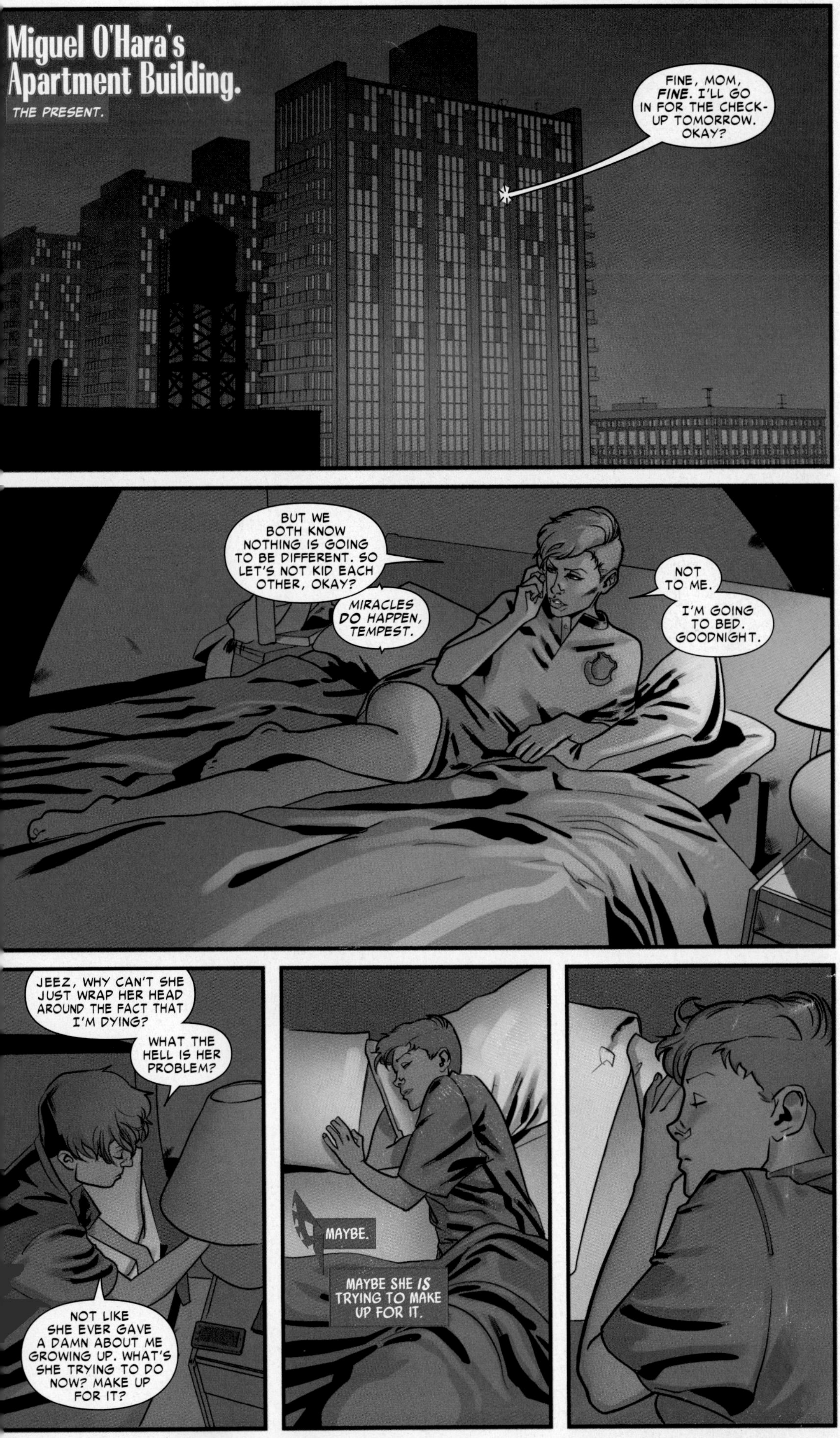
Miguel O'Hara's Apartment Building.
THE PRESENT.
FINE, MOM, *FINE*. I'LL GO IN FOR THE CHECK-UP TOMORROW. OKAY?
BUT WE BOTH KNOW NOTHING IS GOING TO BE DIFFERENT. SO LET'S NOT KID EACH OTHER, OKAY?
MIRACLES *DO* HAPPEN, TEMPEST.
NOT TO ME.
I'M GOING TO BED. GOODNIGHT.
JEEZ, WHY CAN'T SHE JUST WRAP HER HEAD AROUND THE FACT THAT I'M DYING?
WHAT THE HELL IS HER PROBLEM?
NOT LIKE SHE EVER GAVE A DAMN ABOUT ME GROWING UP. WHAT'S SHE TRYING TO DO NOW? MAKE UP FOR IT?
MAYBE.
MAYBE SHE *IS* TRYING TO MAKE UP FOR IT.

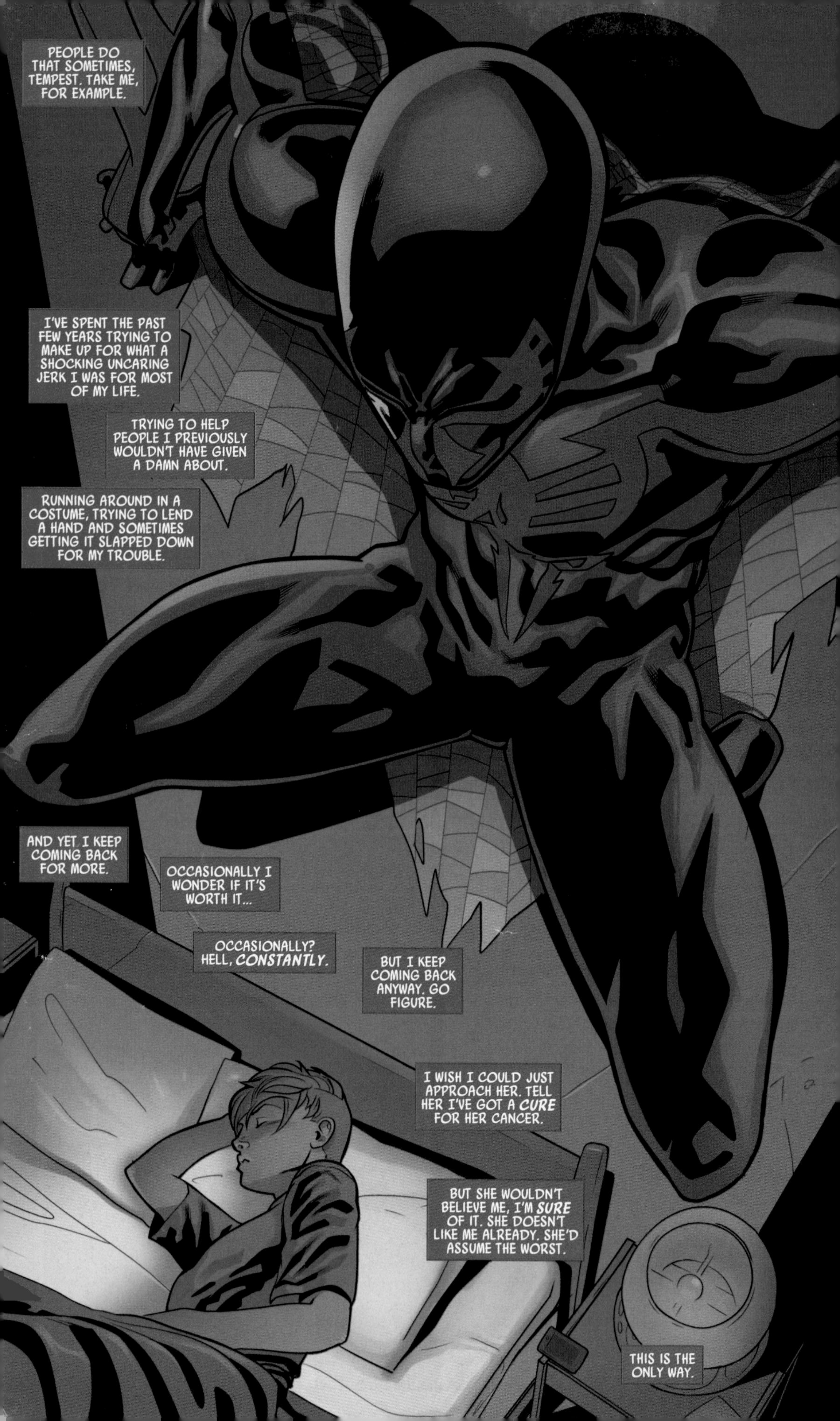
PEOPLE DO THAT SOMETIMES, TEMPEST. TAKE ME, FOR EXAMPLE.
I'VE SPENT THE PAST FEW YEARS TRYING TO MAKE UP FOR WHAT A SHOCKING UNCARING JERK I WAS FOR MOST OF MY LIFE.
TRYING TO HELP PEOPLE I PREVIOUSLY WOULDN'T HAVE GIVEN A DAMN ABOUT.
RUNNING AROUND IN A COSTUME, TRYING TO LEND A HAND AND SOMETIMES GETTING IT SLAPPED DOWN FOR MY TROUBLE.
AND YET I KEEP COMING BACK FOR MORE.
OCCASIONALLY I WONDER IF IT'S WORTH IT...
OCCASIONALLY? HELL, *CONSTANTLY*.
BUT I KEEP COMING BACK ANYWAY. GO FIGURE.
I WISH I COULD JUST APPROACH HER. TELL HER I'VE GOT A *CURE* FOR HER CANCER.
BUT SHE WOULDN'T BELIEVE ME, I'M *SURE* OF IT. SHE DOESN'T LIKE ME ALREADY. SHE'D ASSUME THE WORST.
THIS IS THE ONLY WAY.

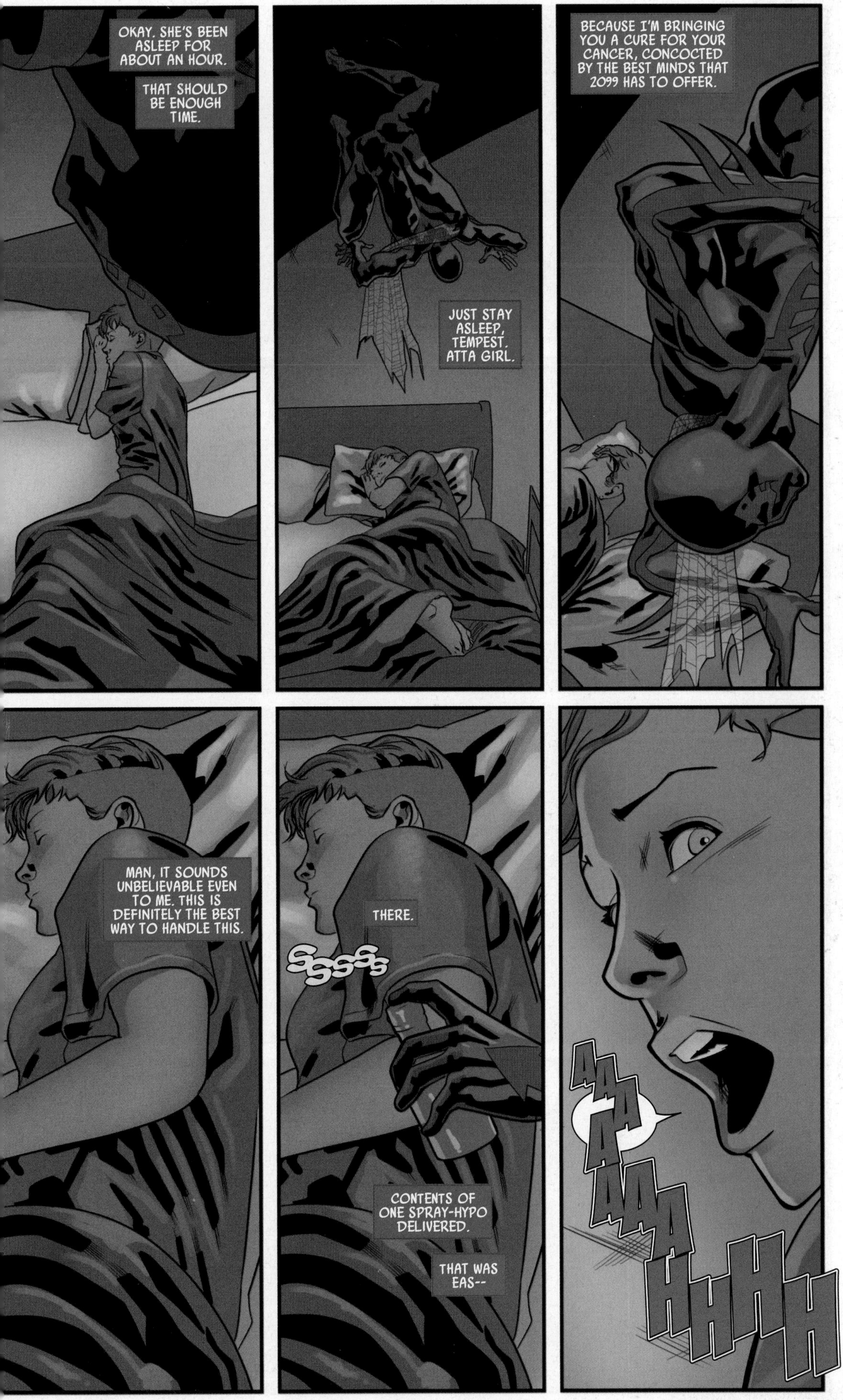
OKAY. SHE'S BEEN ASLEEP FOR ABOUT AN HOUR.
THAT SHOULD BE ENOUGH TIME.
JUST STAY ASLEEP, TEMPEST. ATTA GIRL.
BECAUSE I'M BRINGING YOU A CURE FOR YOUR CANCER, CONCOCTED BY THE BEST MINDS THAT 2099 HAS TO OFFER.
MAN, IT SOUNDS UNBELIEVABLE EVEN TO ME. THIS IS DEFINITELY THE BEST WAY TO HANDLE THIS.
THERE.
SSSSS
CONTENTS OF ONE SPRAY-HYPO DELIVERED.
THAT WAS EAS--
AAAAAAAHHHHH

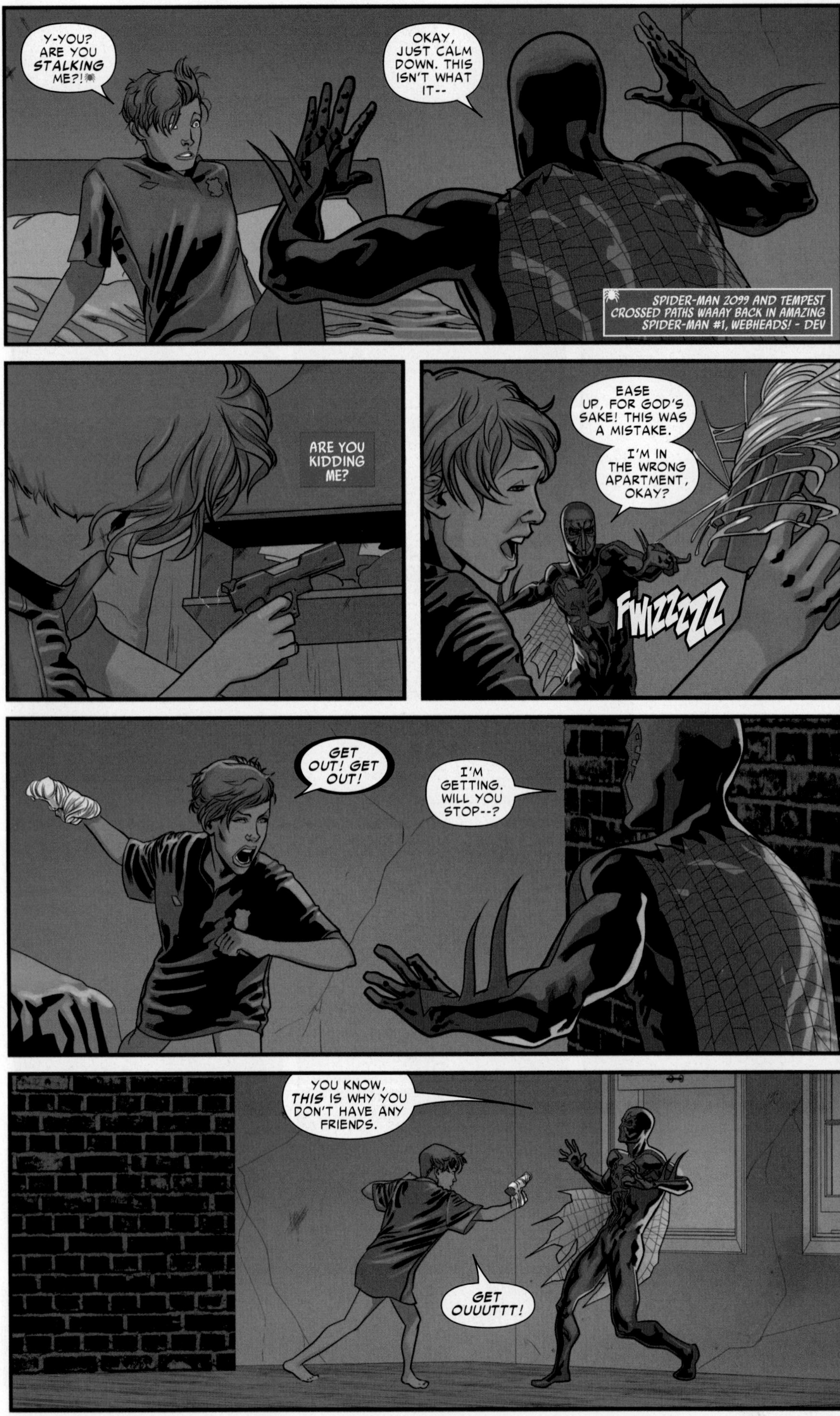
Y-YOU? ARE YOU STALKING ME?!
OKAY, JUST CALM DOWN. THIS ISN'T WHAT IT--
SPIDER-MAN 2099 AND TEMPEST CROSSED PATHS WAAAY BACK IN AMAZING SPIDER-MAN #1, WEBHEADS! - DEV
ARE YOU KIDDING ME?
EASE UP, FOR GOD'S SAKE! THIS WAS A MISTAKE.
I'M IN THE WRONG APARTMENT, OKAY?
FWIZZZZZ
GET OUT! GET OUT!
I'M GETTING. WILL YOU STOP--?
YOU KNOW, THIS IS WHY YOU DON'T HAVE ANY FRIENDS.
GET OUUUTTT!

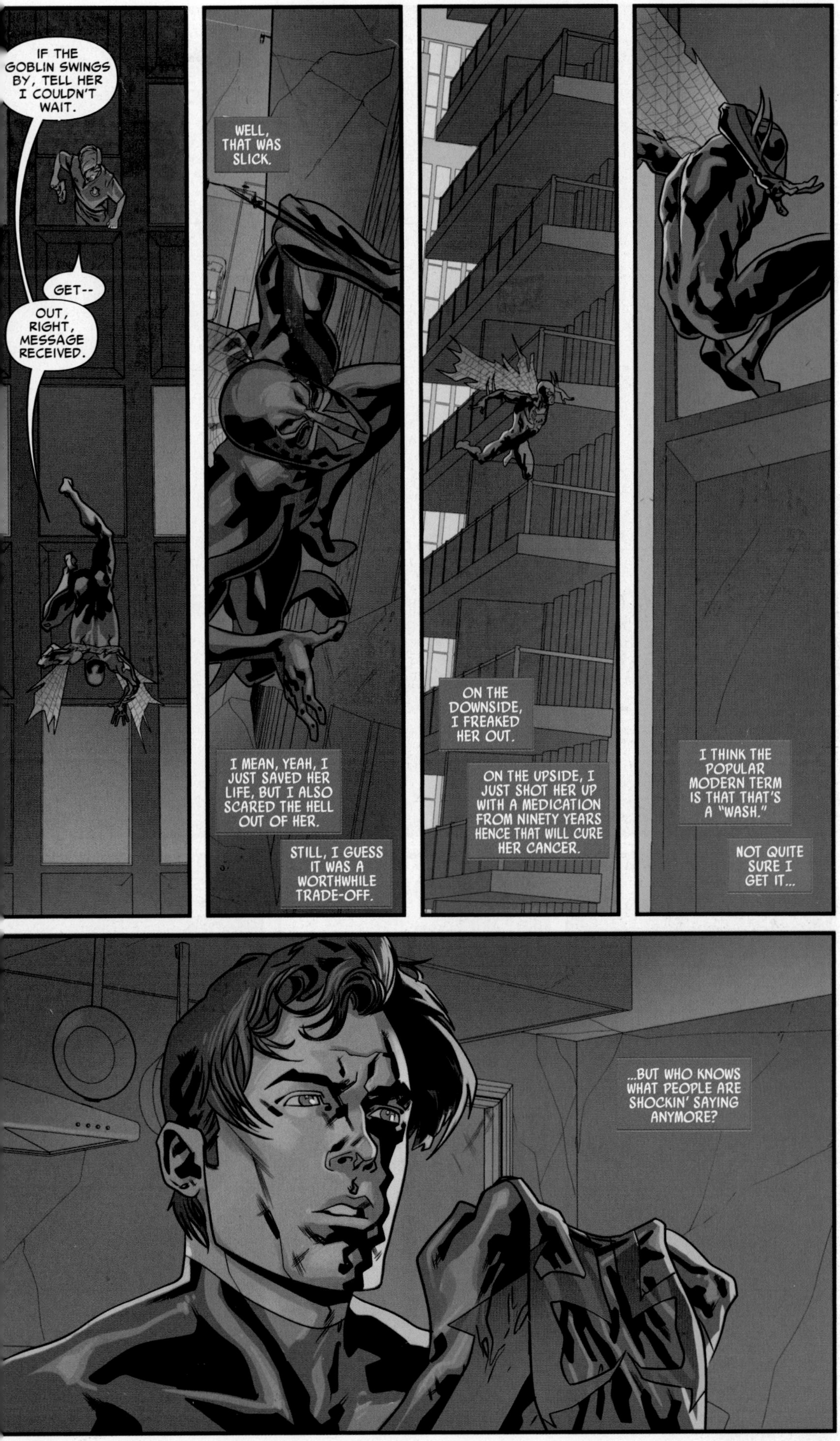
IF THE GOBLIN SWINGS BY, TELL HER I COULDN'T WAIT.
GET--
OUT, RIGHT, MESSAGE RECEIVED.
WELL, THAT WAS SLICK.
I MEAN, YEAH, I JUST SAVED HER LIFE, BUT I ALSO SCARED THE HELL OUT OF HER.
STILL, I GUESS IT WAS A WORTHWHILE TRADE-OFF.
ON THE DOWNSIDE, I FREAKED HER OUT.
ON THE UPSIDE, I JUST SHOT HER UP WITH A MEDICATION FROM NINETY YEARS HENCE THAT WILL CURE HER CANCER.
I THINK THE POPULAR MODERN TERM IS THAT THAT'S A "WASH."
NOT QUITE SURE I GET IT...
...BUT WHO KNOWS WHAT PEOPLE ARE SHOCKIN' SAYING ANYMORE?

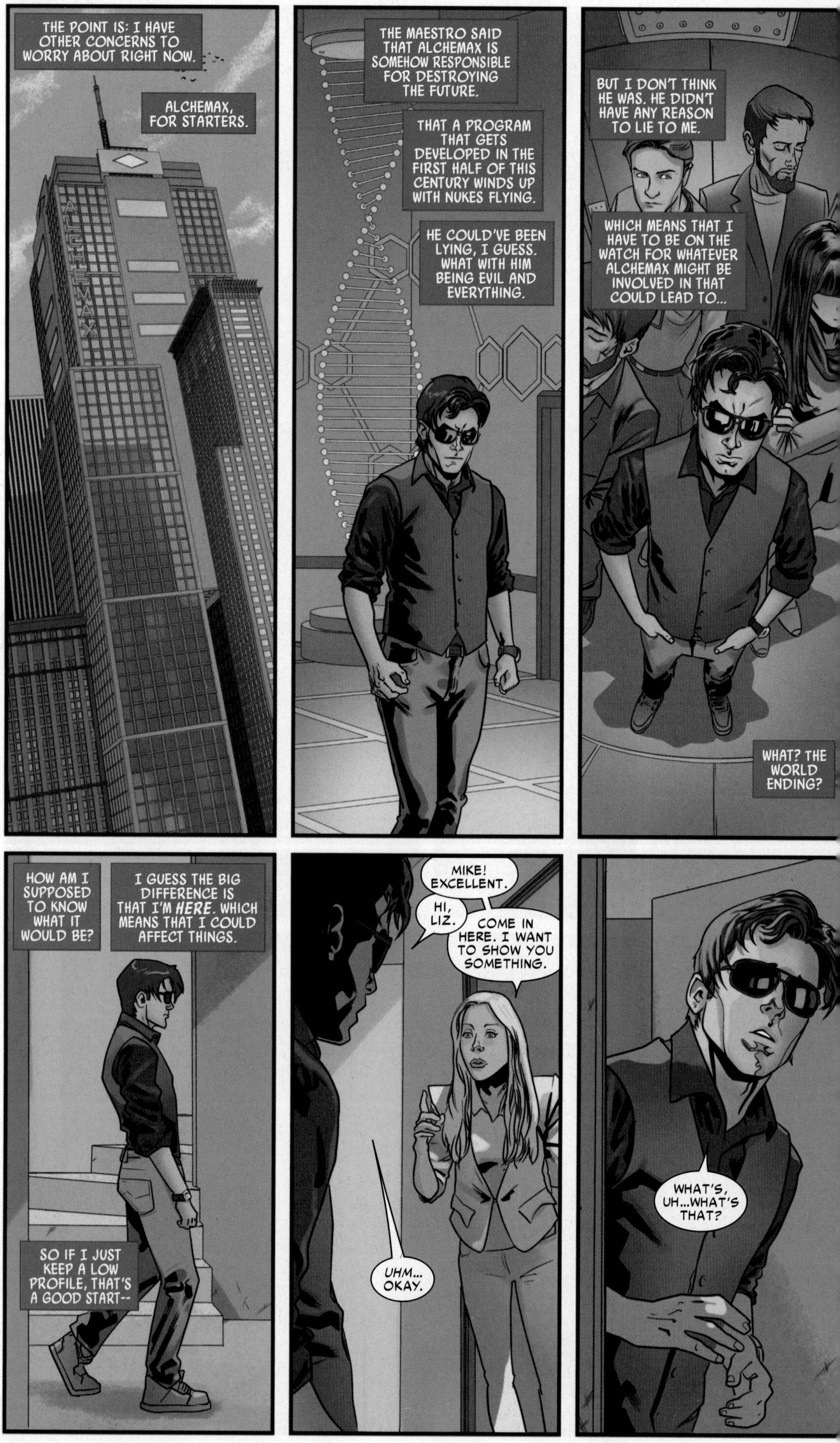
THE POINT IS: I HAVE OTHER CONCERNS TO WORRY ABOUT RIGHT NOW.
ALCHEMAX, FOR STARTERS.
ALCHEMAX
THE MAESTRO SAID THAT ALCHEMAX IS SOMEHOW RESPONSIBLE FOR DESTROYING THE FUTURE.
THAT A PROGRAM THAT GETS DEVELOPED IN THE FIRST HALF OF THIS CENTURY WINDS UP WITH NUKES FLYING.
HE COULD'VE BEEN LYING, I GUESS. WHAT WITH HIM BEING EVIL AND EVERYTHING.
BUT I DON'T THINK HE WAS. HE DIDN'T HAVE ANY REASON TO LIE TO ME.
WHICH MEANS THAT I HAVE TO BE ON THE WATCH FOR WHATEVER ALCHEMAX MIGHT BE INVOLVED IN THAT COULD LEAD TO...
WHAT? THE WORLD ENDING?
HOW AM I SUPPOSED TO KNOW WHAT IT WOULD BE?
I GUESS THE BIG DIFFERENCE IS THAT I'M *HERE*. WHICH MEANS THAT I COULD AFFECT THINGS.
SO IF I JUST KEEP A LOW PROFILE, THAT'S A GOOD START--
MIKE! EXCELLENT.
HI, LIZ.
COME IN HERE. I WANT TO SHOW YOU SOMETHING.
UHM... OKAY.
WHAT'S, UH...WHAT'S THAT?

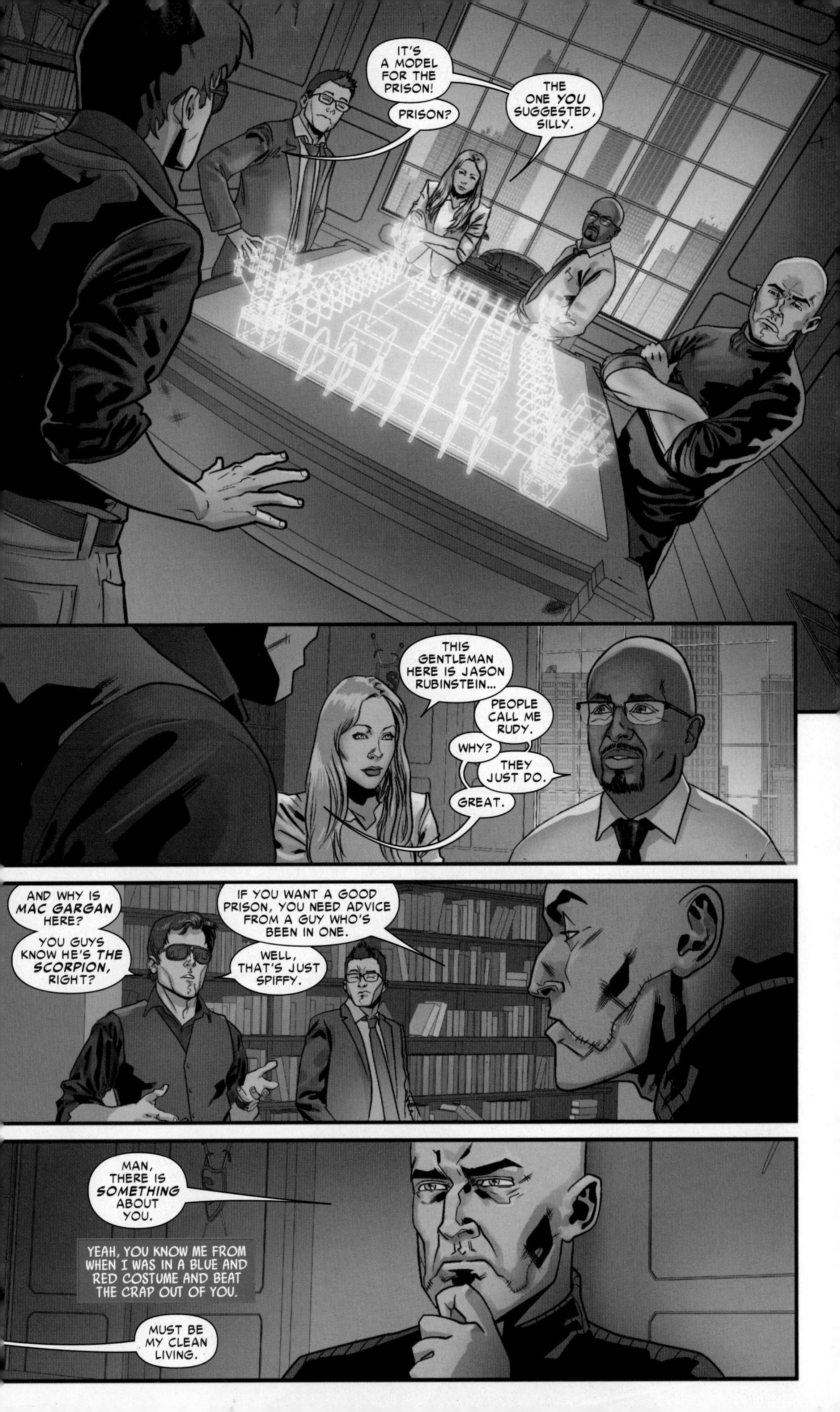
IT'S A MODEL FOR THE PRISON!
PRISON?
THE ONE YOU SUGGESTED, SILLY.
THIS GENTLEMAN HERE IS JASON RUBINSTEIN...
PEOPLE CALL ME RUDY.
WHY?
THEY JUST DO.
GREAT.
AND WHY IS MAC GARGAN HERE?
YOU GUYS KNOW HE'S THE SCORPION, RIGHT?
IF YOU WANT A GOOD PRISON, YOU NEED ADVICE FROM A GUY WHO'S BEEN IN ONE.
WELL, THAT'S JUST SPIFFY.
MAN, THERE IS SOMETHING ABOUT YOU.
YEAH, YOU KNOW ME FROM WHEN I WAS IN A BLUE AND RED COSTUME AND BEAT THE CRAP OUT OF YOU.
MUST BE MY CLEAN LIVING.

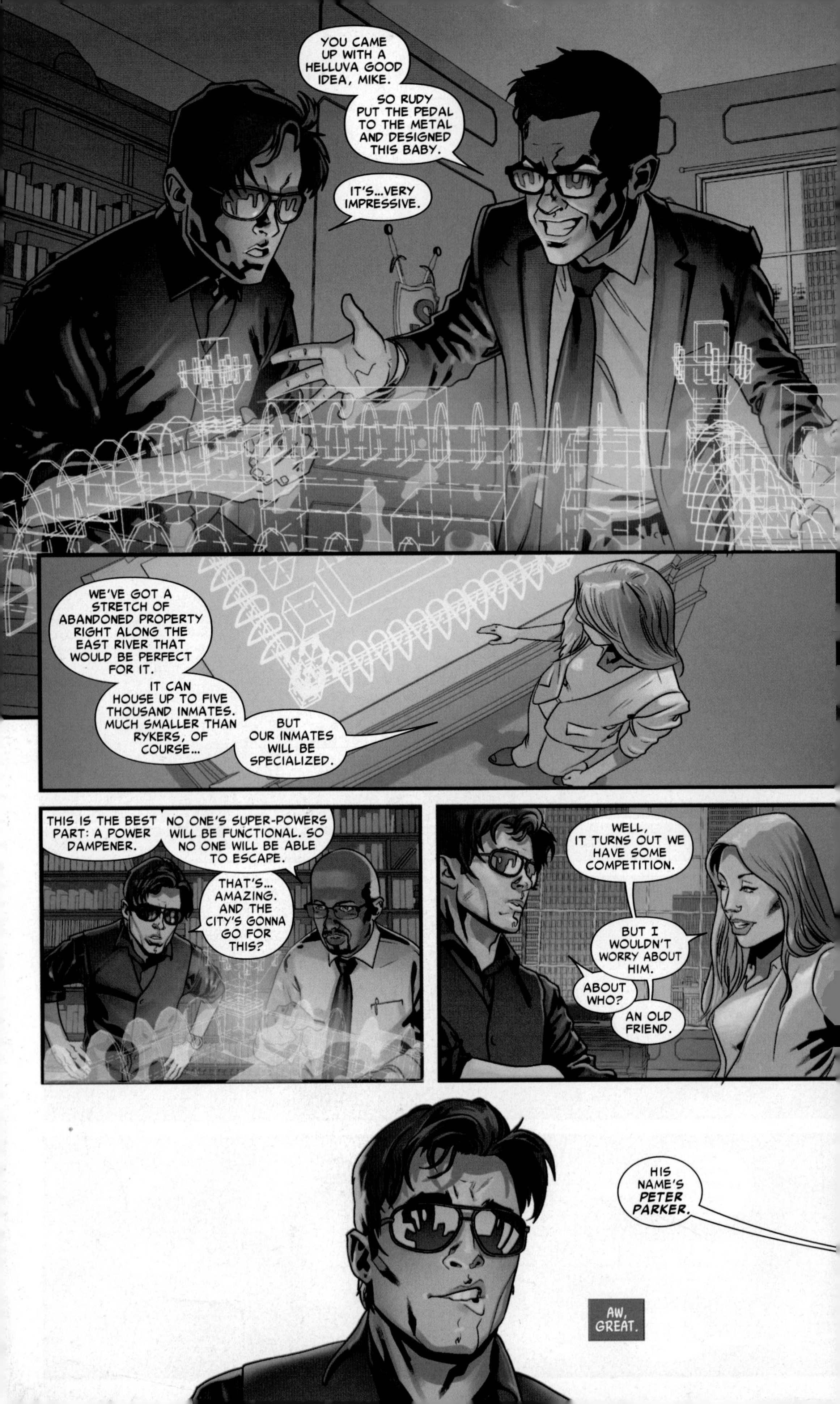
YOU CAME UP WITH A HELLUVA GOOD IDEA, MIKE.
SO RUDY PUT THE PEDAL TO THE METAL AND DESIGNED THIS BABY.
IT'S...VERY IMPRESSIVE.
WE'VE GOT A STRETCH OF ABANDONED PROPERTY RIGHT ALONG THE EAST RIVER THAT WOULD BE PERFECT FOR IT.
IT CAN HOUSE UP TO FIVE THOUSAND INMATES. MUCH SMALLER THAN RYKERS, OF COURSE...
BUT OUR INMATES WILL BE SPECIALIZED.
THIS IS THE BEST PART: A POWER DAMPENER.
NO ONE'S SUPER-POWERS WILL BE FUNCTIONAL. SO NO ONE WILL BE ABLE TO ESCAPE.
THAT'S... AMAZING. AND THE CITY'S GONNA GO FOR THIS?
WELL, IT TURNS OUT WE HAVE SOME COMPETITION.
BUT I WOULDN'T WORRY ABOUT HIM.
ABOUT WHO?
AN OLD FRIEND.
HIS NAME'S PETER PARKER.
AW, GREAT.

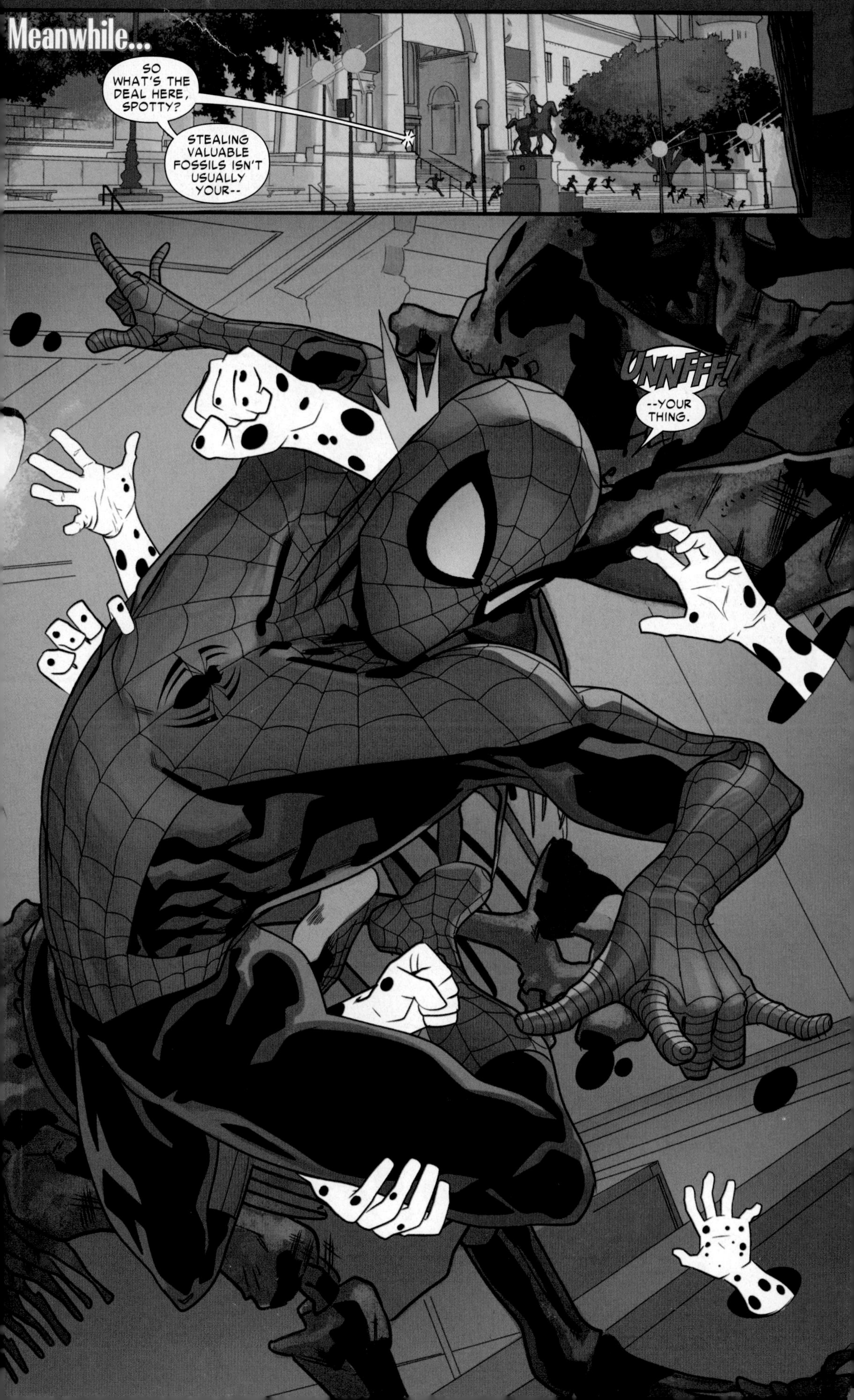

Meanwhile...
SO WHAT'S THE DEAL HERE, SPOTTY?
STEALING VALUABLE FOSSILS ISN'T USUALLY YOUR--
UNNFFF!
--YOUR THING.

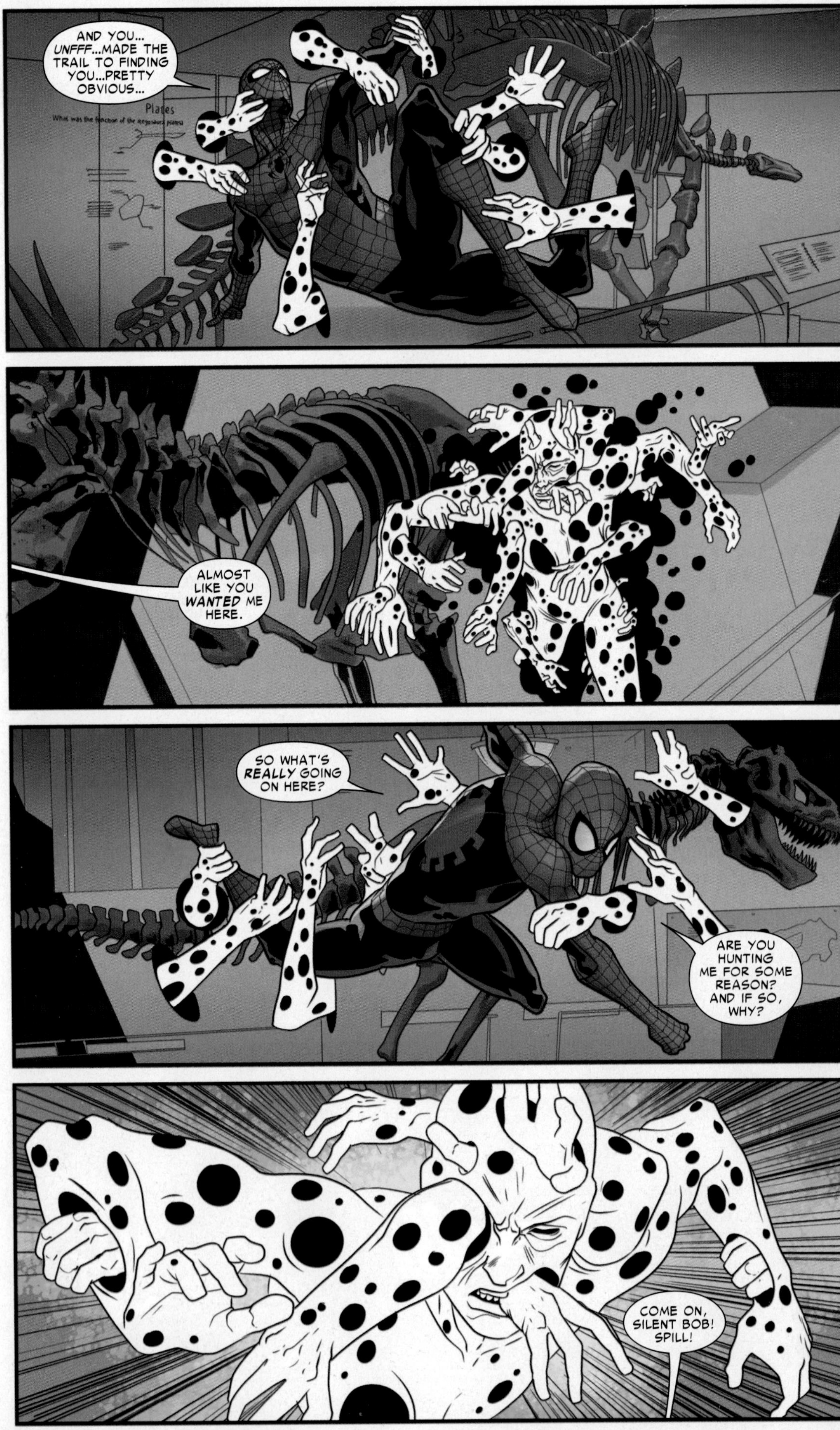
AND YOU... UNFFF...MADE THE TRAIL TO FINDING YOU...PRETTY OBVIOUS...
Plates
ALMOST LIKE YOU WANTED ME HERE.
SO WHAT'S REALLY GOING ON HERE?
ARE YOU HUNTING ME FOR SOME REASON? AND IF SO, WHY?
COME ON, SILENT BOB! SPILL!

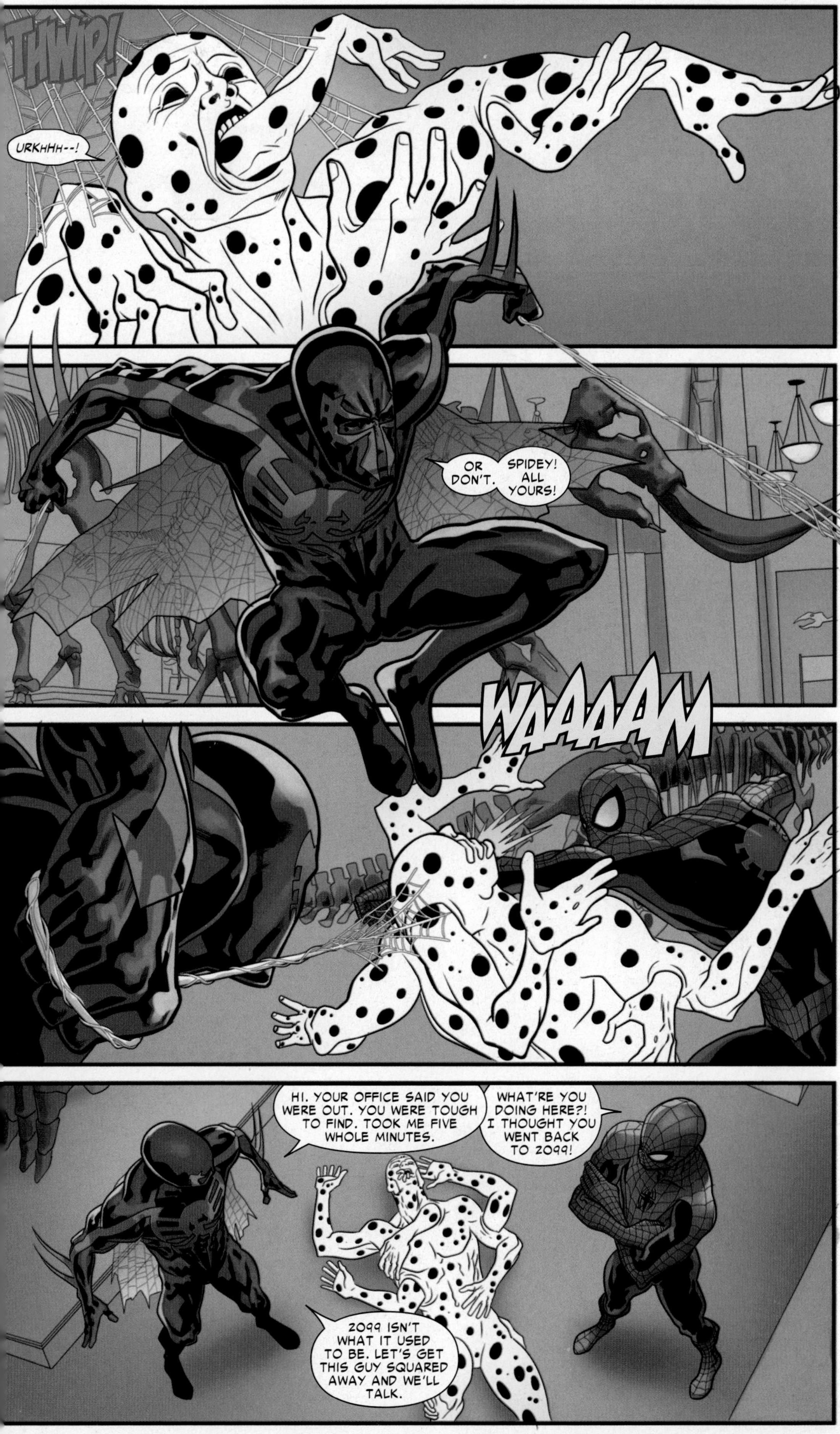
THWIP!
URKHHH--!
OR DON'T.
SPIDEY! ALL YOURS!
WAAAAM
HI. YOUR OFFICE SAID YOU WERE OUT. YOU WERE TOUGH TO FIND. TOOK ME FIVE WHOLE MINUTES.
WHAT'RE YOU DOING HERE?! I THOUGHT YOU WENT BACK TO 2099!
2099 ISN'T WHAT IT USED TO BE. LET'S GET THIS GUY SQUARED AWAY AND WE'LL TALK.

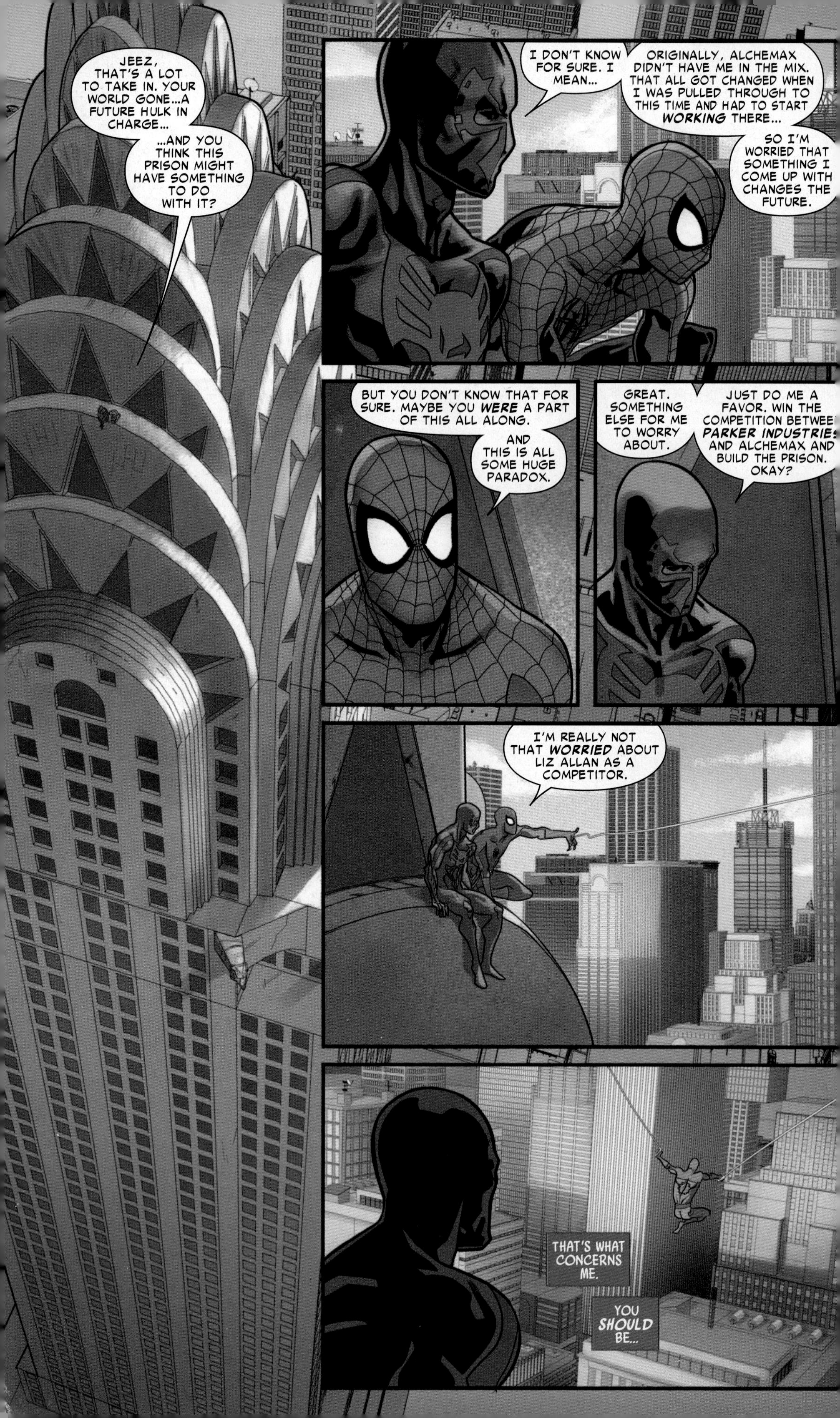
JEEZ, THAT'S A LOT TO TAKE IN. YOUR WORLD GONE...A FUTURE HULK IN CHARGE...
...AND YOU THINK THIS PRISON MIGHT HAVE SOMETHING TO DO WITH IT?
I DON'T KNOW FOR SURE. I MEAN...
ORIGINALLY, ALCHEMAX DIDN'T HAVE ME IN THE MIX. THAT ALL GOT CHANGED WHEN I WAS PULLED THROUGH TO THIS TIME AND HAD TO START WORKING THERE...
SO I'M WORRIED THAT SOMETHING I COME UP WITH CHANGES THE FUTURE.
BUT YOU DON'T KNOW THAT FOR SURE. MAYBE YOU WERE A PART OF THIS ALL ALONG.
AND THIS IS ALL SOME HUGE PARADOX.
GREAT. SOMETHING ELSE FOR ME TO WORRY ABOUT.
JUST DO ME A FAVOR. WIN THE COMPETITION BETWEEN PARKER INDUSTRIES AND ALCHEMAX AND BUILD THE PRISON. OKAY?
I'M REALLY NOT THAT WORRIED ABOUT LIZ ALLAN AS A COMPETITOR.
THAT'S WHAT CONCERNS ME.
YOU SHOULD BE...

Later...

WELL, THIS HAS BEEN A DAY.

I MAY BE TAKING MY LIFE IN MY HANDS, BUT I SHOULD TOUCH BASE WITH TEMPEST.

I WONDER IF SHE KNOWS YET.

HEY, HEY! IT'S MICHELLE!

MIGUEL, ACTUALLY. IS, UH...IS THIS A BAD TIME?

THIS IS A GREAT TIME! JUST GOT BACK FROM A DINNER WITH MY MOTHER. WHATTAYA NEED FIXED?

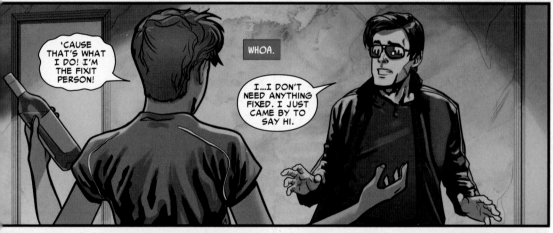

'CAUSE THAT'S WHAT I DO! I'M THE FIXIT PERSON!

WHOA.

I...I DON'T NEED ANYTHING FIXED. I JUST CAME BY TO SAY HI.

THAT'S FATANSTIC!

FANTASTIC.

THAT TOO! WELCOME IN!

WUUUMF!

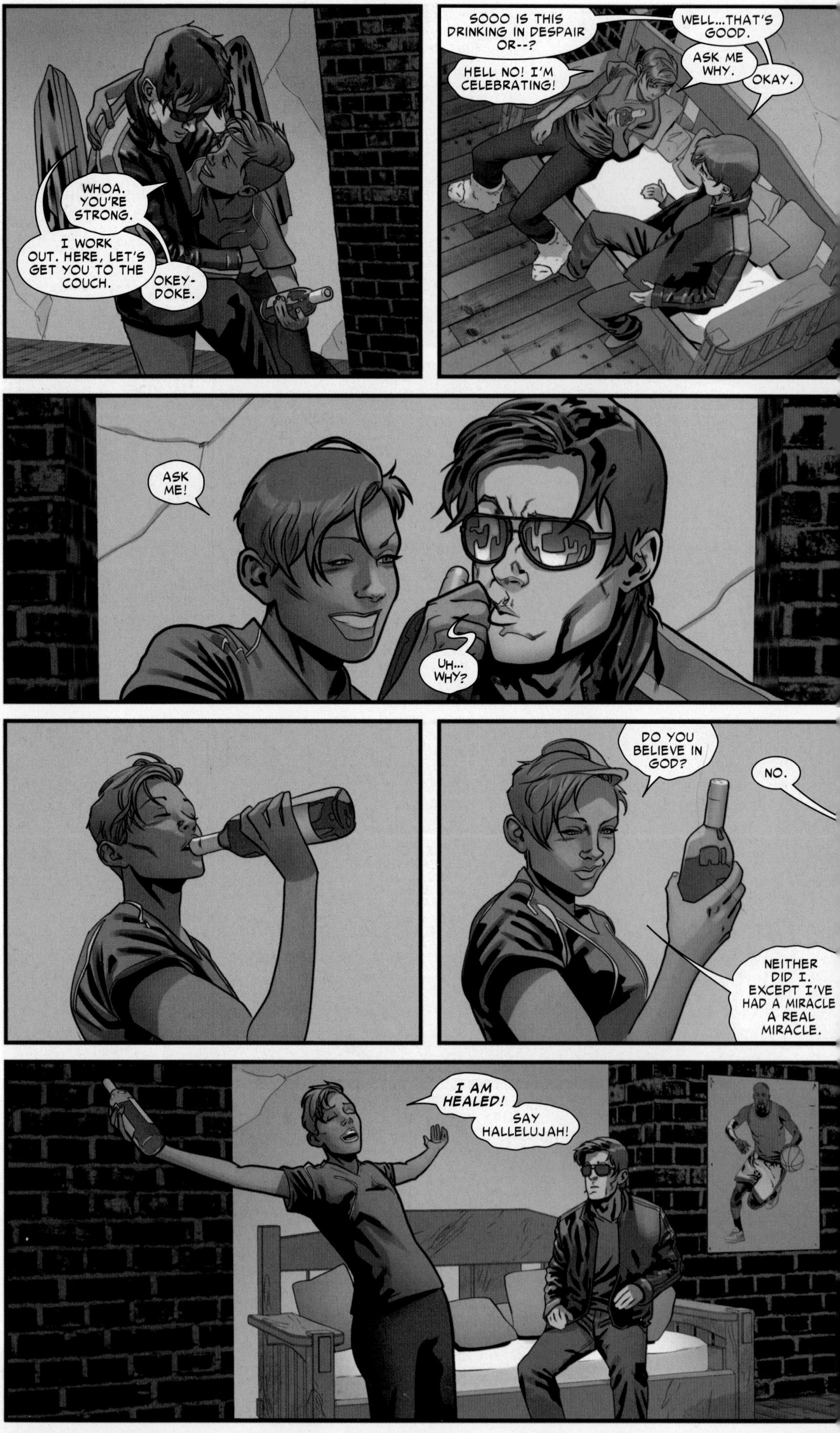
WHOA. YOU'RE STRONG.
I WORK OUT. HERE, LET'S GET YOU TO THE COUCH.
OKEY-DOKE.
SOOO IS THIS DRINKING IN DESPAIR OR--?
HELL NO! I'M CELEBRATING!
WELL...THAT'S GOOD.
ASK ME WHY.
OKAY.
ASK ME!
UH... WHY?
DO YOU BELIEVE IN GOD?
NO.
NEITHER DID I. EXCEPT I'VE HAD A MIRACLE A REAL MIRACLE.
I AM HEALED!
SAY HALLELUJAH!

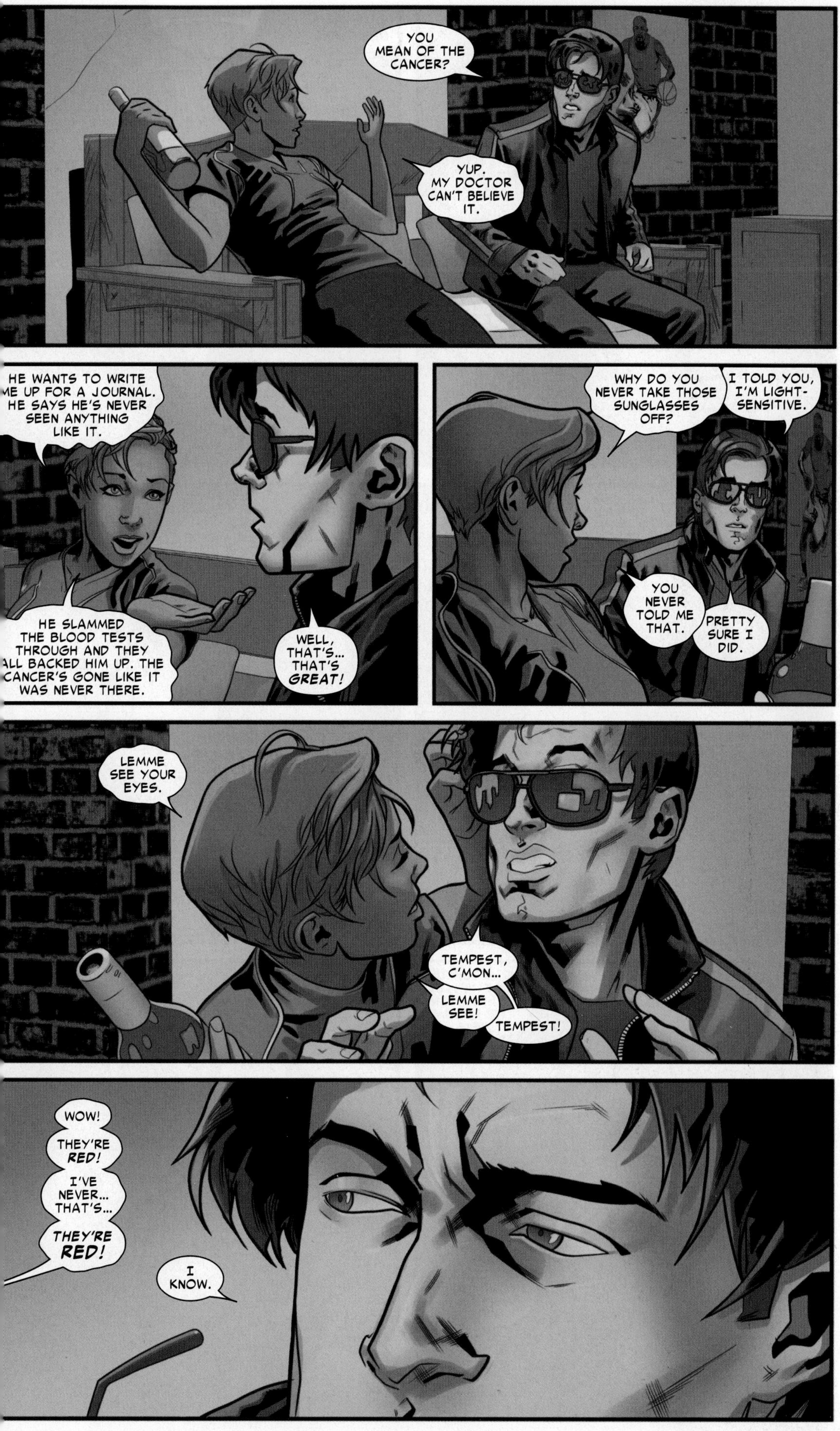
YOU MEAN OF THE CANCER?
YUP. MY DOCTOR CAN'T BELIEVE IT.
HE WANTS TO WRITE ME UP FOR A JOURNAL. HE SAYS HE'S NEVER SEEN ANYTHING LIKE IT.
HE SLAMMED THE BLOOD TESTS THROUGH AND THEY ALL BACKED HIM UP. THE CANCER'S GONE LIKE IT WAS NEVER THERE.
WELL, THAT'S... THAT'S GREAT!
WHY DO YOU NEVER TAKE THOSE SUNGLASSES OFF?
I TOLD YOU, I'M LIGHT-SENSITIVE.
YOU NEVER TOLD ME THAT.
PRETTY SURE I DID.
LEMME SEE YOUR EYES.
TEMPEST, C'MON...
LEMME SEE!
TEMPEST!
WOW!
THEY'RE RED!
I'VE NEVER... THAT'S...
THEY'RE RED!
I KNOW.

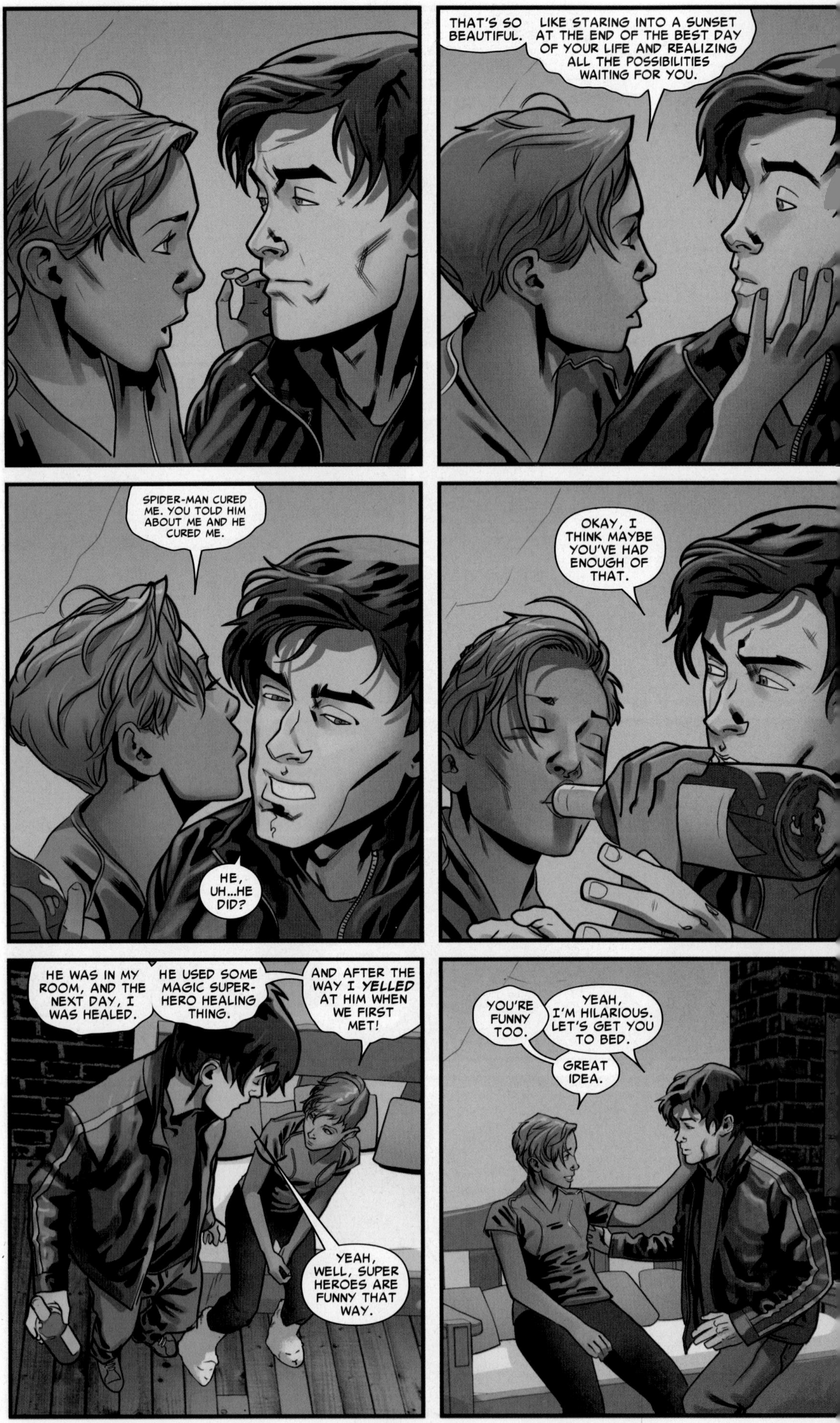
THAT'S SO BEAUTIFUL.
LIKE STARING INTO A SUNSET AT THE END OF THE BEST DAY OF YOUR LIFE AND REALIZING ALL THE POSSIBILITIES WAITING FOR YOU.
SPIDER-MAN CURED ME. YOU TOLD HIM ABOUT ME AND HE CURED ME.
HE, UH...HE DID?
OKAY, I THINK MAYBE YOU'VE HAD ENOUGH OF THAT.
HE WAS IN MY ROOM, AND THE NEXT DAY, I WAS HEALED.
HE USED SOME MAGIC SUPER-HERO HEALING THING.
AND AFTER THE WAY I *YELLED* AT HIM WHEN WE FIRST MET!
YEAH, WELL, SUPER HEROES ARE FUNNY THAT WAY.
YOU'RE FUNNY TOO.
YEAH, I'M HILARIOUS. LET'S GET YOU TO BED.
GREAT IDEA.

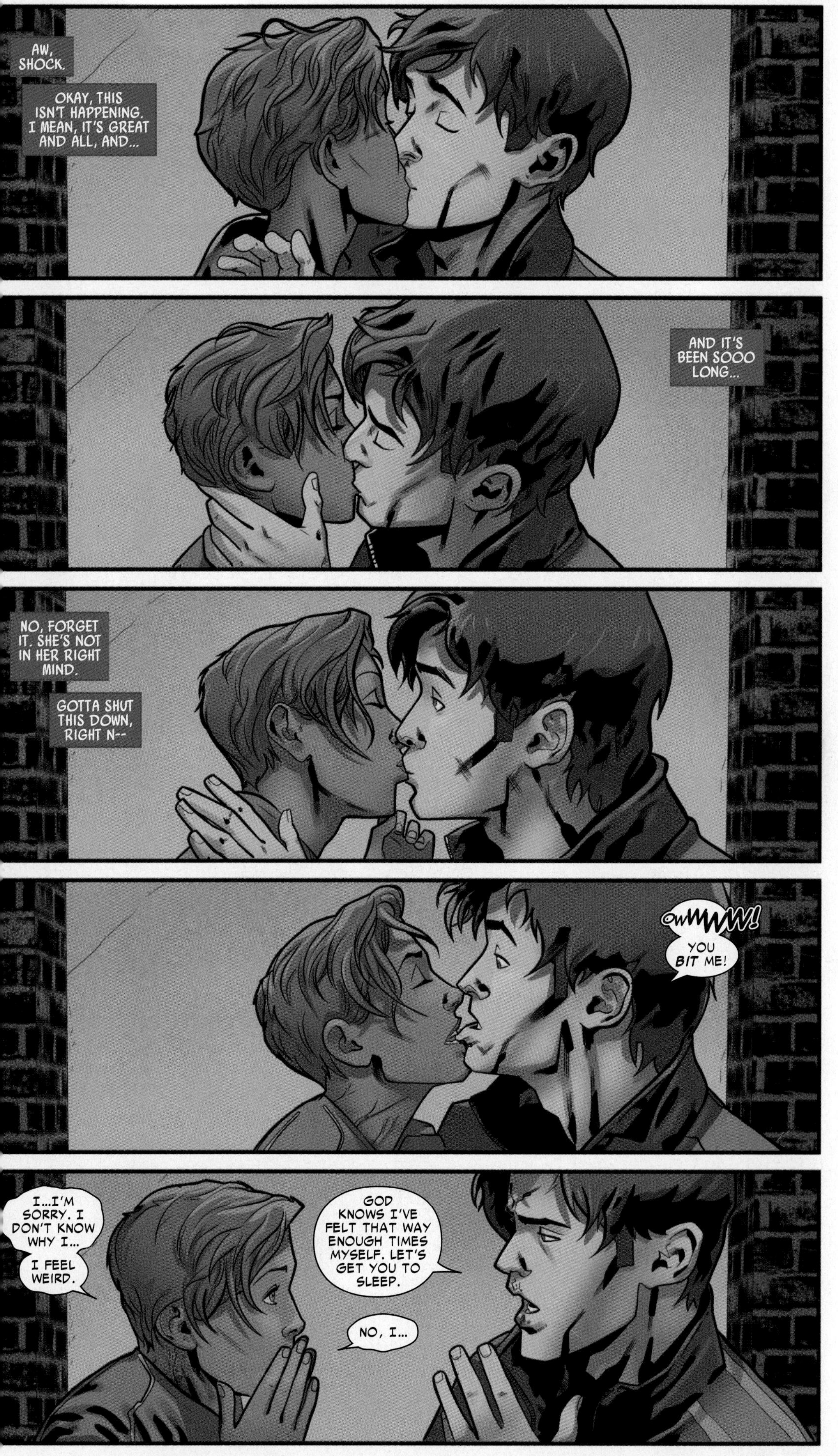
AW, SHOCK.
OKAY, THIS ISN'T HAPPENING. I MEAN, IT'S GREAT AND ALL, AND...
AND IT'S BEEN SOOO LONG...
NO, FORGET IT. SHE'S NOT IN HER RIGHT MIND.
GOTTA SHUT THIS DOWN, RIGHT N--
OWWWW!
YOU BIT ME!
I...I'M SORRY. I DON'T KNOW WHY I...
I FEEL WEIRD.
GOD KNOWS I'VE FELT THAT WAY ENOUGH TIMES MYSELF. LET'S GET YOU TO SLEEP.
NO, I...

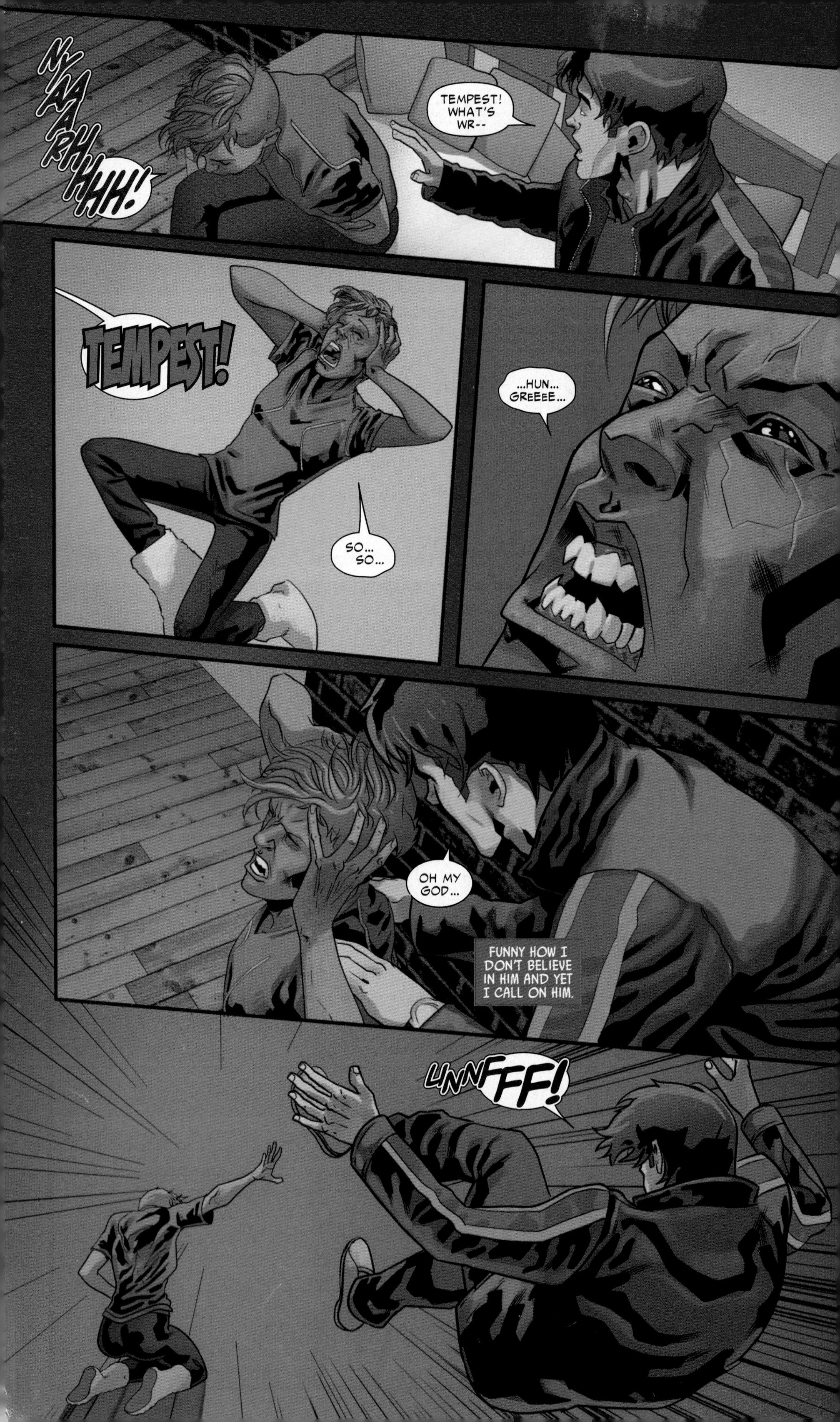
NYAAARHHHH!
TEMPEST! WHAT'S WR--
TEMPEST!
SO... SO...
...HUN... GREEEE...
OH MY GOD...
FUNNY HOW I DON'T BELIEVE IN HIM AND YET I CALL ON HIM.
UNNFFF!

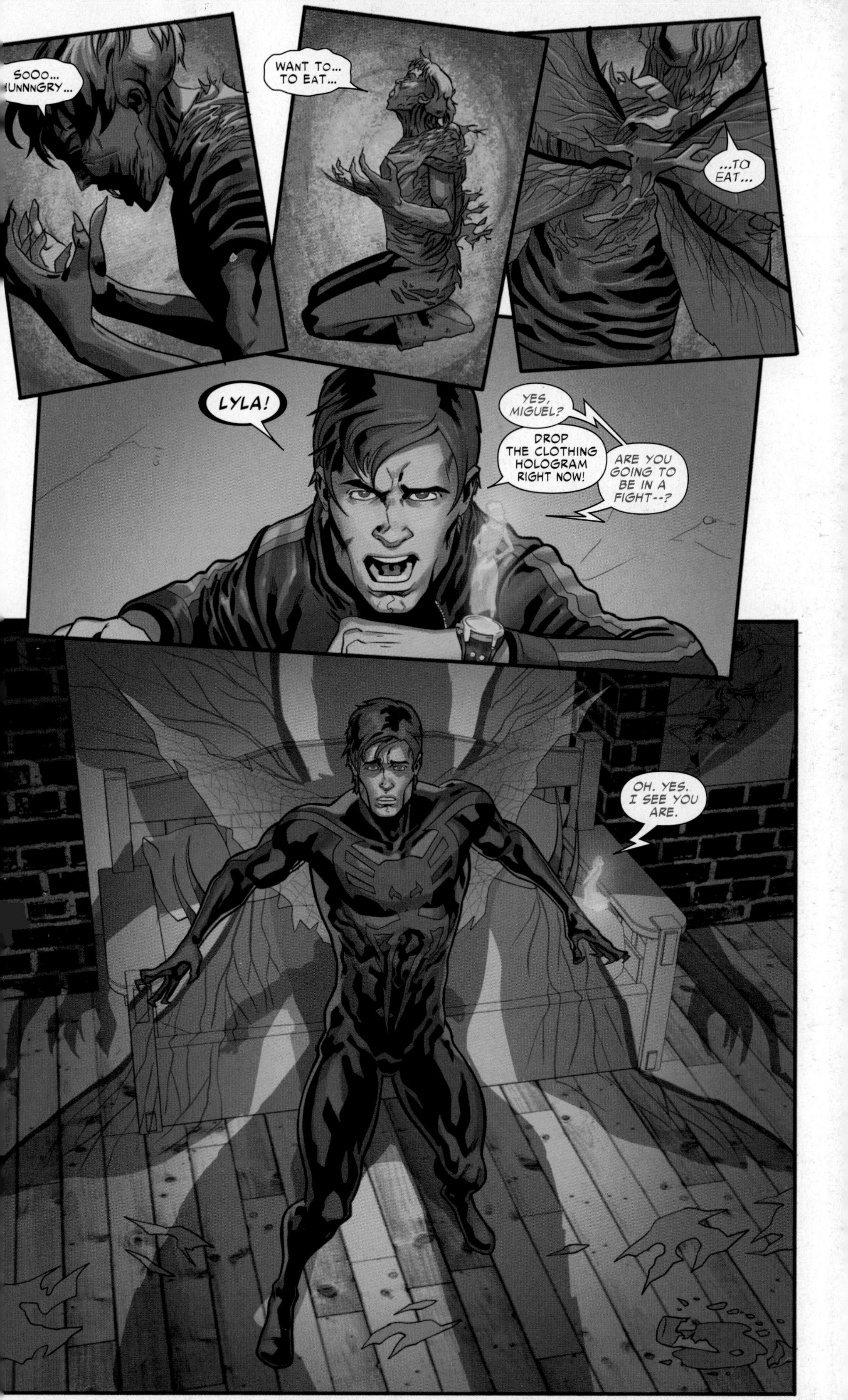
SOOO... HUNNNGRY...
WANT TO... TO EAT...
...TO EAT...
LYLA!
YES, MIGUEL?
DROP THE CLOTHING HOLOGRAM RIGHT NOW!
ARE YOU GOING TO BE IN A FIGHT--?
OH. YES. I SEE YOU ARE.

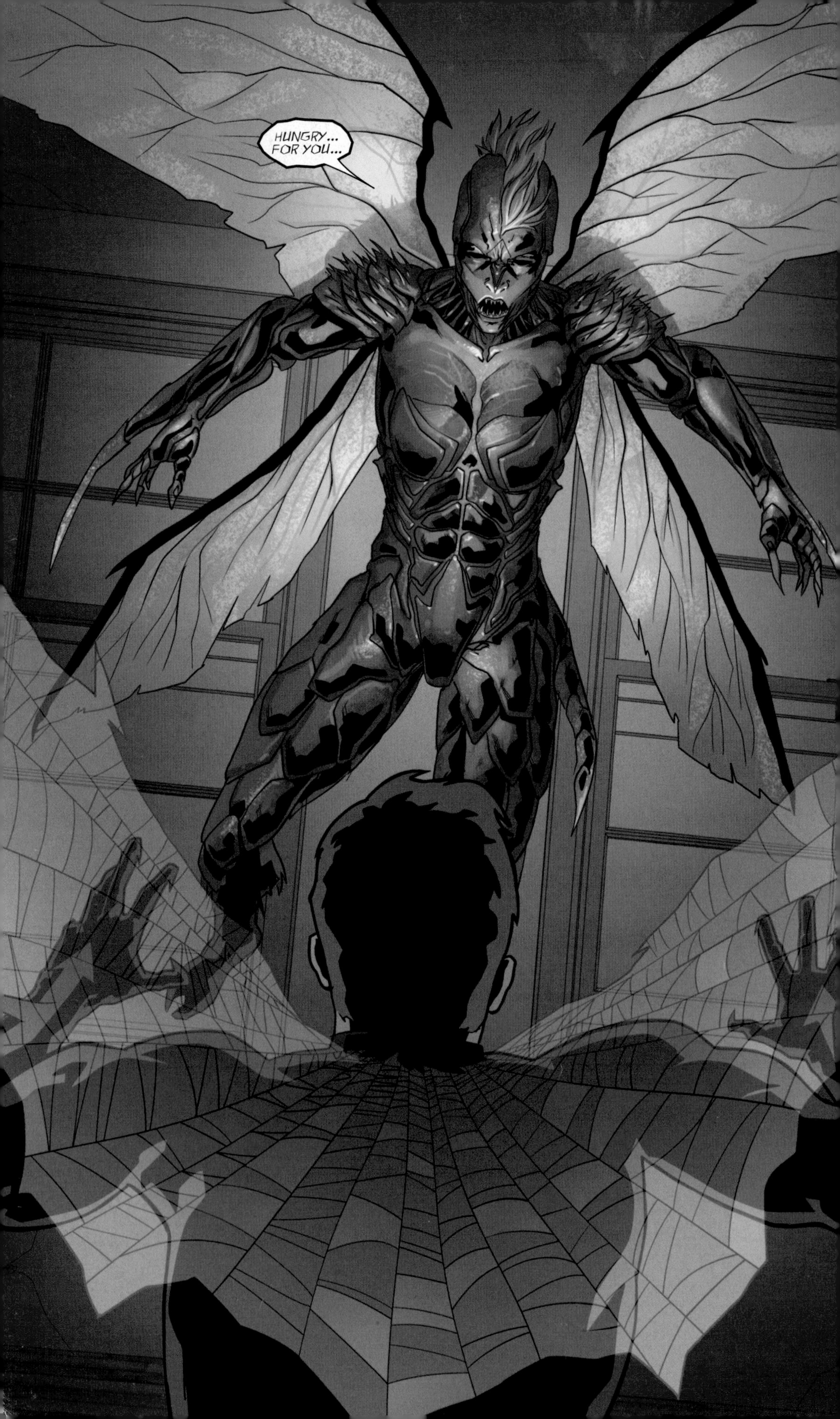
HUNGRY... FOR YOU...

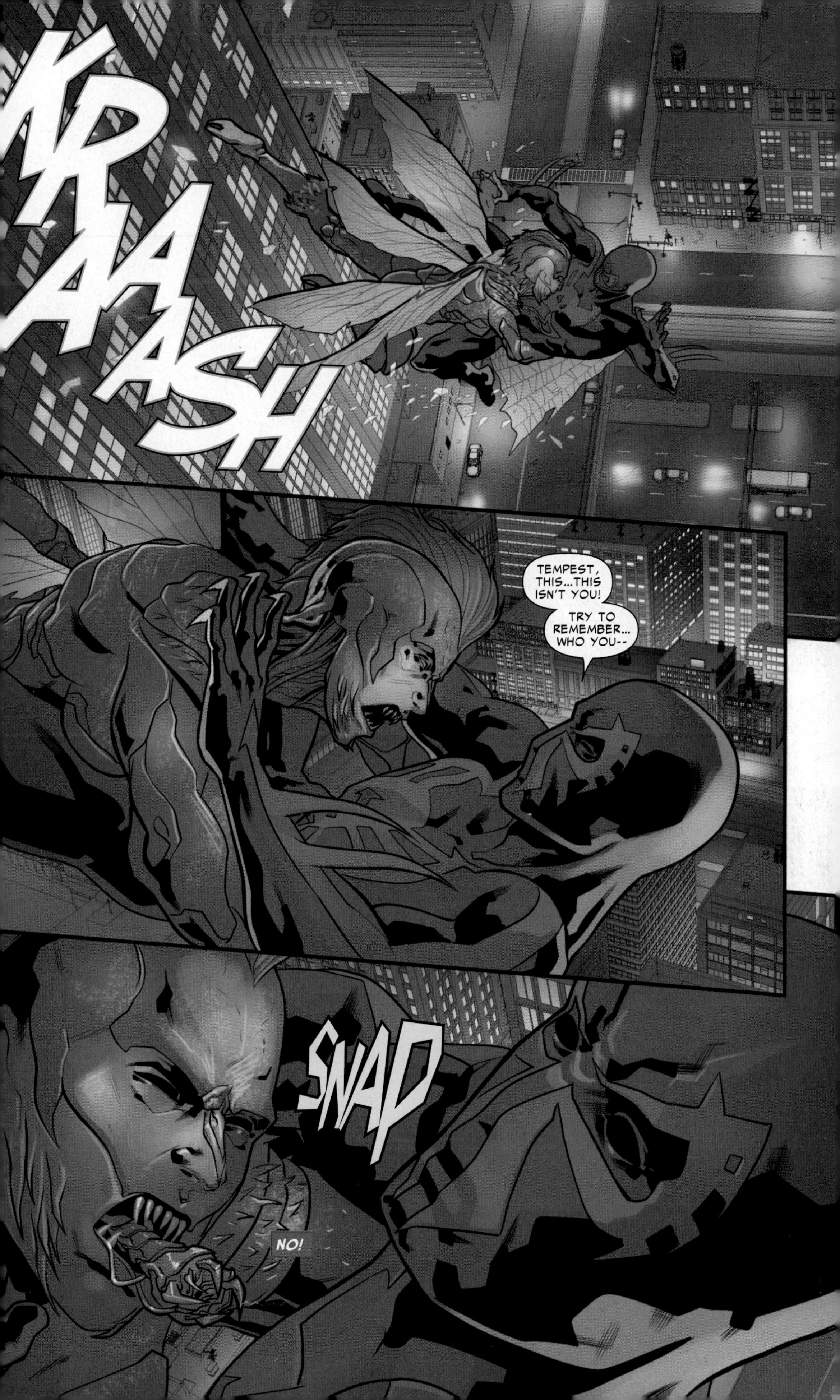
KRAAASH
TEMPEST, THIS...THIS ISN'T YOU!
TRY TO REMEMBER... WHO YOU--
SNAP
NO!

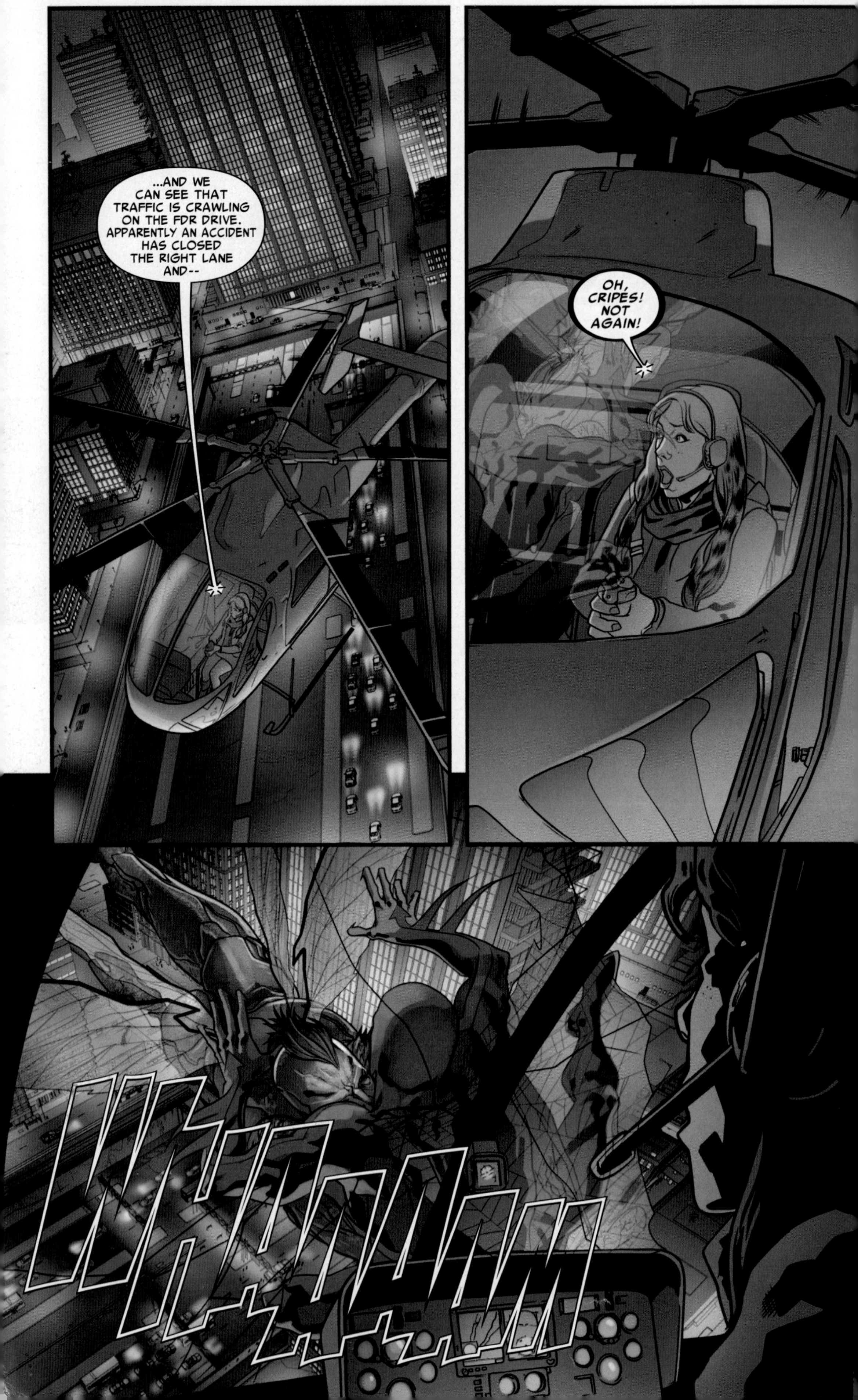
...AND WE CAN SEE THAT TRAFFIC IS CRAWLING ON THE FDR DRIVE. APPARENTLY AN ACCIDENT HAS CLOSED THE RIGHT LANE AND--
OH, CRIPES! NOT AGAIN!
WHAAAM

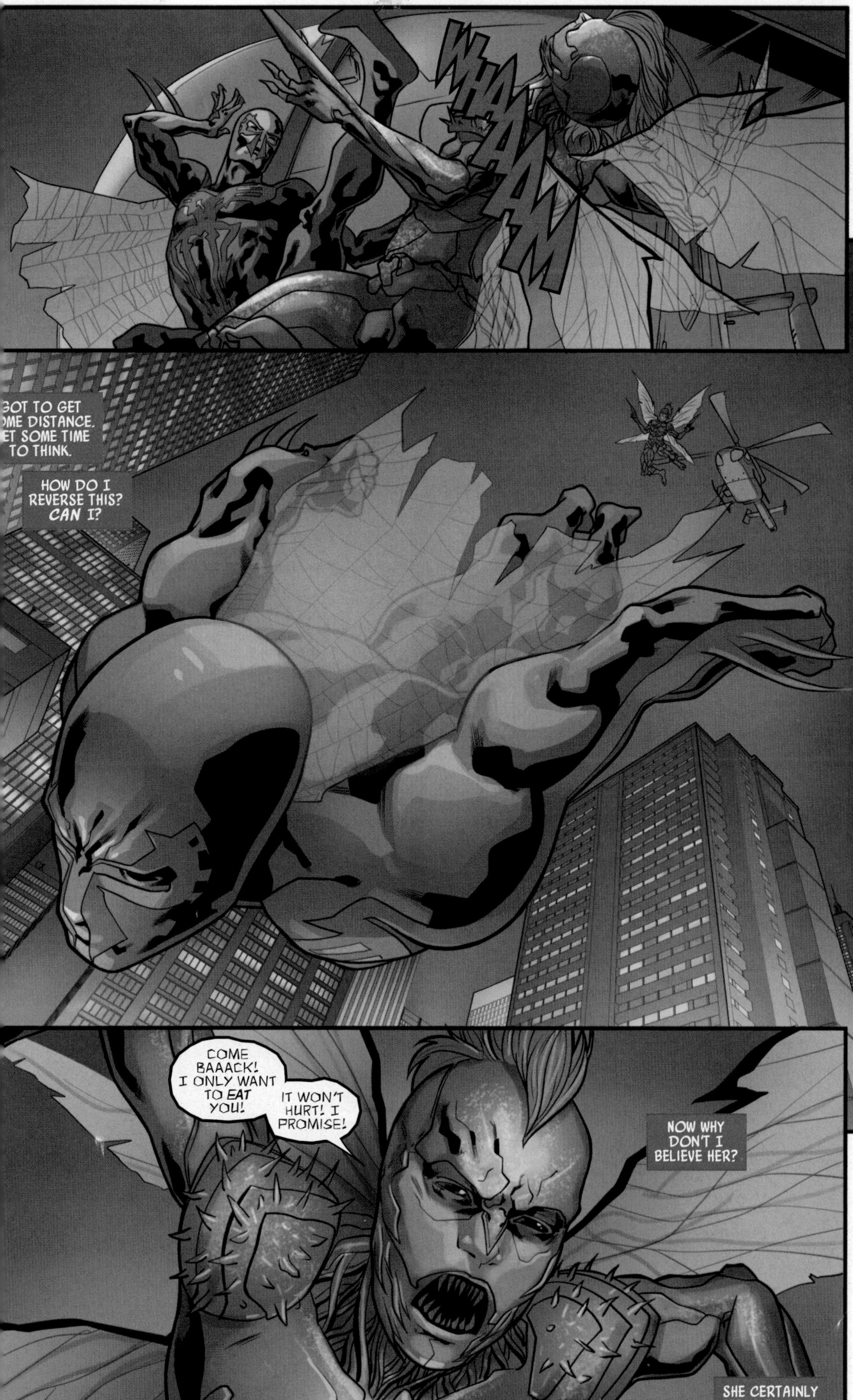
WHAAAM
GOT TO GET
OME DISTANCE.
ET SOME TIME
TO THINK.
HOW DO I REVERSE THIS? CAN I?
COME BAAACK! I ONLY WANT TO EAT YOU!
IT WON'T HURT! I PROMISE!
NOW WHY DON'T I BELIEVE HER?
SHE CERTAINLY SEEMS TO LACK CREDIBILITY.

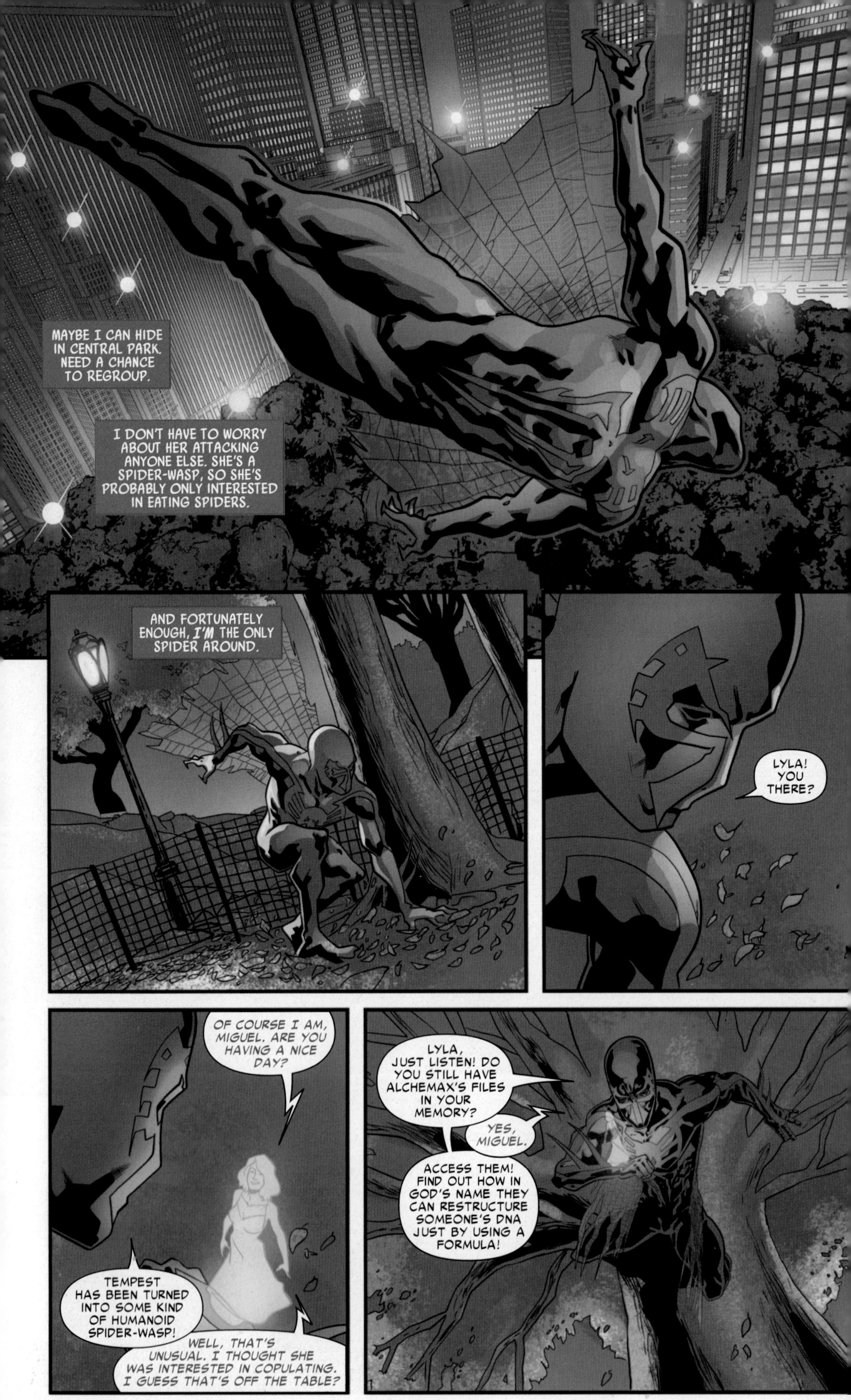
MAYBE I CAN HIDE IN CENTRAL PARK. NEED A CHANCE TO REGROUP.
I DON'T HAVE TO WORRY ABOUT HER ATTACKING ANYONE ELSE. SHE'S A SPIDER-WASP, SO SHE'S PROBABLY ONLY INTERESTED IN EATING SPIDERS.
AND FORTUNATELY ENOUGH, I'M THE ONLY SPIDER AROUND.
LYLA! YOU THERE?
OF COURSE I AM, MIGUEL. ARE YOU HAVING A NICE DAY?
TEMPEST HAS BEEN TURNED INTO SOME KIND OF HUMANOID SPIDER-WASP!
WELL, THAT'S UNUSUAL. I THOUGHT SHE WAS INTERESTED IN COPULATING. I GUESS THAT'S OFF THE TABLE?
LYLA, JUST LISTEN! DO YOU STILL HAVE ALCHEMAX'S FILES IN YOUR MEMORY?
YES, MIGUEL.
ACCESS THEM! FIND OUT HOW IN GOD'S NAME THEY CAN RESTRUCTURE SOMEONE'S DNA JUST BY USING A FORMULA!

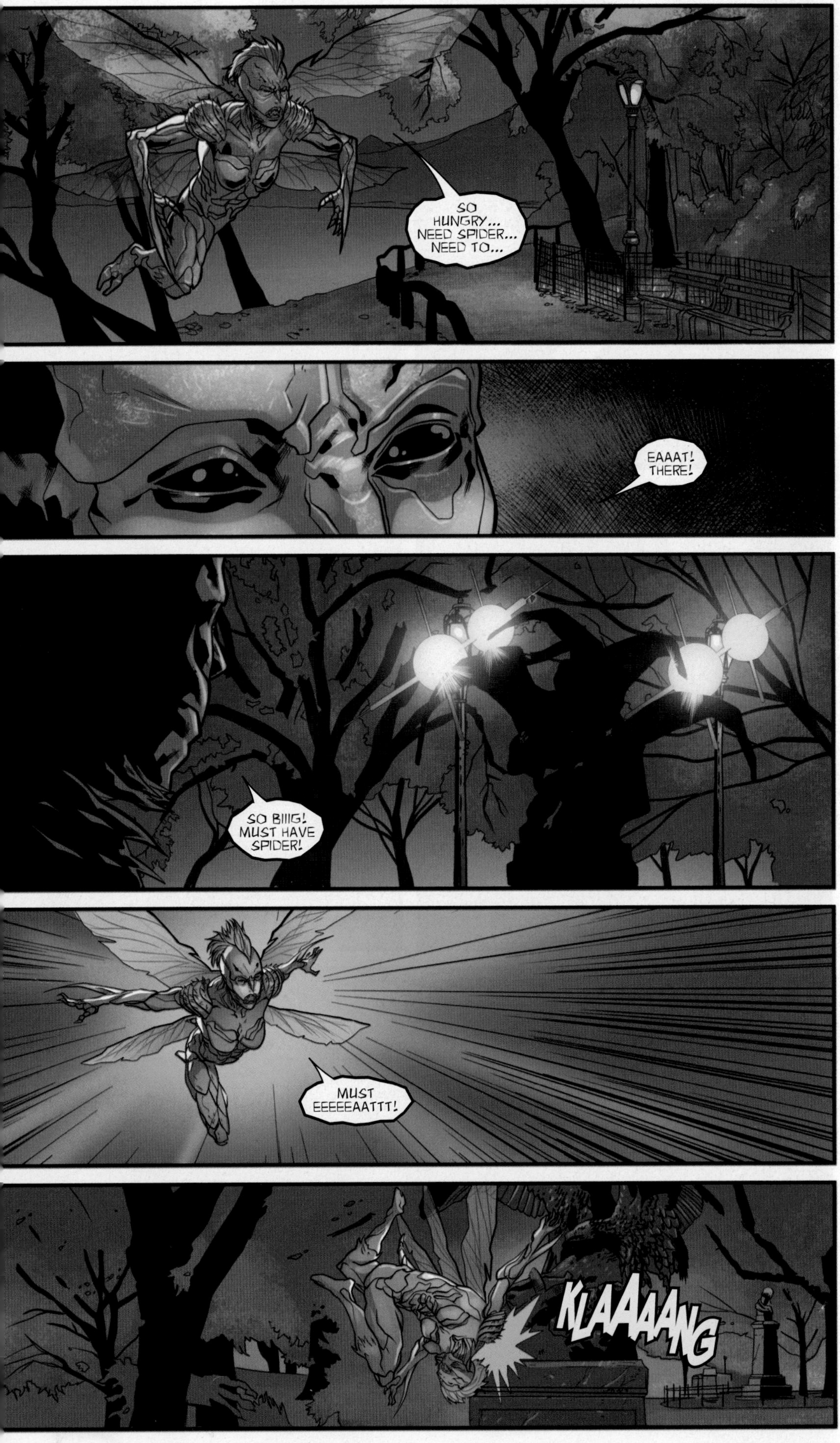
SO HUNGRY... NEED SPIDER... NEED TO...
EAAAT! THERE!
SO BIIIG! MUST HAVE SPIDER!
MUST EEEEEAATTT!
KLAAAAANG

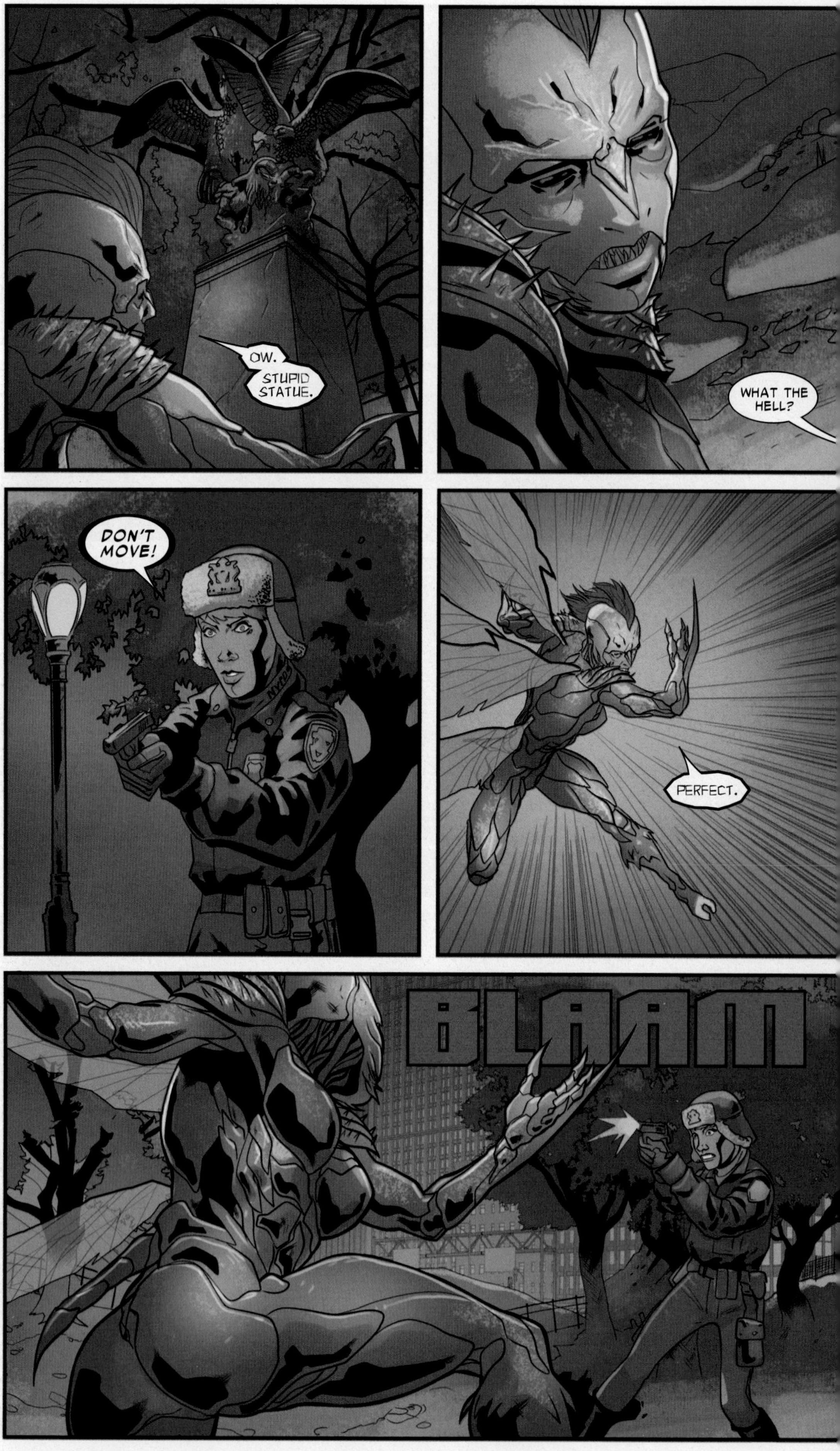
OW.
STUPID STATUE.
WHAT THE HELL?
DON'T MOVE!
PERFECT.
BLAAM

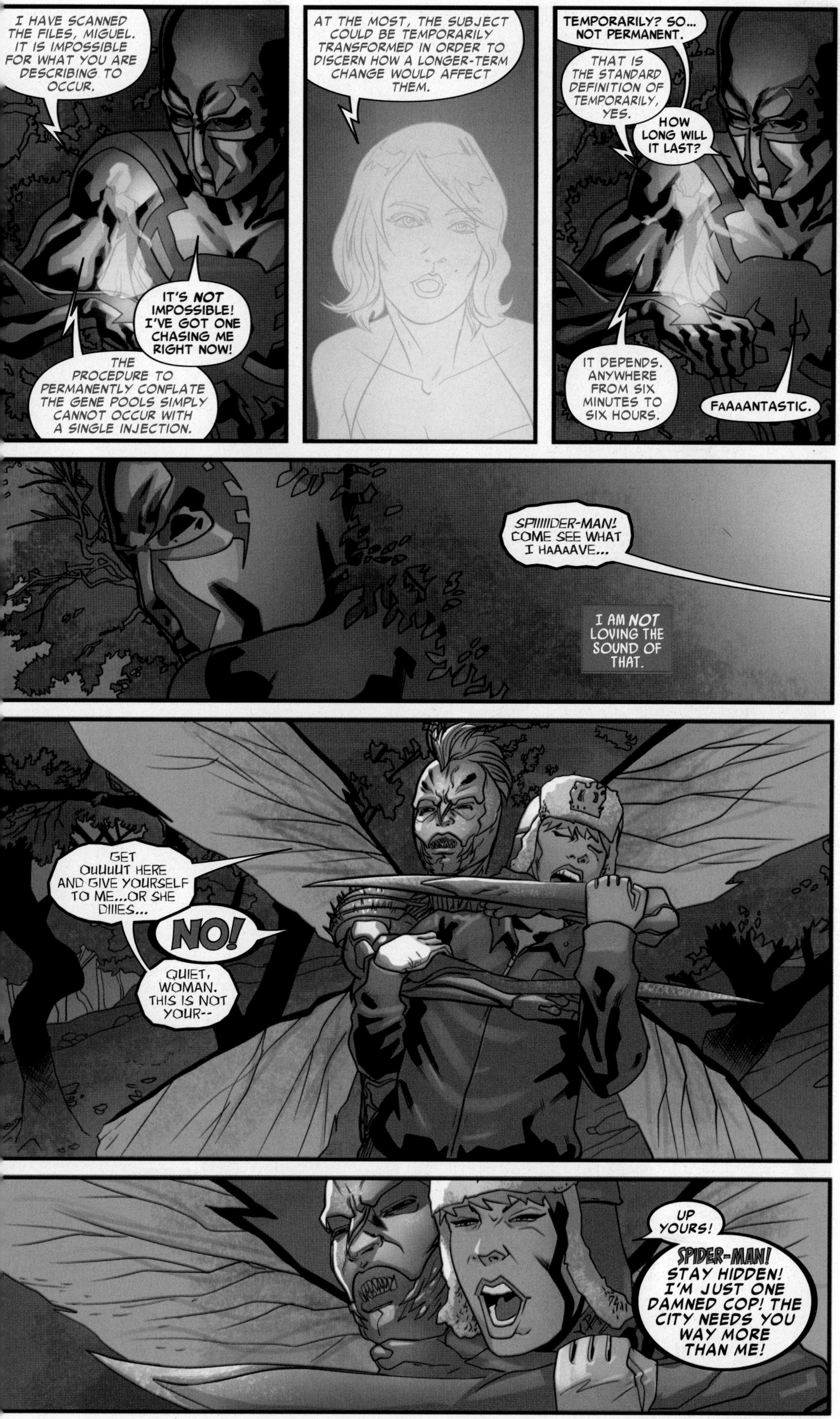
I HAVE SCANNED THE FILES, MIGUEL. IT IS IMPOSSIBLE FOR WHAT YOU ARE DESCRIBING TO OCCUR.
IT'S NOT IMPOSSIBLE! I'VE GOT ONE CHASING ME RIGHT NOW!
THE PROCEDURE TO PERMANENTLY CONFLATE THE GENE POOLS SIMPLY CANNOT OCCUR WITH A SINGLE INJECTION.
AT THE MOST, THE SUBJECT COULD BE TEMPORARILY TRANSFORMED IN ORDER TO DISCERN HOW A LONGER-TERM CHANGE WOULD AFFECT THEM.
TEMPORARILY? SO... NOT PERMANENT.
THAT IS THE STANDARD DEFINITION OF TEMPORARILY, YES.
HOW LONG WILL IT LAST?
IT DEPENDS. ANYWHERE FROM SIX MINUTES TO SIX HOURS.
FAAAANTASTIC.
SPIIIIIDER-MAN! COME SEE WHAT I HAAAAVE...
I AM NOT LOVING THE SOUND OF THAT.
GET OUUUUT HERE AND GIVE YOURSELF TO ME...OR SHE DIIIES...
NO!
QUIET, WOMAN. THIS IS NOT YOUR--
UP YOURS!
SPIDER-MAN! STAY HIDDEN! I'M JUST ONE DAMNED COP! THE CITY NEEDS YOU WAY MORE THAN ME!

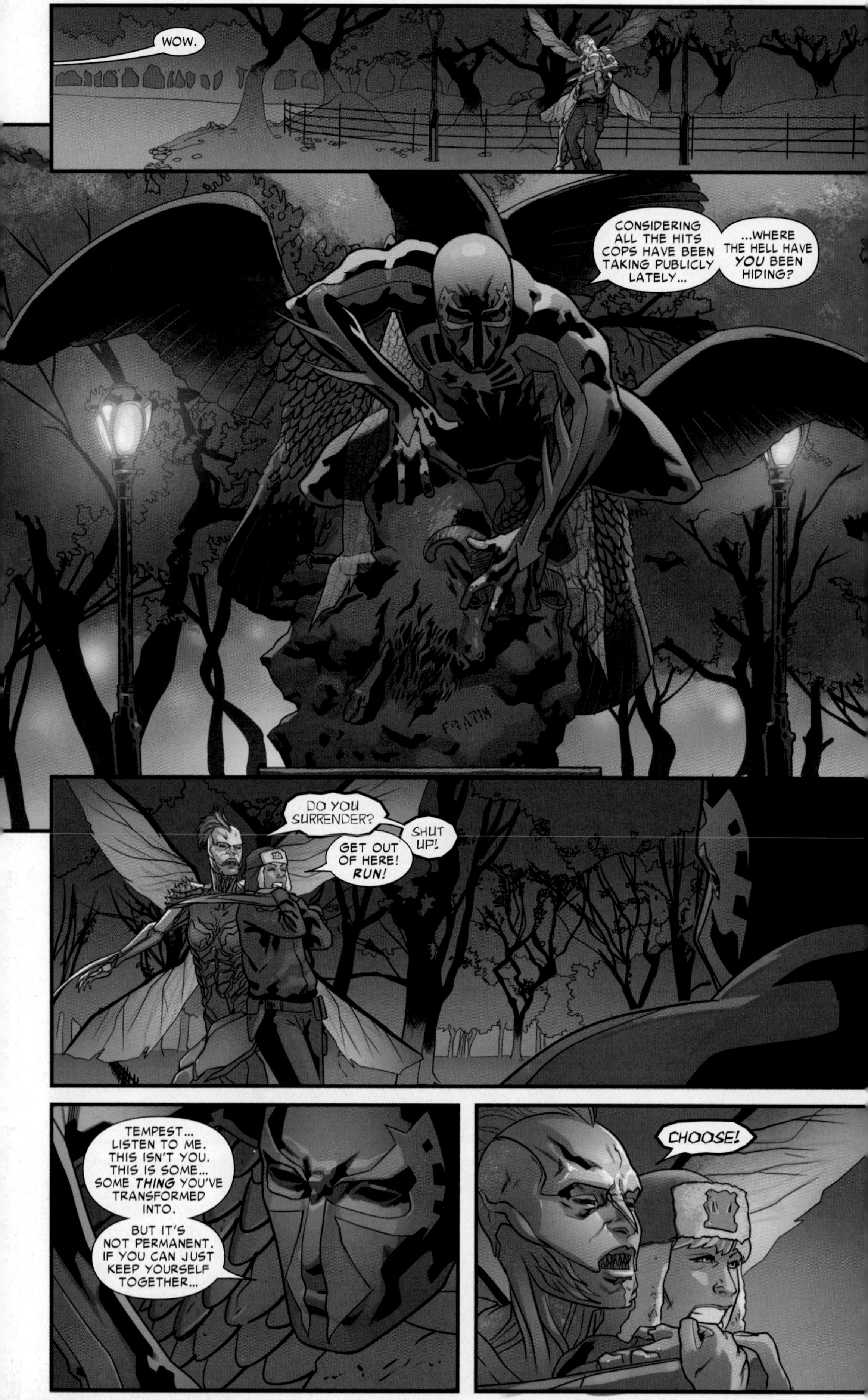
WOW.
CONSIDERING ALL THE HITS COPS HAVE BEEN TAKING PUBLICLY LATELY...
...WHERE THE HELL HAVE *YOU* BEEN HIDING?
DO YOU SURRENDER?
SHUT UP!
GET OUT OF HERE! *RUN!*
TEMPEST... LISTEN TO ME. THIS ISN'T YOU. THIS IS SOME... SOME *THING* YOU'VE TRANSFORMED INTO.
BUT IT'S NOT PERMANENT. IF YOU CAN JUST KEEP YOURSELF TOGETHER...
CHOOSE!

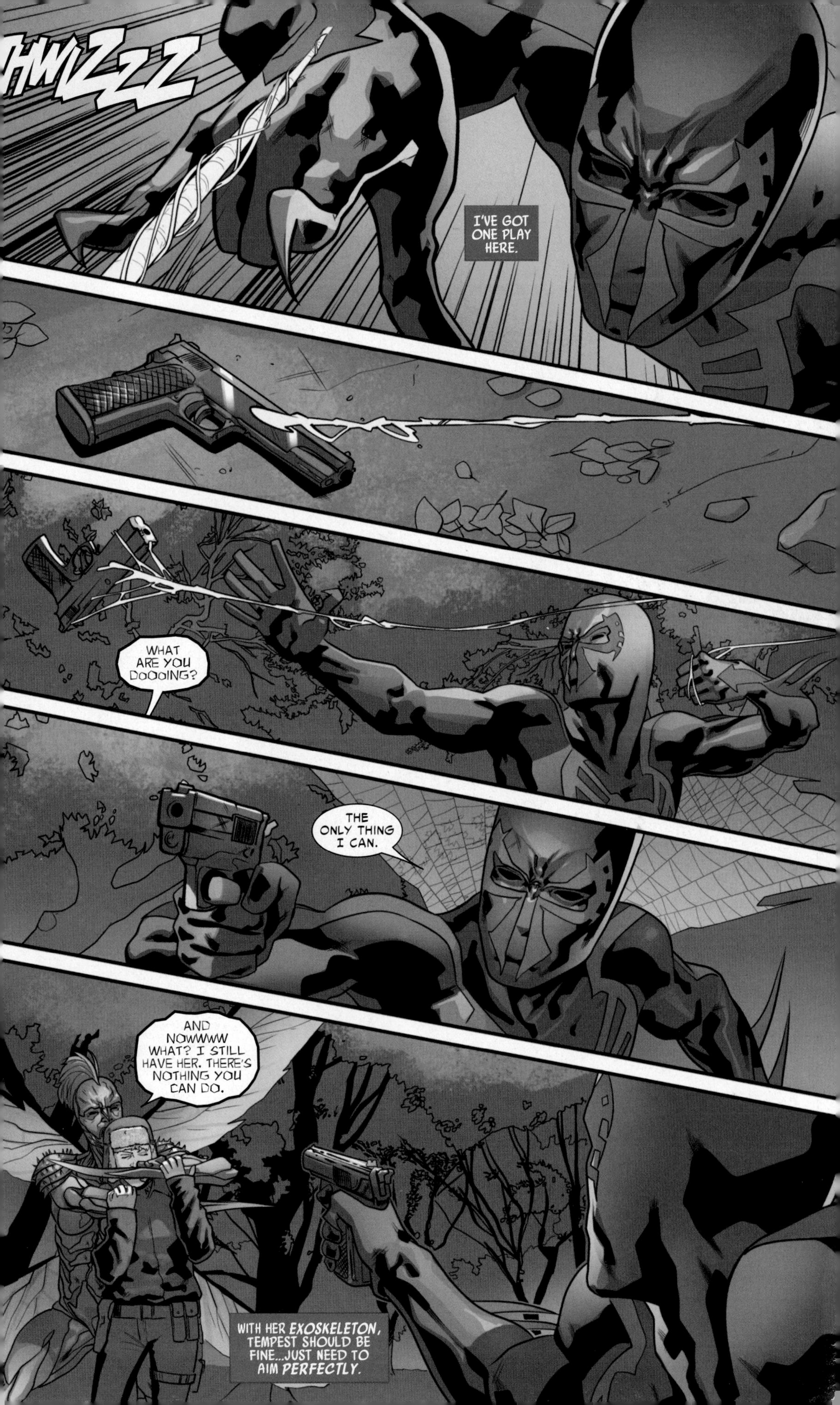
THWIZZZ
I'VE GOT ONE PLAY HERE.
WHAT ARE YOU DOOOING?
THE ONLY THING I CAN.
AND NOWWWW WHAT? I STILL HAVE HER. THERE'S NOTHING YOU CAN DO.
WITH HER EXOSKELETON, TEMPEST SHOULD BE FINE...JUST NEED TO AIM PERFECTLY.

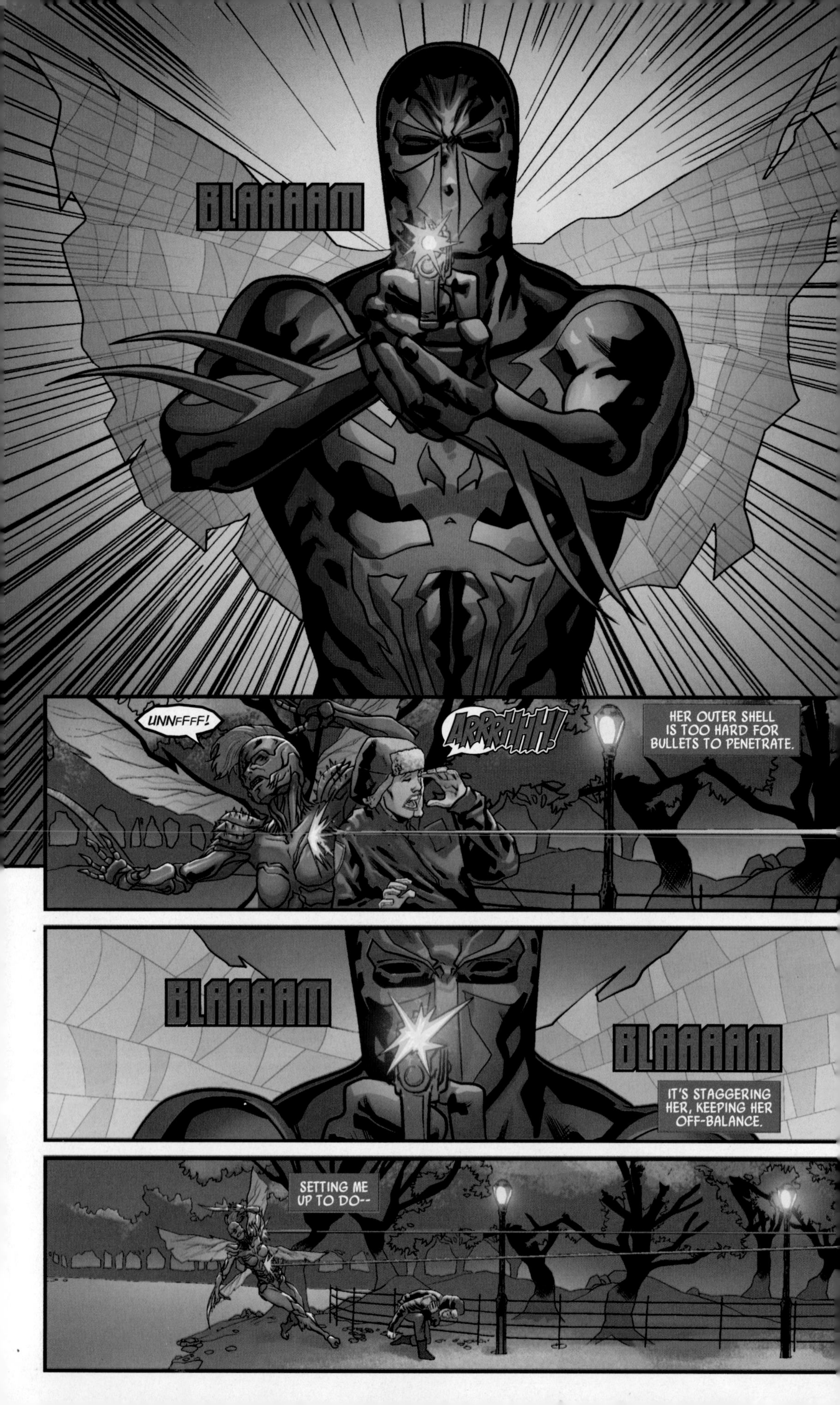
BLAAAAM
UNNFFFF!
ARRRHHH!
HER OUTER SHELL IS TOO HARD FOR BULLETS TO PENETRATE.
BLAAAAM
BLAAAAM
IT'S STAGGERING HER, KEEPING HER OFF-BALANCE.
SETTING ME UP TO DO--

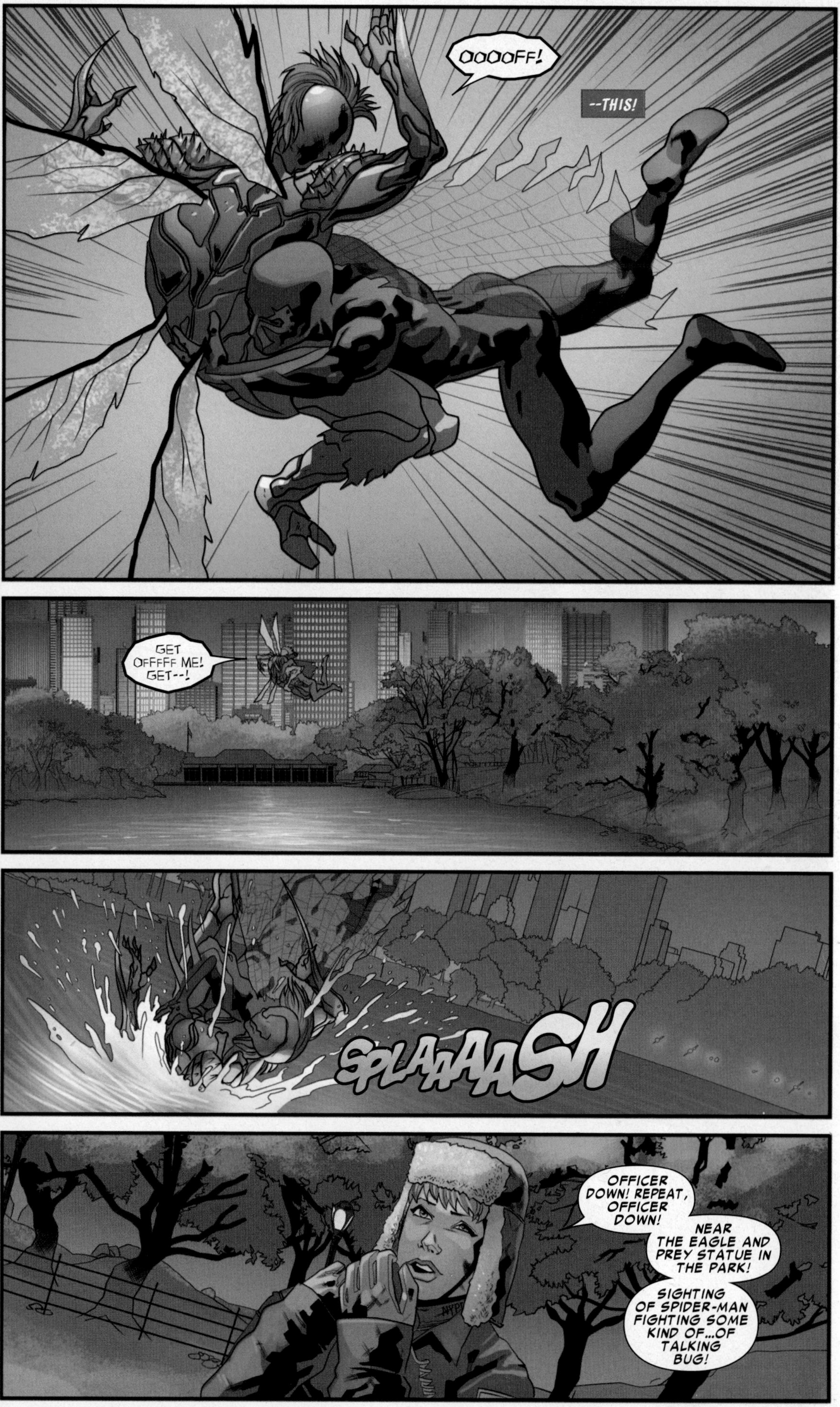
OOOOFF!
--THIS!
GET OFFFFF ME! GET--!
SPLAAAAASH
OFFICER DOWN! REPEAT, OFFICER DOWN!
NEAR THE EAGLE AND PREY STATUE IN THE PARK!
SIGHTING OF SPIDER-MAN FIGHTING SOME KIND OF...OF TALKING BUG!

UNDER WATER, HER WINGS AREN'T GOING TO DO HER ANY GOOD.
IF I CAN JUST FIND A WAY TO KNOCK HER OUT COLD FOR--
ARRHHH! SHOCK IT!
FORTUNATELY HER TEETH CAN'T PENETRATE MY COSTUME, BUT THEY STILL HURT LIKE A MOTHER!
I KEEP HOLDING BACK BECAUSE I DON'T WANT TO RISK HURTING HER.
UNFORTUNATELY SHE DOESN'T HAVE THE SAME ATTITUDE TOWARDS ME.
THUD!
OW! OKAY, FORGET THE GUT PUNCH.
SHE'S STILL TOO HEAVILY ARMORED.

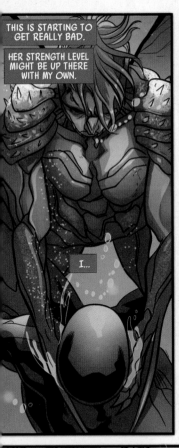

THIS IS STARTING TO GET REALLY BAD.

HER STRENGTH LEVEL MIGHT BE UP THERE WITH MY OWN.

I...

I CAN'T...GET HER OFF ME...

STARTING TO...RUN OUT OF AIR...

HAVE TO... TO...

...TO GET THROUGH... TO...

Tempest... it's...it's... me...

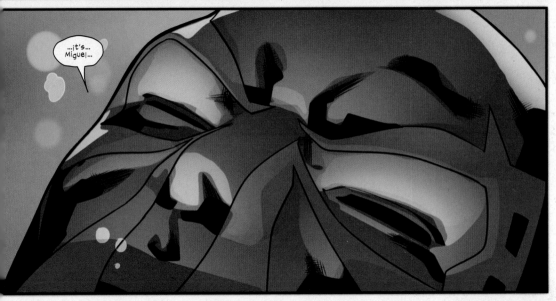

...it's... Miguel...

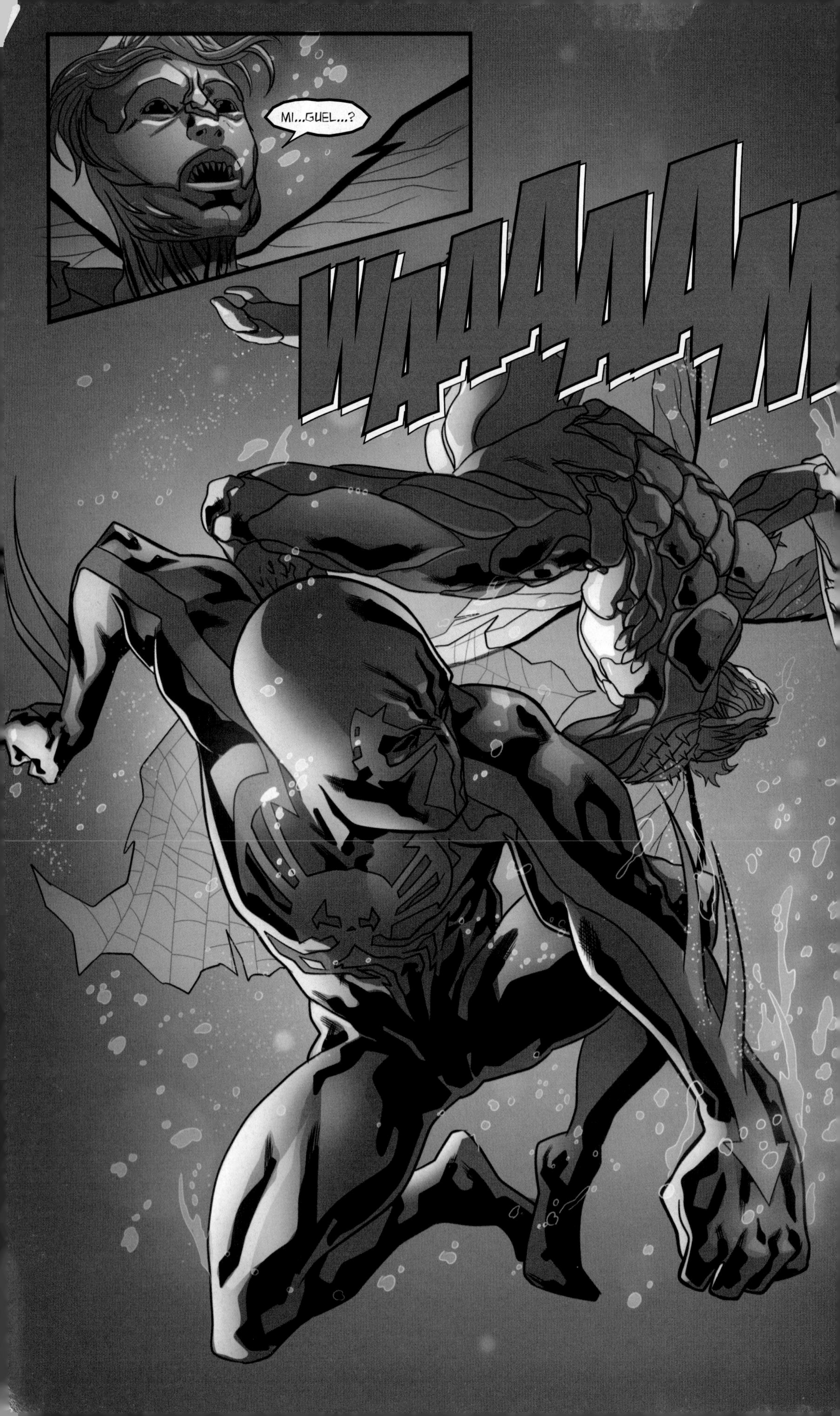
MI...GUEL...?
WAAAAAAM

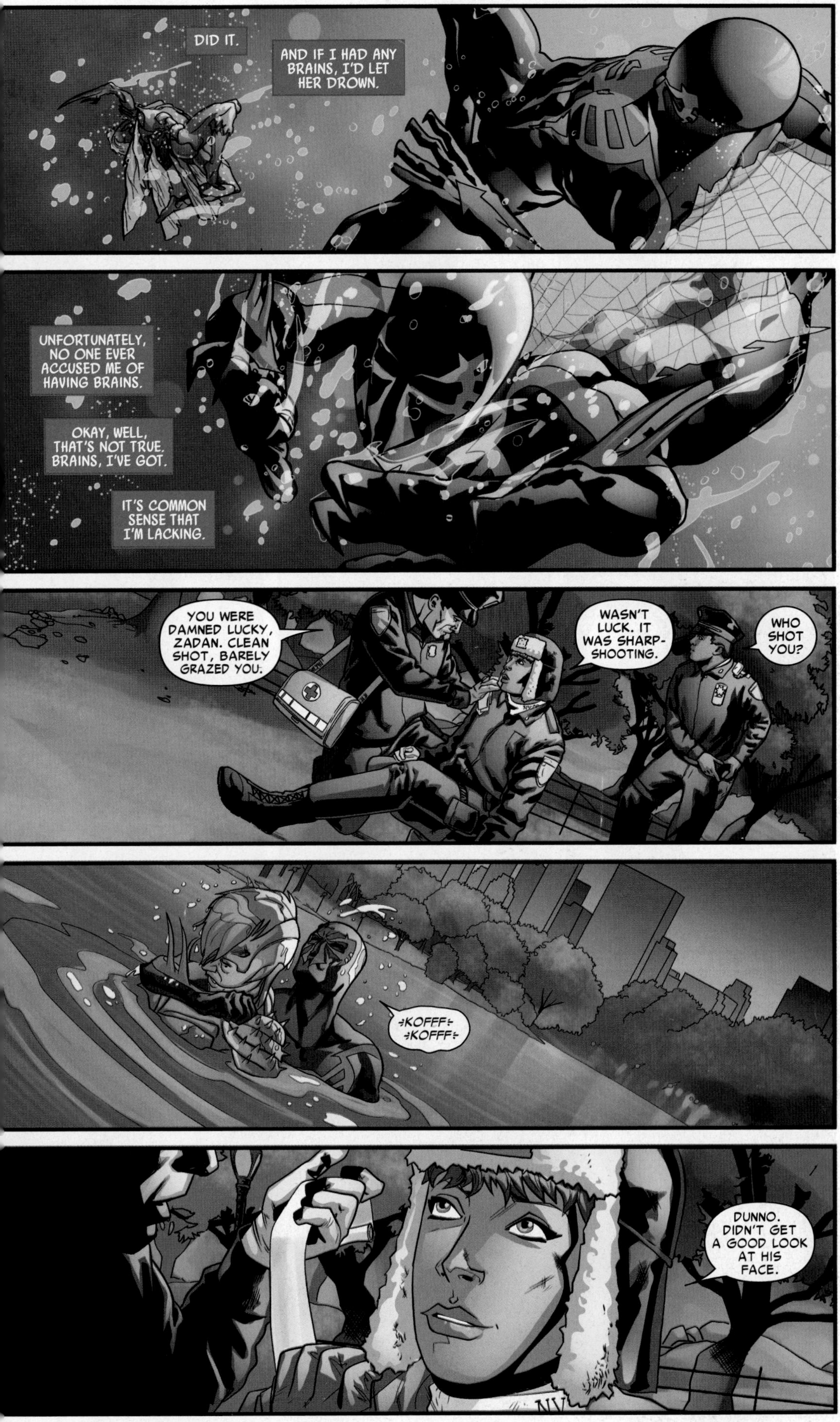
DID IT.
AND IF I HAD ANY BRAINS, I'D LET HER DROWN.
UNFORTUNATELY, NO ONE EVER ACCUSED ME OF HAVING BRAINS.
OKAY, WELL, THAT'S NOT TRUE. BRAINS, I'VE GOT.
IT'S COMMON SENSE THAT I'M LACKING.
YOU WERE DAMNED LUCKY, ZADAN. CLEAN SHOT, BARELY GRAZED YOU.
WASN'T LUCK. IT WAS SHARP-SHOOTING.
WHO SHOT YOU?
KOFFF KOFFF
DUNNO. DIDN'T GET A GOOD LOOK AT HIS FACE.

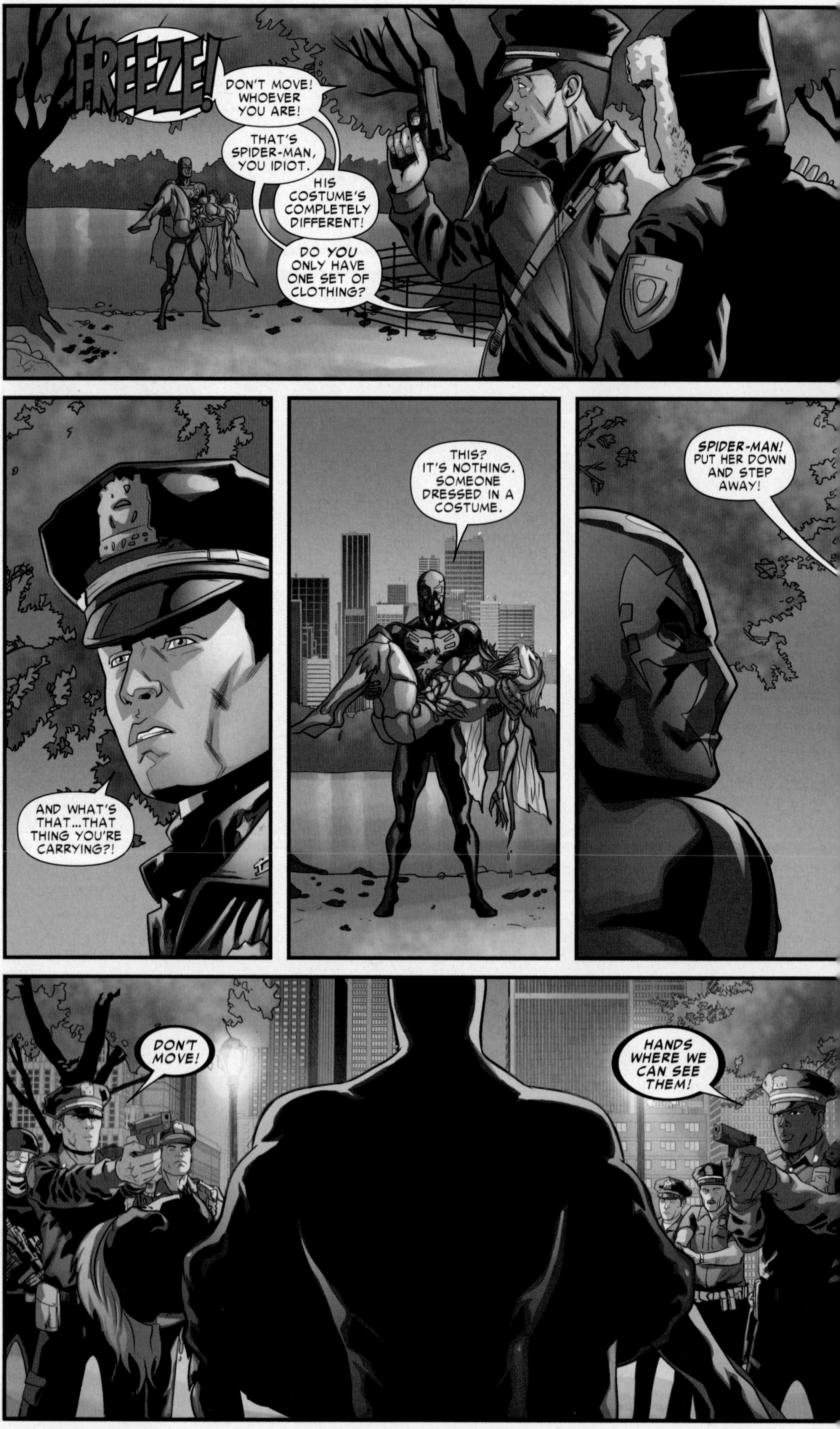
FREEZE!
DON'T MOVE! WHOEVER YOU ARE!
THAT'S SPIDER-MAN, YOU IDIOT.
HIS COSTUME'S COMPLETELY DIFFERENT!
DO YOU ONLY HAVE ONE SET OF CLOTHING?
AND WHAT'S THAT...THAT THING YOU'RE CARRYING?!
THIS? IT'S NOTHING. SOMEONE DRESSED IN A COSTUME.
SPIDER-MAN! PUT HER DOWN AND STEP AWAY!
DON'T MOVE!
HANDS WHERE WE CAN SEE THEM!

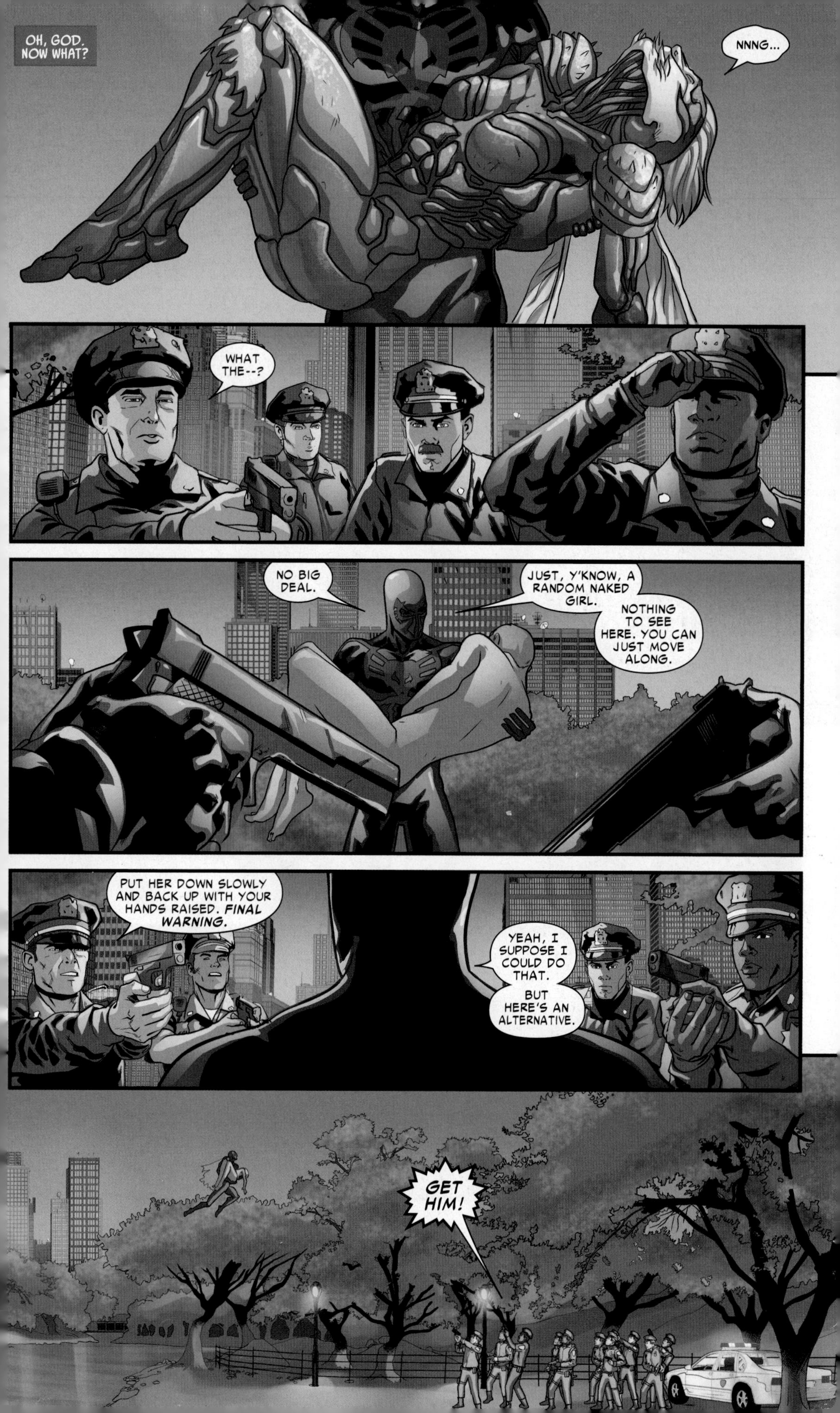
OH, GOD. NOW WHAT?
NNNG...
WHAT THE--?
NO BIG DEAL.
JUST, Y'KNOW, A RANDOM NAKED GIRL.
NOTHING TO SEE HERE. YOU CAN JUST MOVE ALONG.
PUT HER DOWN SLOWLY AND BACK UP WITH YOUR HANDS RAISED. FINAL WARNING.
YEAH, I SUPPOSE I COULD DO THAT.
BUT HERE'S AN ALTERNATIVE.
GET HIM!

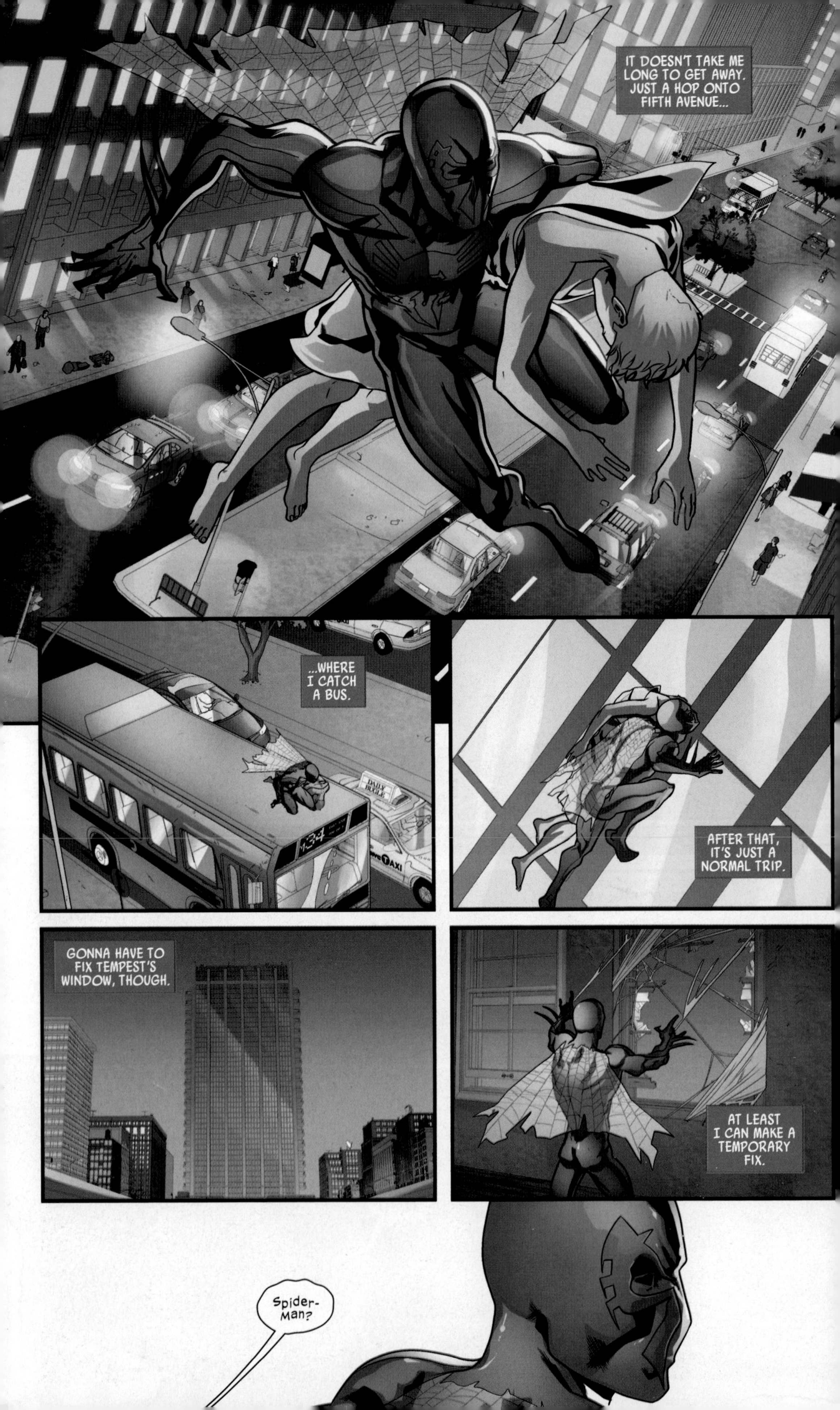
IT DOESN'T TAKE ME LONG TO GET AWAY. JUST A HOP ONTO FIFTH AVENUE...
...WHERE I CATCH A BUS.
DAILY BUGLE
TAXI
AFTER THAT, IT'S JUST A NORMAL TRIP.
GONNA HAVE TO FIX TEMPEST'S WINDOW, THOUGH.
AT LEAST I CAN MAKE A TEMPORARY FIX.
Spider-Man?

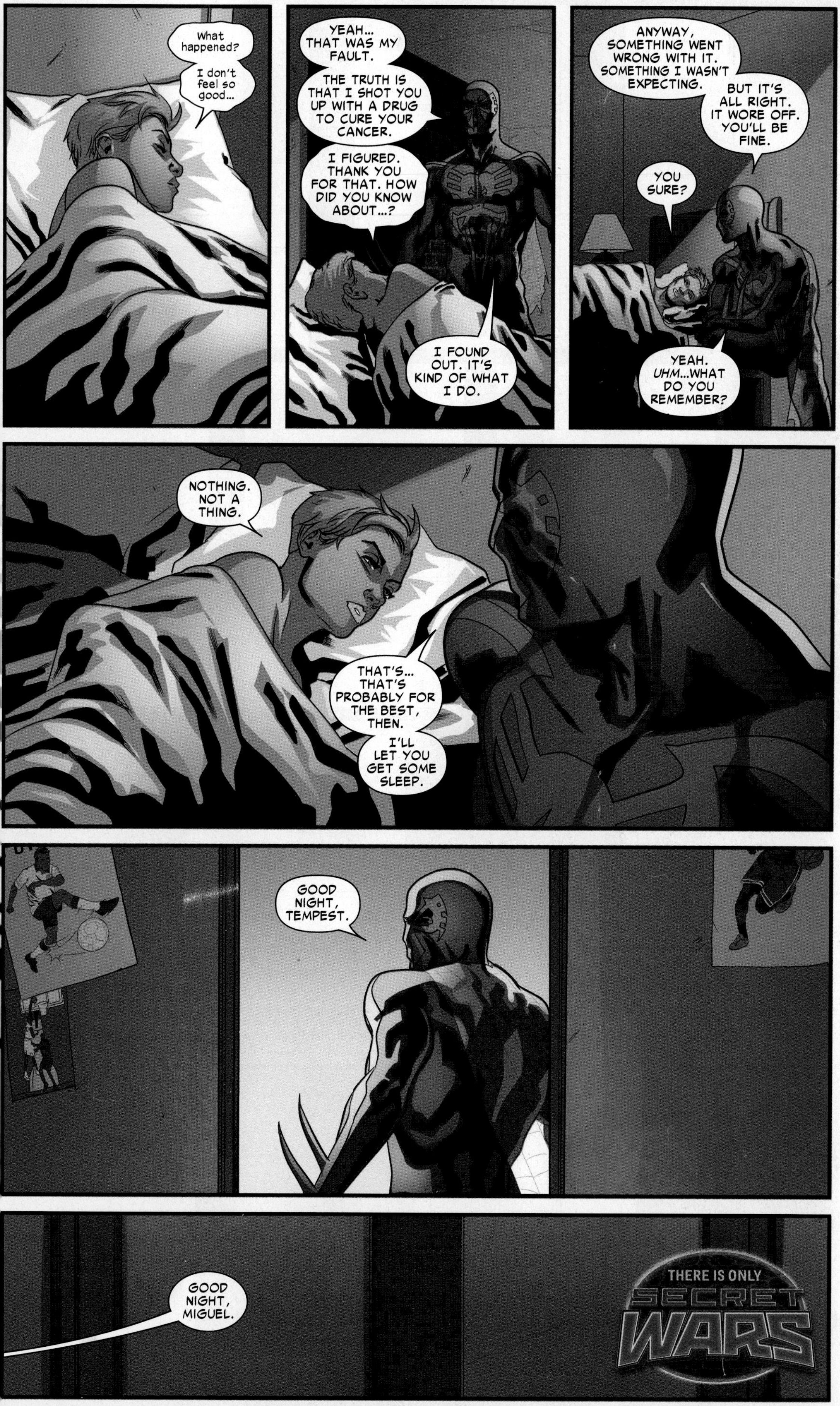
What happened?
I don't feel so good...
YEAH... THAT WAS MY FAULT.
THE TRUTH IS THAT I SHOT YOU UP WITH A DRUG TO CURE YOUR CANCER.
I FIGURED. THANK YOU FOR THAT. HOW DID YOU KNOW ABOUT...?
I FOUND OUT. IT'S KIND OF WHAT I DO.
ANYWAY, SOMETHING WENT WRONG WITH IT. SOMETHING I WASN'T EXPECTING.
BUT IT'S ALL RIGHT. IT WORE OFF. YOU'LL BE FINE.
YOU SURE?
YEAH. *UHM*...WHAT DO YOU REMEMBER?
NOTHING. NOT A THING.
THAT'S... THAT'S PROBABLY FOR THE BEST, THEN.
I'LL LET YOU GET SOME SLEEP.
GOOD NIGHT, TEMPEST.
GOOD NIGHT, MIGUEL.
THERE IS ONLY SECRET WARS

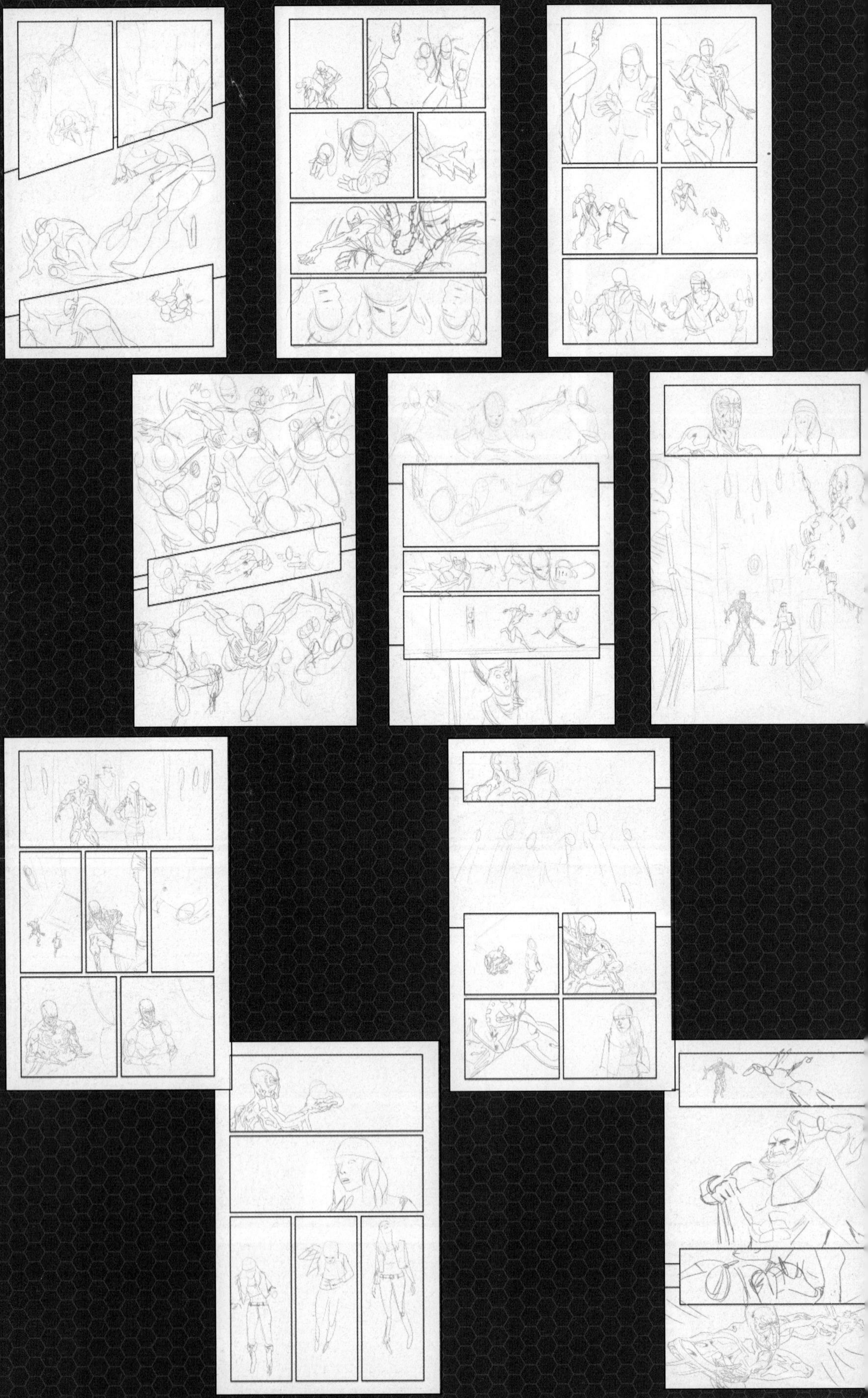

#10 PAGES 6-15 THUMBNAIL SKETCHES BY **WILL SLINEY**

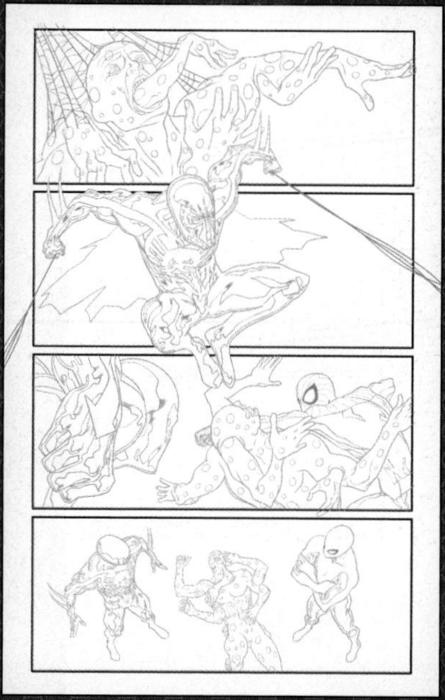

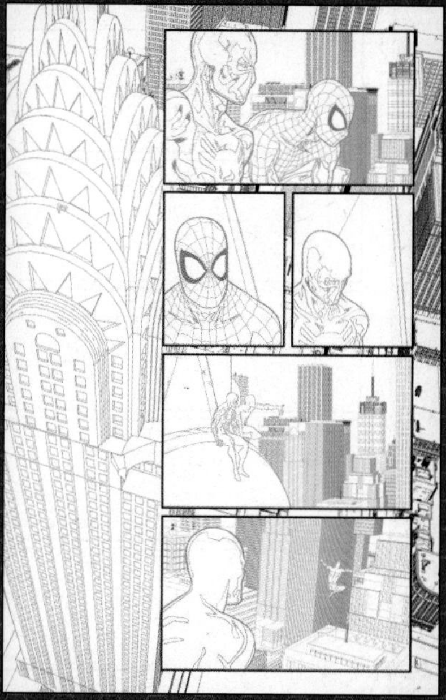

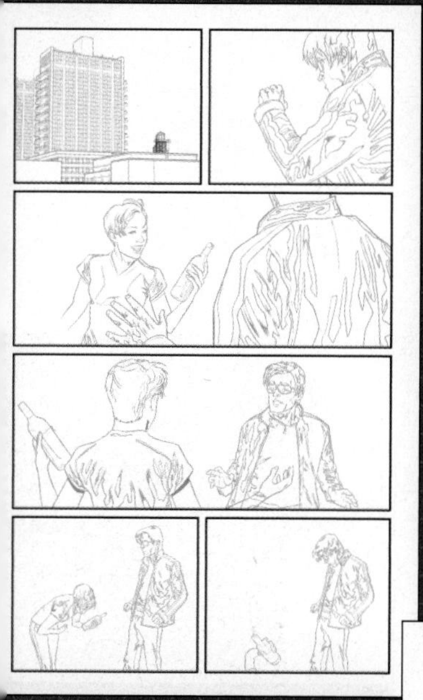

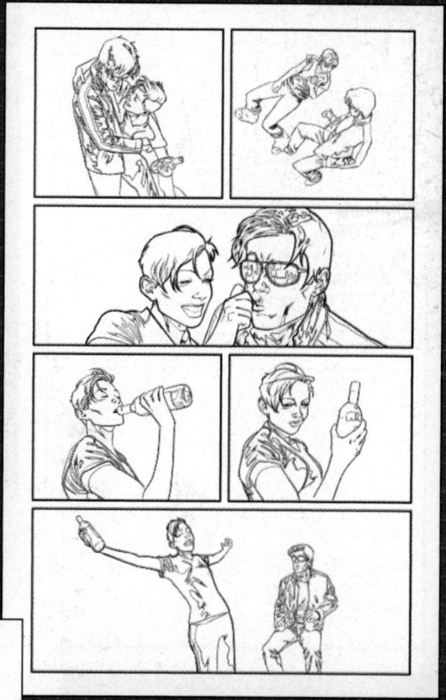

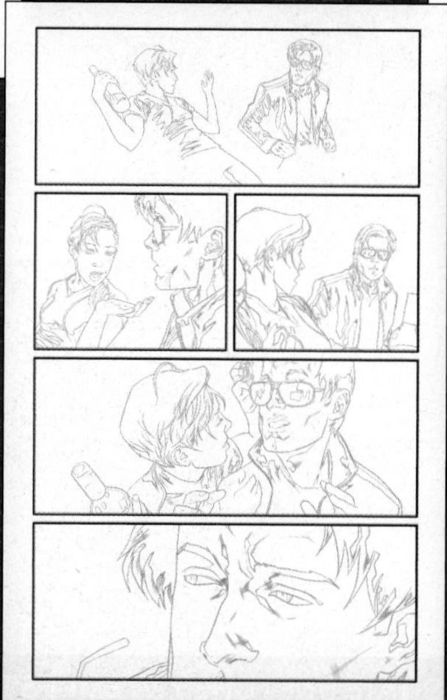

11 PAGES 11-15 THUMBNAIL SKETCHES BY **WILL SLINEY**

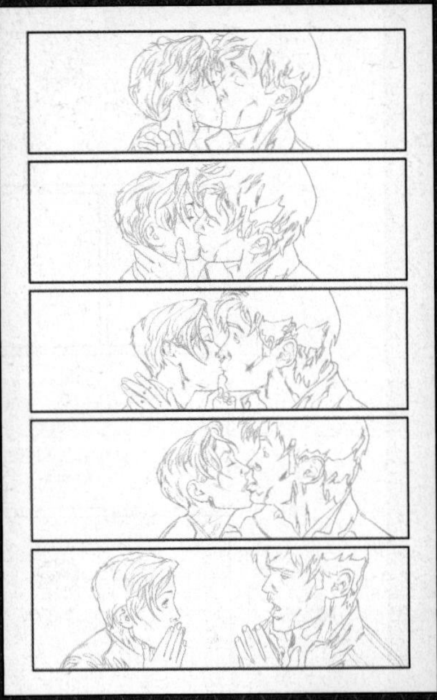

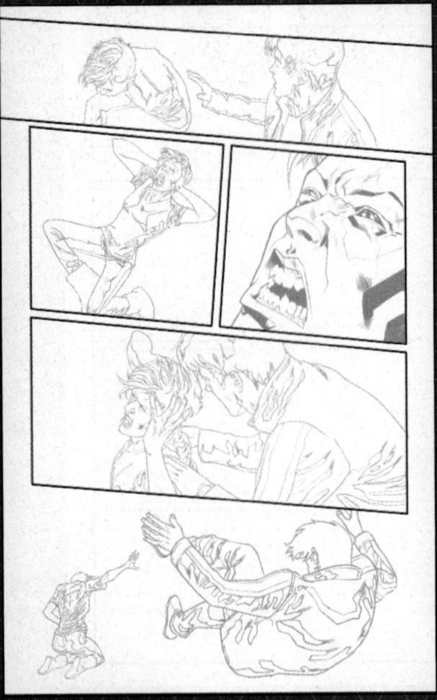

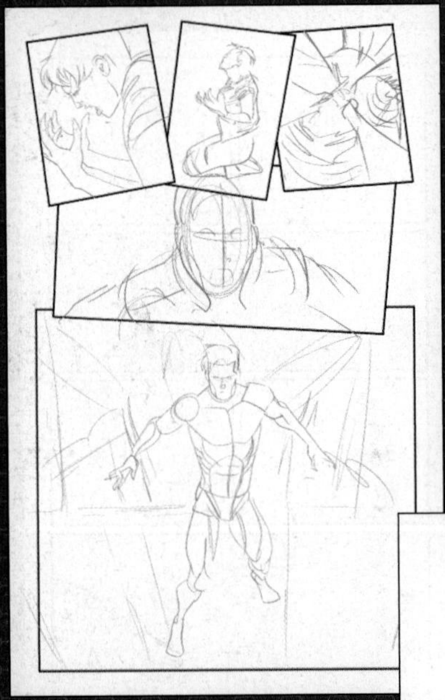

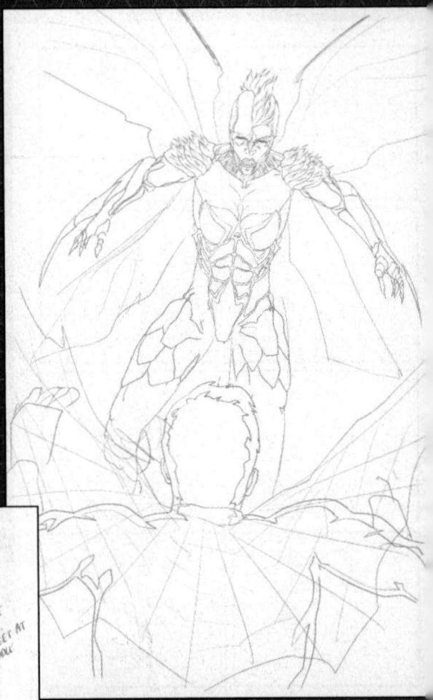

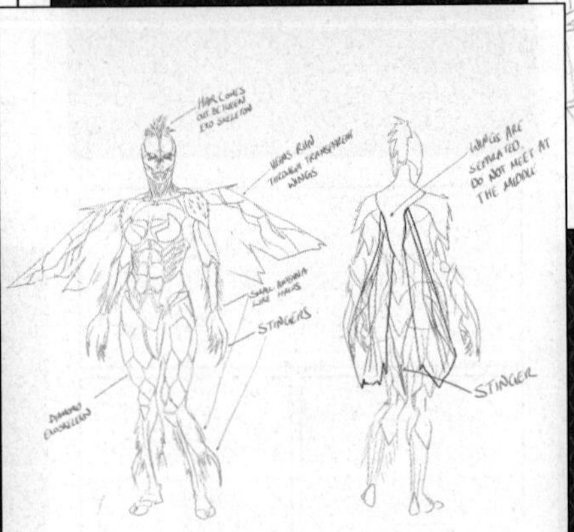
HAIR COMES OUT BETWEEN EXO SKELETON
VEINS RUN THROUGH TRANSPARENT WINGS
WINGS ARE SEPARATED. DO NOT MEET AT THE MIDDLE
STINGERS
STINGER
PALETTE IS SLIGHTLY RAISED OFF FACE

#11 PAGES 16-20 THUMBNAIL SKETCHES & TEMPEST/SPIDER-WASP DESIGNS

BY **WILL SLINEY**

FULL PAGE of Daemos slamming into the forcefield of the cage holding him with all his strength. Energy is crackling around him. Spidey and Lady Spider are standing on the other side, watching him.

Lady Spider 1: Is there any chance he could break out?

Spidey 2: None. The energy level holding him multiplies exponentially the more he shoves against it.

Spidey 3: He'd have to take out the entire Eastern seaboard power grid to even make a dent in it. And even then it would still hold against him.

Spidey 4: Like I said, he's not going anywhere.

Panel A: And then Spidey turns away.

Spidey 1: But we are. Come on.

Lady Spider 2: Where are we going?

Spidey 3: We have an appointment.

Lady Spider 4: How? We just got here. And with whom?

Panel B: Interior, Tyler's office. He is seated behind his desk, Winston next to him.

Caption 5: "With the guy who runs this place. Tyler Stone.

Caption 6: "He's my...old friend."

Panel C: The doors burst open as Spidey knocks them open. Lady Spider is following.

Spidey 7: Tyler. It's been a while.

Tyler 8: Spider-Man. Good to see you again.

Spidey 9: Somehow I kind of doubt that.

Tyler 10: I would stop where you are at the moment.

Spidey 11: Why?

Panel D: And gun muzzles are suddenly sticking out of the entire upper rim of the office, all targeting Spidey.

Tyler 12: I've redecorated.

Caption 13: Lasers. I hate lasers.

Tyler 14: According to what you said on your way over, you were willing to let bygones be bygones.

Panel E: Spidey gestures angrily.

Spidey 15: You sent me to 2014 and dumped me there!

Tyler 16: And yet here you are. Not quite sure what you have to be upset about.

Tyler 17: By the way, who's your friend?

Spidey 18: Lady Spider. She doesn't matter.

Panel F: She looks at him in irritation. He's rolling his eyes, or at least we try to convey that.

Lady Spider 19: Ex-cuse me?

Spidey 20: You know what I mean.

Lady Spider 21: Not really, no.

Page 3

Panel A: He turns to face Tyler.

Spidey 1: I need you to clear out the lab adjacent to where we have Daemos bottled up.

Tyler 2: Clear it out why?

Spidey 3: For my use. I need to dissect something.

Tyler 4: Dissect--?

Spidey 5: A previous body of the guy we're currently holding. And I need you to send someone to go pick it up from where I stashed it.

Tyler 6: And I'm to provide you this out of the goodness of my heart?

Panel B: Angle on Spidey.

Spidey 7: You can't stay here forever, Tyler. Sooner or later, you have to go home

Spidey 8: Sooner or later, if you piss me off...I will get you.

Spidey 9: You want to test me on that?

Spidey 7: You can't stay here forever, Tyler. Sooner or later, you have to go home

Spidey 8: Sooner or later, if you piss me off...I will get you.